BRITISH RAILWAY HISTORY IN COLOUR

Volume 4B:
GLOUCESTER MIDLAND LINES
Part 3: SOUTH
STONEHOUSE to WESTERLEIGH and BRANCHES

Stanier 'Jubilee No. 45658 *Keyes* appears to be making fairly light work of its ten-coach train as it climbs towards Wickwar station beneath a somewhat threatening sky on 8th August 1964. The ascent of the southern end of the Cotswold escarpment begins at Berkeley Road and apart from a brief downward dip shortly after, the climb is non-stop all the way through Charfield and Wickwar to just south of Yate. However, it is at a manageble and steady 1 in 281 gradient for most of the way, with short sections less than that, so banking engines were never required. New from Derby Works on 18th December 1934, No. 45658 was a long time resident of Leeds Holbeck shed and carries its 55A shedplate on the smokebox door. The train is a summer Saturday holiday express but is not carrying a reporting number; however, it is likely to have originated at Bradford and may be the 10.36am to Paignton, which was due past Wickwar at around 3.35pm. The 'Jubilee' would hand over to a WR locomotive at Bristol Temple Meads, although this was not a platform stop, which would haul it the rest of the way. *Keyes* was withdrawn from service in September 1965. NPC

PREVIOUS PAGE: Class '4F' No. 44534 passes over Station Road Crossing at Iron Acton with the branch goods for Grovesend Quarry and Thornbury train circa 1960. The view is looking south, with the siding and disused station being to the right. Any shunting here would be carried out on the return journey. DAVID POLLARD/NPC

BRITISH RAILWAY HISTORY IN COLOUR

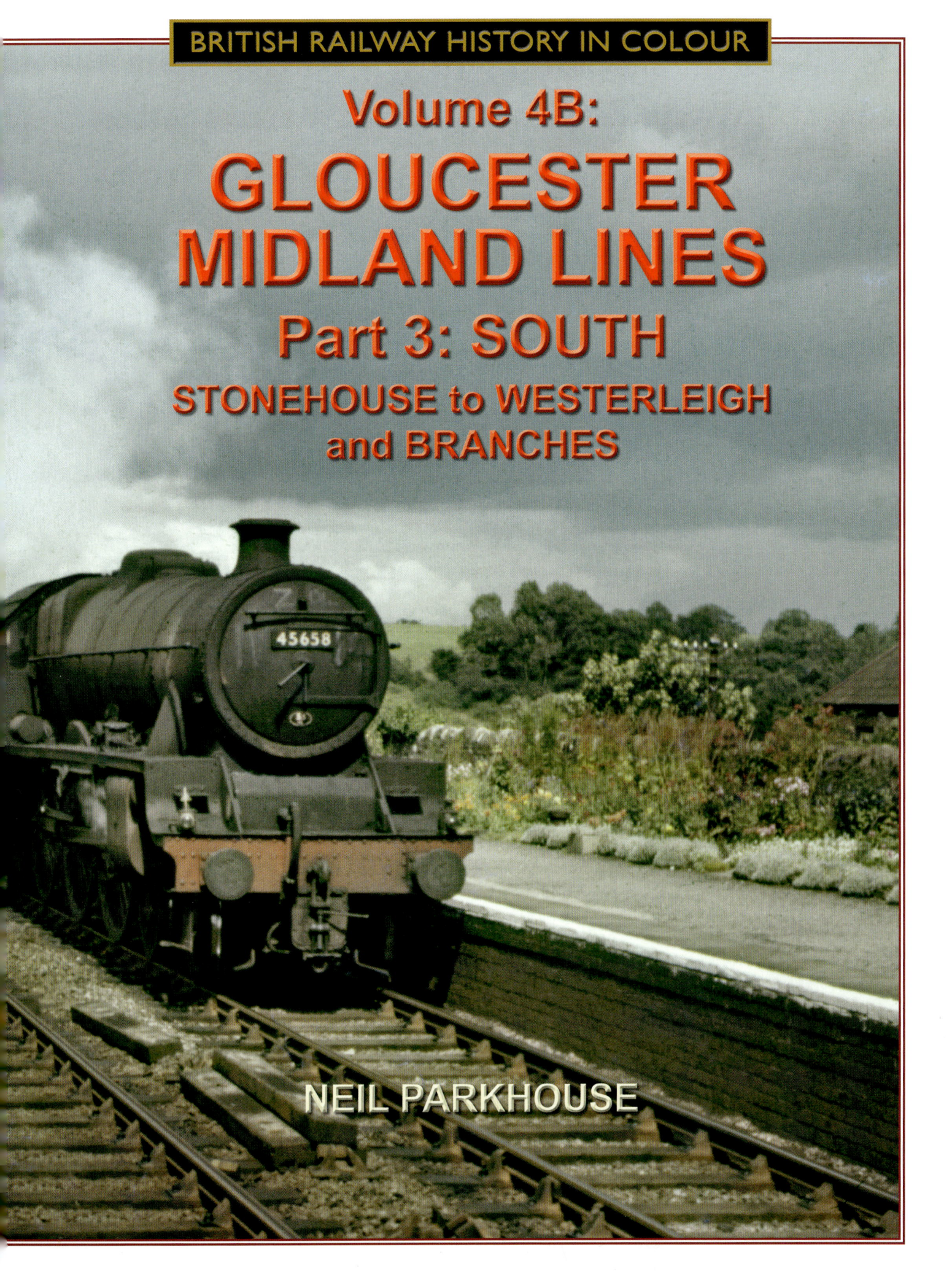

Volume 4B:
GLOUCESTER MIDLAND LINES
Part 3: SOUTH
STONEHOUSE to WESTERLEIGH and BRANCHES

NEIL PARKHOUSE

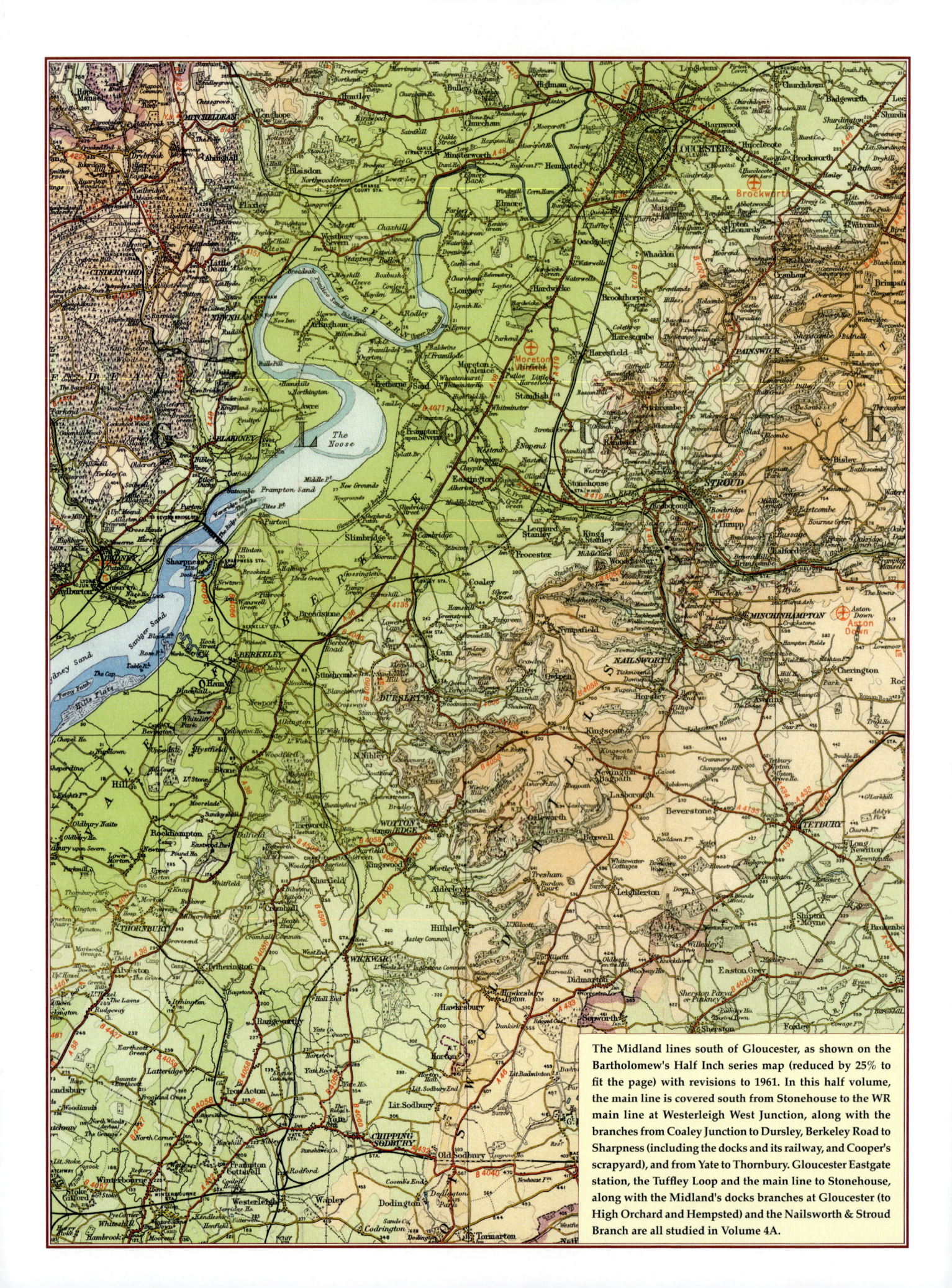

The Midland lines south of Gloucester, as shown on the Bartholomew's Half Inch series map (reduced by 25% to fit the page) with revisions to 1961. In this half volume, the main line is covered south from Stonehouse to the WR main line at Westerleigh West Junction, along with the branches from Coaley Junction to Dursley, Berkeley Road to Sharpness (including the docks and its railway, and Cooper's scrapyard), and from Yate to Thornbury. Gloucester Eastgate station, the Tuffley Loop and the main line to Stonehouse, along with the Midland's docks branches at Gloucester (to High Orchard and Hempsted) and the Nailsworth & Stroud Branch are all studied in Volume 4A.

CONTENTS
VOLUME 4B

Introduction to Volume 4B: .... page VI

Section 7: The Bristol & Gloucester Line: .... page 209
Stonehouse to Coaley Junction

Section 8: The Dursley Branch .... page 227

Section 9: The Bristol & Gloucester Line: .... page 269
Coaley Junction to Berkeley Road

Section 10: The Sharpness Branch .... page 295

Section 10: Sharpness Docks and Railway, and Cooper's Metals Scrapyard .... page 343

Section 11: The Bristol & Gloucester Line: .... page 371
Berkeley Road to Yate

Section 12: The Thornbury Branch .... page 423

Section 13: The Bristol & Gloucester Line: .... page 441
Yate to Westerleigh West Junction

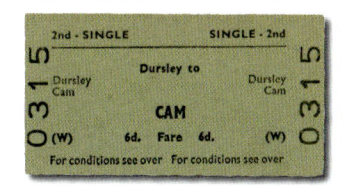

Published by LIGHTMOOR PRESS
© Lightmoor Press & Neil Parkhouse 2019
Designed by Neil Parkhouse

British Library Cataloguing-in-Publication Data. A catalogue record for this book is available from the British Library

ISBN: 9781911038 67 2

All rights reserved. No part of this publication may be reproduced, stored in a retrieval system or transmitted in any form or by any means, electronic, mechanical, photocopying, recording or otherwise, without the written permission of the publisher.

LIGHTMOOR PRESS
Unit 144B, Harbour Road Trading Estate,
Lydney, Gloucestershire GL15 4EJ
website: www.lightmoor.co.uk
email: info@lightmoor.co.uk

Lightmoor Press is an imprint of
Black Dwarf Lightmoor Publications Ltd

Printed in Poland
www.lfbookservices.co.uk

Signalman Gilroy Kerr captured this scene at Coaley, with the goods shed peeping out from behind a snowdrift, in the bitter winter of early 1963. GILROY KERR

INTRODUCTION TO VOLUME 4B

As explained in the Introduction to Volume 4A, the first part of the journey south from Gloucester Eastgate on Midland metals, the original intention was that this was going to be one book. That plan fell apart once it became apparent that the sheer volume of material available meant that any single volume was going to be in excess of 450 pages – not a popular size with bedtime readers especially, who tend to find their legs going to sleep before the rest of them! However, having made that decision and also decided that both should be published at the same time, I then had to look at the introductory pages to the two volumes that resulted. Should I repeat the full introduction, the Bristol & Gloucester Railway background history and the acknowledgement sections in both, which would add an extra nine or ten pages to this volume?

The answer I decided had to be no, so my first duty here is to apologise to those of you who have only purchased this volume and have no interest in the other one. However, as my intention was to publish this as one book, telling the story of the Bristol & Gloucester Railway and the various branches that it connected with, I have remained as close to that original concept as possible, with the page numbering continuing on from where Volume 4A ended. In coming to this decision I have also taken in to account that there are a vast number of loyal readers of this series who are buying every one as they come out, so essentially it is to them and their loyalty that I am pandering, as much as I am to my original plan.

And yes I could have chopped things out, cut it all down to fit in one volume but consider what you would have missed. If you never spent time lineside on a summer Saturday at somewhere like Wickwar, or Rangeworthy just to the north of Yate, or even in the depths of winter at Nibley just to the south, then it is difficult to appreciate now what those days were like. The sheer variety of trains and with no clue as to what locomotive would be at the head of the next one, coupled with the sounds and smell of steam, along with the changing seasons and their effect on the smoke and steam produced by an engine working hard in the icy cold of winter or the heat of summer. For those who miss such days or were never fortunate enough to experience them – and I only ever did once or twice – then the pictures within these pages will at least give you a flavour of what it was about, why watching and photographing trains was such an engrossing hobby and why it can never be repeated.

If you want to quickly flip from place to place, moving on at a much faster pace than we do here, then these volumes will not be for you. But if you prefer to tarry awhile, pull up a chair, poor a cup of strong tea from your flask and break out a doorstep cheese and ham sandwich, then slowly turn the pages as you wait to see what is coming past next, well then I dedicate these books and this series to you. We are of a mind.

Finally, whilst I have omitted a full Acknowledgements section, I have included an alphabetical list here of all those who should be thanked again for their contributions and assistance, many unknowing as they are photographers no longer with us but without whose talents and foresight these books would not be possible: Ben Ashworth, Audie Baker (KRM), Chris Baldwin, Andy Barton, Pete Berry, David Bick, Malcolm Bobbitt, Tony Bowles (Archiving & Restoration Trust), Fred Butler, Paul Chancellor (Colour-Rail), Derek Chaplin, Mike Christensen, John Dagley-Morris, Maurice Deane, Roy Denison, Tony Dyer, Mike Fenton, Pete Fidczuk, Dr Simon Fosbury, Nick Freezer, John Grainger, Michael Hale, Alan Jarvis, Gilroy Kerr, Don Mann, Derek Markey, Gerry Nicholls, Trevor Owen, Blake Patterson, Gerald Peacock, David Pollard, David Postle (KRM), Bill Potter, Paul Riley, John Ryan, Alan Sainty, Mike Squire, Nigel Stennett-Cox, David Stowell, Paul Strong, John Strange, John Tarrant, Mark Warburton and Paul Woollard.

Neil Parkhouse, Lydney 2019

A platform lamp at Berkeley Road on 12th October 1963, against a backdrop of beautifully tended flower beds so typical of stations prior to the end of steam. It is these incidentals that went to make up a pre-Beeching era railway station which made them so attractive to enthusiasts and now today to collectors, who keenly search out these accoutrements of a bygone age.
BLAKE PATTERSON/ COURTESY THE RESTORATION & ARCHIVING TRUST/REF. BPUK1R18

They don't write 'em like this any more! Enamelled sign on Berkeley Road footbridge, 15th August 1959. TREVOR OWEN

SECTION 7

THE BRISTOL & GLOUCESTER LINE STONEHOUSE TO COALEY JUNCTION

Ex-GWR 'Grange' Class 4-6-0 No. 6803 *Bucklebury Grange* coasts through Stonehouse Bristol Road with a summer Saturday express from the West Country bound for Wolverhampton on 17th July 1965. 'Bristol Road' had been appended to the station name by BR from 17th September 1951, to distinguish it from the ex-GWR station nearby, which had 'Burdett Road' added to its name. The locomotive, new in September 1936, was weeks away from withdrawal from Wolverhampton Oxley shed, a service life of exactly twenty-nine years. Stonehouse signal box, a 20ft Midland Type '2b' cabin, opened on 5th September 1897, replacing an earlier box sited a few yards to the south. It was closed on 14th October 1968. The gated entrance to Hoffman's private siding features again on the right. The car near the signal box is an Austin A30 of circa 1953-54, distinguishable from the succeeding A35 by the much smaller rear window. BILL POTTER/KRM

The main line between Gloucester and Bristol was – and to an extent still is – a succession of junctions, so our next short journey along it takes us south from Stonehouse for around three miles to Coaley, junction for the Dursley Branch. This section of railway is relatively level but executes a gentle curve from south to west all the way to Coaley and it includes one major engineering structure, Stonehouse Viaduct (No. 85), carrying the line over the low valley of the River Frome about half a mile south of the station. Also known locally as or Beard's Mill Viaduct, the first structure was designed by Brunel and comprised ten timber spans on timber fan supports. With trains getting heavier, the Midland rebuilt it in 1883-84, the new bridge having five lattice girder spans supported on substantial blue brick piers. It was rebuilt again by BR in 1970, the lattice girders replaced by new wrought iron spans, with concrete walkways, resting on the brick piers. The three centre spans are 45 feet in length and the shorter two outer spans are 27ft 9ins.

There was one intermediate station, at Frocester, serving a small village that in 1891 numbered 247 souls. The coming of the railway failed to make any impact on the growth of the village, which at the 2001 census had dropped to 194 and by 2011 was down again to just 155. The station, opened with the line on 6th July 1844, was a pre-Beeching closure on 11th December 1961.

In 1917, the demand for concrete in connection with the First World War effort led to the building of a three and a half mile long mineral branch from Frocester to gravel pits at Frampton on Severn. A nitro-cellulose factory was being built at Henbury but when this project was abandoned prior to completion, work on the unfinished railway also ceased. However, it was resurrected the following year in connection with the construction of a new army ordnance depot at Bramley in Berkshire and the line was completed by German prisoners of war working under the Royal Defence Corps. Trains began running on the line in June 1918.

Leaving the main line via a double junction just to the north-east of the road bridge at the Gloucester end of the station, the branch ran in a north-westerly direction to reach the gravel pits, with a level crossing of the Bristol Road (now the A38) on the way. The

A fine panorama of Stonehouse Bristol Road station, looking north towards Gloucester circa 1964. The nameboard seems overly large but up until 1947 had read 'STONEHOUSE CHANGE HERE FOR STROUD AND THE NAILSWORTH BRANCH'. As built for the opening of the line north to here in 1844, the station comprised the small Brunellian style building at the far end of the Down platform and a smaller shelter on the Up side. Following the opening of the Nailsworth Branch in 1867, facilities were expanded with the addition of the building in the centre on the Down side, in a similar style to the original, which was to an extent mirrored by the new shelter provided on the Up platform, and the construction of the station master's house. It would seem a possibility that the platforms would have been extended at the same time and the goods shed was also doubled in size, although the extension, on the nearer end here, had a lower roof. The station footbridge (No. 88A) was a standard structure, comprising lattice girders supported on cast iron columns. The span was 48ft and it was provided in 1893. The station remained gas lit until closure, on 4th January 1965. A 2017 proposal to reopen a station here has made no progress to date. NPC

RIGHT: This rather indifferent quality view of the signal box and station, taken on 19th July 1968, is included because it is the only colour view seen to date of the coal depot that was opened in the yard here on 7th October 1966, under the auspices of the Stonehouse Coal Concentration Co. Ltd. It remained in use until 1989. DAVID STOWELL

BELOW: The Stonehouse to Coaley Junction section of the Br&GR line, as shown on the 1961 edition 1 inch OS. Stonehouse Viaduct spans the more southerly tributary of the River Frome. The gravel pits branch left the main line immediately north of the road bridge by Frocester station and ran close to the road to Eastington, there turning west to cross the A38 near the '(T)'. It then turned north to the clay pits seen here as lakes beneath the words 'Frampton on Severn'. Although only in existence for a few years, it was fully detailed on the 1921 25 inch OS.

line included a short branch to a loading wharf on the canal at Frampton and up to seven industrial locomotives worked there, for which there was an engine shed and repair shop at the terminus. Further need locally for concrete, for the new National Shipyards under construction at Chepstow and Portbury, and for the manufacture of 1,000 ton barges out of concrete at Gloucester, kept the line in operation beyond the end of the war. For a short period the traffic generated was quite intense but the failure of the shipyards and the termination of the concrete barge contract meant the need for large quantities of gravel quickly dwindled and it is thought that trains had ceased to run by the end of 1920, although the junction with the main line was not removed until the end of April 1924. Overall, along with the hastily built shipyards, it must have been an enormous waste of money, albeit spent at a time of huge shipping losses, shortages of steel and a belief that the war would last until 1921 at least. A short section of wooded cutting curving away from the main line at Frocester is the most visible reminder today, much of the route having been ploughed back into the fields over which it ran. The gravel pits, in the area known as Perryway, are now flooded and surrounded by woodland.

LEFT: The station forecourt in 1963. The larger building was the station master's house. For many years it was the only railway building remaining here, albeit hidden from road view behind a large modern industrial unit but, sadly, word was received as this section was being written in June 2019 that it had quietly been demolished. NPC

Another view of the forecourt, with the original Br&GR station building nearest the camera. The unknown photographer was standing with his back to the Nailsworth & Stroud Branch platform, the foot route to which is here marked by a rail, half hidden in the ground, leading from the Down platform exit. NPC

Taken on the same day as a Down train departs on the far left towards Bristol, this is a nice study of the 1867-built shelter on the Up platform. In the background are some of the buildings of the large Hoffman's factory. NPC

OPPOSITE PAGE BOTTOM: BR 'Standard', Class '4' No. 75023, makes spirited progress as it pulls away from Frocester with an Up 'Stopper' on a clear cold day circa 1961. Completed at Swindon in December 1953 and smartly turned out in lined green BR passenger livery, the locomotive was stationed at Gloucester Barnwood for three years, from late summer 1958 to the autumn of 1961, when it transferred away to Templecombe. The train has just passed through the arch of Eastington Road Bridge (No. 83), whilst Frocester station is just about discernible through the arch of the second bridge in the distance. NPC

BRITISH RAILWAY HISTORY IN COLOUR: 4B. GLOUCESTER MIDLAND LINES SOUTH – STONEHOUSE TO WESTERLEIGH   213

BR 'Standard' Class '5' No. 73003 heads south towards Frocester with a Down express circa 1964. New from Derby Works in May 1951, the engine had been reallocated from Shrewsbury to Bristol Barrow Road in September 1963, where it stayed until the summer of 1965 and from where it was withdrawn at the end of WR steam. NPC

BR '9F' No. 92051 heads a southbound mixed freight towards Frocester on 25th July 1964. The view is from Frocester Bridge (No. 82), looking back to Eastington Road Bridge, and the trees on the left obscure the cutting at the start of the long closed Frampton gravel pits branch. In the right background is Bourne House and the adjacent smithy, which had been in use since 1839, although by the time of this view most of the work was apparently on-site farriery, so very little traditional blacksmithing was being carried out there. No. 92051 was based at Kirkby in Ashfield shed, one of several East Midlands allocations since entering service in August 1955. Moving to Newton Heath just over two months after the picture was taken, it was withdrawn from Carlisle Kingmoor in October 1967. TONY BOWLES/COURTESY THE RESTORATION & ARCHIVING TRUST/REF. ARC00272

Right: Looking in the opposite direction from Frocester Bridge, as Saltley-based 'Black Five' No. 45447 starts a four-coach Bristol-Gloucester local away from the Up platform on a damp but sunny evening in 1961. The station closed on 11th December that year and this view is likely to be very close to that date, whilst the train is probably the 9.15am ex-Temple Meads which stopped all stations from Mangotsfield, calling here at 10.20am. Although situated essentially in open countryside when the line was built, the small goods yard was placed on the north side of the station, on a cramped site between the end of the Down platform and the road bridge, neccessitating the use of a wagon turntable to access four short sidings fanning out from it, one of which ran inside the goods shed, whilst another served livestock pens. This antiquated arrangement remained in use to the end, the station closing to both goods and passengers on the same day. No. 45447 was to make it almost to the very end of steam on British Railways, being withdrawn from Rose Grove shed in Lancashire at the beginning of August 1968. JOHN STRANGE/NPC

Below: Almost certainly taken an hour or so later, an unidentified 'Castle' Class 4-6-0 thunders through Frocester Bridge with the Down 'The Cornishman' express, still at this date composed mostly of chocolate and cream liveried stock. Starting from Wolverhampton Low Level at 9.55am, the express called at Cheltenham Malvern Road at 11.02am and then travelled via the Gloucester Avoiding Line, so was due past here at around 11.25am. Plymouth was reached at 3.30pm and the final destination of Penzance at 6.45pm. A couple of steel mineral wagons, no doubt having brought in coal for the local merchant, straddle the wagon turntable. The goods yards at Charfield and Yate were served by similar arrangements, although the former had been removed in 1956. JOHN STRANGE/NPC

A delightful view of a Sunday track gang at work at Frocester on 3rd June 1962, six months after closure. The view is again looking north towards Frocester Bridge, with Eastington Road Bridge visible beyond, shortly after the connection to the goods yard and the four short sidings had been removed, leaving plain track running through the platforms, which were only around four carriages in length. The Brunellian style station building and the waiting shelter on the Up side had both originally been equipped with canopies extending to the platform edges but these had been removed at an unknown date, certainly after 1932 and probably by BR in the early 1950s. The buildings and platforms had all been demolished by 1964, leaving the signal box standing in splendid isolation until it too closed on 11th May 1966 and was removed soon after. The station master's house, a stone building provided some time after the station first opened, is out of sight here off to the right. It remains today, now a private residence and largely hidden from view, as the only reminder of Frocester station's existence. ROY DENISON

No. 1445 works 'light engine' to Berkeley Road to work the Sharpness Branch on 16th April 1964. The picture is taken from what the Midland referred to as Harmer's Mill Bridge (No. 78), half a mile to the south of Frocester station. Incidentally, Harmer's Mill seems to have been an MR misnomer, as the OS names it as Halmore Mill. The property on the left still remains, although has been extended in the intervening years. Looking in the opposite direction today, one would be gazing down on the platforms of Cam & Dursley station, opened on 29th May 1994. No. 1445 was new in April 1935 and spent its career around Worcestershire and Herefordshire, moving to Horton Road on 10th March 1964 for the last six months of its working life. DON MANN

No. 78001 heads north near Coaley with a rake of empty steel mineral wagons in spring 1964. The train has probably come off the Dursley Branch and the location is likely to be alongside the track on the opposite side of the bridge from which the picture above was taken; not on the same occasion though, as the photographer clearly had a different brand of colour film in his camera! DON MANN

Seen from the junction for the Dursley Branch, Class '4F' No. 44591 makes its only appearance in these pages, heading in to Coaley with a Birmingham to Bristol 'stopper' on 13th May 1961. The locomotive was based at Burton-on-Trent, so was some way from home and hence why it is a rare 'cop' for us, but had clearly been pressed in to use by Saltley shed staff to cover this turn. New in October 1939, it had been allocated to Saltley at the time of Nationalisation, moving to Burton in 1954. It was withdrawn from Kirkby in Ashfield in November 1964. MARK B. WARBURTON

BRITISH RAILWAY HISTORY IN COLOUR: 4B. GLOUCESTER MIDLAND LINES SOUTH – STONEHOUSE TO WESTERLEIGH 219

Few railwaymen had any interest in photography or bothered taking a camera to work but an exception was Gilroy Kerr, who was a signalman at Coaley Junction from 1963, taking over from Derek Markey who had moved to Berkeley Road. On this busy main line, Coaley was a three-shift box, open around the clock except for Sundays during the 1960s, closing at 8.00am on the morning of the Sabbath and re-opening at 6.00am on the Monday; in the 1950s it had closed at 1.50pm on a Sunday afternoon. This view of his place of work was taken by Gilroy in 1963 and we shall see more of his pictures over the next few pages and a little further on. Coincidentally, some slides taken in 1983 by ex-Coaley Junction signalman Derek Markey feature in the Sharpness Docks section. The voices of both men can also be heard on Andy Barton's DursleyGlos website, giving short reminiscences about their time in the box, poignant because Derek is no longer with us. INSET TOP: A view along the length of the lever frame, which faced out on to the branch. BOTH GILROY KERR

STONEHOUSE TO COALEY JUNCTION

Photographed from the box on 20th May 1965, signalman Gilroy Kerr noted that this was Down Class '4' short fitted freight, hauled by ex-GWR '28XX' 2-8-0 No. 3816. The train consist appears to be BR containers on 4-wheeled 'Conflat' wagons. No. 3816 was new in March 1940 and was on its final posting to Severn Tunnel Junction shed, with less than two months left in service. GILROY KERR

Gilroy Kerr started as a junior porter at Coaley in 1961. His duties included checking the various lamps at locations such as the signal boxes at Box Road near Cam, Berkeley Road and Frocester, as well as the station lamps at Coaley. He tended to do this work between the last branch train in the morning (10.30am) and the first train in the afternoon (4.00pm), when the engine was at Dursley shunting the yard there. He also helped with shunting at Coaley, making use of the shunting pole. After some time as a senior porter, in September 1962 he moved to Frocester box to learn the art of signalling from an ex-London tube driver in his 70s. In January 1963, he applied for and got the job of signalman at Coaley Junction, taking over the position from Derek Markey, who moved to Berkeley Road. He worked a three-shift rota, 6am-2pm/2pm-10pm/10pm-6am; the box was closed 10pm Saturday until 6am on Monday, unless there was any engineering work in the vicinity. When Coaley box closed in 1968, he moved to Gloucester Central working as a parcel porter (though on signalman's rates) but eventually took redundancy in 1973. He then worked for Lister's in Dursley until retiring in 2007.

ABOVE: We have already seen a couple of pictures of Sharpness Branch locomotives heading 'light engine' to and from work but here we have the signalman's view of 0-4-2T No. 1472 making its way south on 22nd August 1964. As we shall see a little later on, this engine was a regular on the Sharpness Branch at this time and up until the service was withdrawn a few weeks after this picture was taken. GILROY KERR

LEFT: Gilroy's position allowed him to photograph some of the more unusual weekday workings, such as this view of No. 78006, which had paid a visit to the Dursley Branch with the weedkilling train on Thursday 10th June 1965. With the spray apparatus still in operation, the train is seen pulling back out on to the Down main line and may well have then been bound for the Sharpness Branch next. GILROY KERR

RIGHT: Locally named ex-GWR 'Grange' Class 4-6-0 No. 6848 *Toddington Grange* rattles past the box with a Down Class '4' fitted freight on 19th May 1965. New in October 1937, No. 6848 was on its penultimate posting at the date of this view, to Worcester shed, having transferred there from Pontypool Road in January 1964. In November 1965 it was sent to Oxford shed, from where it was withdrawn at the end of WR steam a few weeks later. Toddington Grange was a large manor house at Toddington, north of Winchcombe, which by the 1960s was in use as a school for maladjusted children. A handsome red brick building, it has now been demolished and a small housing estate occupies the site. Incidentally, the small corrugated iron hut in the foreground of all these pictures was the lamp hut – it was not the shed near the station building, that has erroneously been shown elsewhere as being the lamp hut, which was actually provided for the porters. GILROY KERR

STONEHOUSE TO COALEY JUNCTION

As the fireman leans out the cab window, BR 'Standard' Class '4' 2-6-0 No. 76042 restarts an Up local to Gloucester away from Coaley on 9th September 1964. New from Doncaster Works in August 1954, No. 76042's first posting was to the ex-L&NER shed at Neasden. By the date of this view it was another of Saltley's vast complement of engines, moving on to Bescot in March 1965, then Stourbridge Junction and finally Oxley, from where it was withdrawn in late June 1966. GILROY KERR

We saw '9F' No. 92220 *Evening Star* in Volume 4A north of Standish Junction in April 1965 but here it is again at a slightly earlier date. With brasswork still gleaming, the last steam locomotive built by British Railways is about to pass Coaley Junction signal box with the Down working of train No. 4V50, the 10.40am empty Esso tank wagons from Bromford Bridge to Avonmouth, on 13th July 1964. If running to time, the train was due past Gilroy's box at around 1.38pm. GILROY KERR

Looking northwards from the Up platform at Coaley on 4th August 1961, with Class '16XX' 0-6-0PT No. 1605 standing in the Dursley platform having recently arrived from the terminus with the branch shuttle. As the driver climbs down from his cab, the signalman is either posing for or keeping a close eye on the photographer from the end window of his box. Wagons can be seen in both the Up Refuge siding and the Down side headshunt, and note the dip in the line as it heads beneath Harmer's Mill Bridge in the left middle distance. New from Swindon Works at the start of November 1949, No. 1605 moved to Horton Road in October 1957 and was to remain there until withdrawal in February 1962. Designed by F.W. Hawksworth but built by BR after Nationalisation, the small-wheeled '16XV' Class locomotives were a direct replacement for the '2021' Class pannier tanks constructed in the late 19th and early 20th centuries but had very short service lives – one as little as five years – with all seventy of them having gone by 1966. JOHN RYAN

RIGHT: On the same day as the previous view, Class '4F' No. 44165 calls with the 6.23pm Bristol to Birmingham train. The signalman has pulled the Up Starter off but the driver waits for the guard of the freight train held in the Up Refuge siding to make his way safely across the tracks before proceeding. Presumably he had just visited the box for a word with the signalman, perhaps to find out how long his train was going to be held. With luck, they would be following the local once it had cleared the section. This is the second time we have seen No. 44165, as it featured in Volume 4A calling at Eastgate with a southbound 'stopper'. JOHN RYAN

BELOW: Instruction regarding the use of the Up lie-by siding, from the *Sectional Appendix to the Working Time Table, Gloucester District, October 1960*.

COALEY
When a train requires to set back from the Up Main line into the Up Lie-By and has been brought to a stand ahead of the connection from the Main line the Guard or Shunter, or Fireman in the case of a light engine, must pull over the lever which works an indicator in the signal box to show that it is necessary to set the points for the Lie-By and the lever must remain in the pulled position until the train has been shunted into the siding and the Main line is clear.

'Black Five' No. 45222 stands at Coaley with a northbound Bristol to Birmingham 'stopper' on 4th August 1964. The signalman has given the 'off' but the driver is looking back waiting for the guard's flag before starting away. Built by Armstrong, Whitworth & Co. Ltd for the LM&SR in December 1935, No. 45222 was based at Bescot at the date of this view and still had close to three years left in traffic, with allocations to Banbury, Colwick and Newton Heath yet to come, prior to withdrawal in early February 1967. BLAKE PATERSON/COURTESY THE RESTORATION & ARCHIVING TRUST/REF. BPUK0483

BRITISH RAILWAY HISTORY IN COLOUR: 4B. GLOUCESTER MIDLAND LINES SOUTH – STONEHOUSE TO WESTERLEIGH   225

'Jubilee' No. 45656 *Cochrane* heads non-stop through Coaley in August 1962, with train No. 1E60, from Bristol Temple Meads to Sheffield. New in to service from Derby Works on 17th December 1934, the 4-6-0 spent most of the 1950s and early '60s based at Sheffield Millhouses shed, moving to Canklow at the start of 1962. It was transferred back to Sheffield but this time to Darnall shed in mid June 1962, which proved to be its final posting, withdrawal taking place in late December, just over four months after this picture was taken. The photographer had clearly gained permission from the signalman – Gilroy Kerr perhaps? – to walk a little way up the track to take this fine overall view of the junction, his position having been noted by the driver of *Cochrane*. DAVID POLLARD/NPC

LEFT: 'Royal Scot' Class No. 46132 *The King's Regiment Liverpool* coasts through Coaley Junction with a Down express in 1960. New from the North British Locomotive Co. in September 1927, the 4-6-0 was based in London at Kentish Town shed at this date, so was clearly an unexpected sight at this location. It transferred to Saltley in 1961, so would likely then have worked this way again on occasion, before moving north to Carlisle in June 1962, first to Upperby and then across to Kingmoor the following year, from where it was withdrawn in January 1964.

BELOW: Ex-LM&SR 'Crab' 2-6-0 No. 42823 with an Up Bristol to Birmingham 'stopper' on the same day. New in October 1929 the locomotive was based at Saltley shed for the last eight year's of its working life, prior to withdrawal in February 1964. Note the photographer's shadow in the foreground.
BOTH M.E.J. DEANE, COURTESY DR SIMON FOSBURY

BELOW: Situated in the 'Vee' of the junction, the operating floor of the box at Coaley had windows all round, as this view of the rear of it shows. It was opened by the LM&SR on 31st March 1935, which explains its being different in design to the ex-Midland boxes we have seen to date, replacing a Midland box of 1891. In the background, No. 78001 is in the process of leaving the branch with a freight from Dursley. The facing crossover which would have permitted the train to run directly from the branch to the Up main (seen in the picture on page 210, near the rear of the train) had been taken out in October 1963. BILL POTTER/KRM

SECTION 8

THE DURSLEY BRANCH

Looking back at the junction from the front carriage of the branch train, as a connecting Bristol to Birmingham service, headed by Saltley-based '4F' No. 44165, heads away on 4th August 1961. Beyond, a freight waits in the Up Refuge siding for it to pass before proceeding northwards. JOHN RYAN

Unlike its near neighbour the Nailsworth Branch, the Dursley Branch never had any pretensions to be part of a grander through scheme. This was entirely the result of geography, the town of Dursley lying at the head of the short Cam Valley, a deep cleft at the southern end of the Costwold escarpment which precluded any possible extension of the line. In common with Stroud and Nailsworth, the predominant local trade during the 19th century was the woollen industry but, at a time of boom, the Bristol & Gloucester Railway passed by over two miles away from the town. On approaching the Midland Railway with a petition for a station in the town shortly after they had absorbed the Br&GR in 1845, the inhabitants of Dursley were informed that the stations at Frocester or Berkeley Road were close enough to serve their needs.

A public meeting of 1852 resolved to pursue the idea more forcibly, which resulted in the formation of the Dursley & Midland Junction Railway (D&MJR) on 25th May 1855. The route chosen was to run from a new junction on the Midland Railway, almost due south in a fairly straight line following relatively easy terrain for a distance of 2½ miles, serving the village of Cam before reaching a terminus on the north side of Dursley, albeit within easy walking distance of the town centre. Fund raising began, the line having the support of prosperous local mill owners who were desperate for it to be built and John Thornhill Harrison of Frocester Court was brought in to carry out the survey and prepare an estimate of costs. Born in 1815, Harrison was in semi-retirement farming 500 acres of land at Frocester but had worked as assistant engineer to Brunel on the construction of the C&GWUR and Br&GR lines in the 1840s and subsequently as resident engineer on the South Devon Railway, so the tiny little Dursley Company were fortunate indeed to gain the services of so eminent a personage to survey their route.

The D&MJR gained its Act on 25th May 1855, the chairman and deputy being Edward Bloxham and George Lister respectively, the latter being the owner of Rivers Mill, Dursley and the father of Robert Ashton Lister, who set up R.A. Lister & Co. in 1867, a company which was to become synonymous with the branch. Despite the support for the line, finance was always tight and neither the chairman or his deputy, nor the company secretary, ever took any remuneration for their roles. Harrison's initial estimate of £12,000 for construction had to be increased by £2,100 to allow for an additional bridge over a road and due to the opposition of a local landowner, who demanded an exorbitant price for his land. The money raised towards the construction included a sum of £4,000 borrowed from the Midland Railway, indicating from an early stage that the line was almost certainly destined to end up as part of their system but without the hassle of them actually having to build it.

In August 1855, the directors accepted the lowest tender for the

Class '4F' No. 43853 of Gloucester Barnwood shed was probably no stranger to the Dursley Branch but would have been a rare 'cop' here in the summer of 1959 working the passenger service, which was normally in the hands of tank engines. Built by the Midland at Derby in 1918, No. 43853 was at Barnwood from September 1952 to January 1963, when it transferred down to Bath Green Park to work on the Somerset & Dorset line for its last four and a bit months of service. The station was built by the Dursley & Midland Junction Railway Company and thus the building was in a completely different style to all the other Br&GR stations. It did, however, bear a strong family resemblance to the station building at Dursley, although it faced in to the 'Vee' of the lines here at Coaley rather than on to either platform and had been given a flat roofed extension, seen here nearest the camera, by BR shortly after Nationalisation. Interesting motor cars seem also to have been a feature of the station forecourt, as we shall see; on the left here is a 1939 Austin 8hp tourer, with the back-end of a likewise circa 1939 Vauxhall 10hp Model 'H' on the right, the British car industry's very first chassis-less production car. The registration of JL 6395 denotes a Boston, Lincolnshire issue of that year. JOHN CHAMPION/COLOUR-RAIL.

One of the auto-fitted ex-GWR Class '64XX' pannier tanks, No. 6437, poses alongside the branch platform on 4th February 1961, coupled to an ex-LM&SR motor driving brake carriage. Unlike the GWR, the LM&SR did not build auto coaches but simply converted some of their standard 57ft non-corridor stock for this purpose. Sadly the number of this vehicle is not known, so little can be gleaned about its history but it is likely to be of mid-1930s vintage. There is also some lettering on the side which is not discernible. There is no evidence that the branch service was ever a 'Pull & Push' operation, as the LM&SR termed auto trains but I am wondering if this was some sort of trial by Gloucester to run it as an auto or motor service, although no mention could be found in the railway press of the day. No. 6437, which is in the attractive British Railways lined green passenger livery which many of the class were given, was new from Swindon in April 1937 and had been allocated to Horton Road in May 1960, where it stayed until withdrawal in July 1963. ROY DENISON

THE DURSLEY BRANCH

RIGHT AND BELOW: Two views showing No. 1630 arriving at Coaley in the summer of 1961 and then running round its two coach train. These smaller GWR-designed but BR-built pannier tanks had taken over working of the branch passenger services from ex-Midland types in 1956, although as the pictures show, they by know means had exclusive control certainly in the final few years. No. 1630 went new in to service at Horton Road from Swindon Works on 13th January 1951, where it stayed – apart from a couple of very short sojourns, to first Swindon in 1955 and then Worcester in 1961 – until March 1962, when it transferred to Swindon. By the end of that year it had moved to Oxford and it was officially withdrawn in June 1964, although may have been in store for some months prior to that.
BOTH GERALD PEACOCK

LEFT: The Dursley Branch, as shown on the 1961 edition 1 inch OS.

line's construction but the contractor then promptly withdrew and it was awarded instead to H.D. Yateman of Gloucester; work on building the line began almost immediately. The Midland supplied second-hand rails and chairs to assist with the construction and allowed the company access to the the site chosen for the new junction station, which the D&MJR was to build. The intention was to have the line opened as soon as possible for goods traffic, with passenegrs services to follow once the stations were built. Edward Gazzard, who owned the mill named after him near the intended site of the terminus, resigned from the board in order to undertake the construction of the stations.

The Dursley Branch opened for goods on Monday 25th August 1856 but Col. Yolland's inspection on behalf of the Board of Trade three days earlier prevented the line's use for passenger traffic until certain improvements had been made to the signalling arrangements. The official opening to passenger trains duly followed on Wednesday 17th September 1856. The line was to be worked by the Midland and in a further sign of their influence, staff were appointed by them as well, although most were local and followed recommendations by the D&MJR. However, all did not go smoothly in the relationship and, in August 1857, the larger company were given notice to cease working the line, the D&MJR being in a precarious financial state as a result of the charges imposed by the Midland. The company felt that they could work it more cheaply themselves and bought the contractor's 0-4-0 box tank, although they were forced to borrow a pair of 4-wheeled coaches from the Midland to operate the service; the MR also provided goods stock. However, the finances did not improve, not helped by a general recession in trade, so finally, in 1859, the option of selling out to the Midland was pursued. A price was agreed and the bill authorising the takeover was part of a Midland Railway additional powers Act of 28th June 1861, with the formal date of transfer deemed to be 1st January that year.

The line subsequently enjoyed a quiet but reasonably prosperous existence during the later years of the 19th century and through to the 1920s, when, as elsewhere, road transport began to make inroads. Goods traffic stayed healthy, much of it generated by the agricultural engineering firm R.A. Lister & Co. Ltd, which had premises that eventually extended along the western side of the terminus for a distance of around half a mile, from just beyond the buffer stops all the way to the engine shed. Passenger receipts were sufficient for the service to continue long after those on the nearby Nailsworth & Stroud Branch had been withdrawn but they finally succumbed on 10th September 1962, before Dr Beeching's 1963 report on *The Reshaping of Britain's Railways*. By the end, the terminus station at Dursley had become something of an anachronism, almost overwhelmed by Listers factory buildings but the firm were almost single-handedly responsible for the branch remaining open for a few more years. The ending of general goods traffic on 28th June 1968 was followed by the closure of Coaley Junction signal box

LEFT: Another of the '16XX' Class, No. 1605, about to leave for Dursley in May 1961. Although built by Swindon Works in October 1949, the engine;s first allocation, to Southall shed, was not until January 1950. It was then sent to Worcester in September 1953 and arrived at Horton Road in October 1957. Withdrawal from there took place in February 1962.

BELOW: A month later and one of the larger '64XX' Class was in charge of services. New in November 1934, No. 6415 arrived at Horton Road in March 1958, its final posting, withdrawal from there taking place by November 1961. The train is no doubt waiting for any passengers for Cam or Dursley from the Class '4F' hauled Down connecting service arriving at the main line platform.
BOTH M.E.J. DEANE,
COURTESY DR SIMON FOSBURY

on 14th October, after which the line was operated as a long siding to Lister's works. However, they had been gradually switching what was effectively the most profitable traffic over to road and the inevitable end came with the final closure on 11th July 1970.

The British Railways steam era began with two ex-Midland Class '1F' 0-6-0 tanks still in charge, No's 41720 and 41727, which lasted until 1956. They were replaced on passenger duties by Western Region, BR-built Class '16XX' pannier tanks, whose small wheels were ideally suited to the branch, whilst '2F', '3F' and, occasionally, '4F' 0-6-0s handled the goods traffic, sometimes appearing too on a passenger duty. Latterly, larger '64XX' and '74XX' 0-6-0PTs were used on passenger trains, whilst for the final few months Class '46XXX' 2-6-0 tender engines covered most passenger and goods duties. An '82XXX' was a rare visitor in 1965, with a pair of Ivatt Class '2MT' 2-6-0s in charge by then. After steam had finished, North British diesels and 'D95XX' diesel-hydraulic 0-6-0s worked the goods traffic of the final years.

The main visible relic of the branch today is the old goods shed at Coaley Junction, in commercial use but Grade II listed. The concrete viaduct over the River Cam still stands but nothing remains of Cam station, where Station Road still crosses the old route. Dursley station was obliterated by factory development as Listers expanded further. However, following a protracted period of upheaval from 1986, caused by ownership changes and declining sales, the factory itself closed completely in 2014, as the remaining production was moved to a new site near Gloucester. The works has now been completely erased, its vast site being redeveloped for residential, commercial and social use. At the northern extremity, where the branch arrived at the station, the new Vale Community Hospital now straddles the route and nearby, the old metal footbridge over the track is perhaps the most remarkable survivor of all and cries out for preserving.

THE DURSLEY BRANCH

The '74XX' Class were almost identical to the '64XX' 0-6-0 pannier tanks but with a higher pressure boiler and they were not auto fitted. No's 7400 to 7429 were all built at Swindon Works in 1936-37 but the rest of the class, No's 7430 to 7449, were completed by BR, between 1948 and 1950. No. 7435, seen here running round its train at Coaley, emerging in September 1948. It was noted as being one of three of the class (along with No's 7436 and 7437) that were very late in being fitted with smokebox numberplates, which was not until at least 1958 and maybe even later. Not being auto-fitted, the BR-built members of the class remained in the standard unlined black livery in which they were first turned out. The picture is undated but must have been taken between mid January and early July 1962, which is when it was allocated to Horton Road. It then moved away to Stourbridge Junction and finally to Aberdare, from where it was withdrawn in July 1964. The train had clearly deposited a number of passengers who were now waiting on the Up main platform for a train to Gloucester. NPC

BRITISH RAILWAY HISTORY IN COLOUR: 4B. GLOUCESTER MIDLAND LINES SOUTH – STONEHOUSE TO WESTERLEIGH

A second view of No. 6415 waiting to leave. Note that the short platform could barely accommodate the two coaches that made up most branch services. Although Barnwood shed was ostensibly responsible for the operation of all passenger trains on the ex-Midland lines around Gloucester, from around 1956 the Dursley branch services were worked by ex-GWR and BR/WR types supplied by Horton Road, although they were generally shedded at Barnwood; the Sharpness Branch followed suit in 1960, after the accident to the Severn Bridge. The car on the left is a circa 1946 Hillman Minx Mark 1, a model which ran from late 1939 to late 1947, whilst the moped in front looks to be a French Mobylette of circa 1958; Raleigh later licence-built the design in the UK. The car belonged to the photographer; Maurice Deane was a bank manager with a passion for trains but who had early on realised that lines such as this were unsustainable economically and thus made it his mission to visit and photograph as many as possible. The small porters hut in the centre of the picture, with its decorative barge boards, was a Midland Railway addition, the boards matching those to be found on the Up platform waiting shelter. M.E.J. DEANE, COURTESY DR SIMON FOSBURY

THE DURSLEY BRANCH

Rather strangely, for the last few months of the passenger service, it was handed over to a pair of BR-built Ivatt Class '2MT' 2-6-0s, No's 45626 and 45627, which were in fact the last two of the class built, at Swindon in March 1953. No. 45627 poses beside the grass grown loop and sidings on 7th July 1962. Parked on the left is a circa 1952 Triumph Mayflower, a 'small luxury' car notable for its razor edge styling but which was discontinued in 1953 as it was not a great sales success. COLOUR-RAIL

No. 46526 waits for departure in July 1962. The engine spent six months at Barnwood shed, from March to September 1962, transferring away then to Oswestry. It was withdrawn from Saltley shed in July 1966. In the forecourt on the left is a circa 1959 Ford Prefect 100E model, whilst the delightful relic to its right is a circa 1936-37 Riley Kestrel or Merlin. The WF registration denotes Wakefield in Yorkshire as its town of origin. Note the brake van on the right again, seemingly something of a permanent fixture here. JOHN CHAMPION/COLOUR-RAIL

LEFT: Latterly, weekday services were generally operated with just a single coach, for which the Ivatts were clearly overpowered but still used. Here, on Friday 25th May 1962, No. 46527 waits to head back to Dursley with a service which could more conveniently and cheaply be provided by a bus service and, indeed, soon would be. The two Ivatts arrived at and departed Barnwood together, with No. 46527 also heading to Oswestry but the engine then finished its career at Bescot, near Walsall, in October 1965. NPC

ABOVE: A young lad watches sister engine No. 45626, splendidly turned out in full BR lined green passenger livery, backing on to its short train after running round following arrival on 30th August 1962. B.J. ASHWORTH

RIGHT: Seen from across the grass grown loop and siding, No. 45626 makes ready for its next departure in the summer of 1962. The presence of the Triumph Mayflower again on the left would indicate that the car could have been a regular here – did it perhaps belong to one of the station staff or the signalmen?
DAVID POLLARD/NPC

THE DURSLEY BRANCH

RIGHT: On 3rd September 1962, photographer Mark Warburton paid a visit to the branch to record the passenger service a week before its demise and his sequence of pictures showing the arrival and running round of No. 46527 at Coaley merits reproducing here in full. Despite this being a Saturday, the single coach still sufficed for passengers, the train being strengthened only by the addition of a van for extra parcels traffic. The rear of a Royal Mail Morris Minor post van just creeps in to view on the right.

OPPOSITE PAGE TOP: The wide angle of this view shows the rear of the station building in full again, with its flat-roofed, early 1950s BR-built extension. A white Fiat Nuova 500 and a Morris Mini Minor stand in the station forecourt, the latter's 147 NHY numberplate indicating that it was first registered in Bristol.

OPPOSITE PAGE BOTTOM: This delightful view showing the group of 6-8 year olds taking turns to look in the cab completes the sequence. Too young to appreciate that the age of steam was rapidly coming to a close, at their age the ambition to be a 'train driver' would still have been to the fore, a thought that would baffle today's technology obsessed younger generation.
ALL MARK B. WARBURTON

ABOVE: No. 46527 runs round its train, a move that was signalled by the ground disc in the centre of the picture. Note that there was another ground disc for Up direction movements at the other end of the loop.

RIGHT: Now backed on to its train again, a small crowd of excited young boys converge on No. 46527 to get a glimpse of the footplate – there would be few, if any, chances to do this in the future. Note that the coach, a suburban brake composite, has its luggage doors open almost certainly for the Royal Mail bags, so the box van is likely to have been for Listers traffic.

BRITISH RAILWAY HISTORY IN COLOUR: 4B. GLOUCESTER MIDLAND LINES SOUTH – STONEHOUSE TO WESTERLEIGH 237

THE DURSLEY BRANCH

ABOVE: A very unusual visitor on 10th June 1965 was BR 'Standard' Class '3' 2-6-2T No. 82040, on the Gloucester to Dursley freight. The fireman is about to rejoin his engine after visiting the box to make tea, a perk of branch line life. New in to service on 19th May 1955, No. 82040 had spent much of its career moving round all three of the Bristol sheds – Bath Road, Barrow Road and St. Philips Marsh – but then had eighteen months down on Southern Region territory from October 1963, at Exmouth Junction. Sent back north to Horton Road in late May 1965 and despite looking in fine fettle here, the engine had only three weeks of service left, being withdrawn at the start of July. Note the shunter's pole hung on the rear bufferbeam. GILROY KERR

INSET RIGHT: This snapshot was taken for the driver, whose daughter had gone up on to the footplate with him. GILROY KERR

LEFT: Whilst at Coaley photographing the ex-SR 'Merchant Navy' Class 'Spam Can' on 13th September 1967 (page 279), Bill also captured North British Class '22' No. D6329 of Bristol Bath Road shed returning with the branch goods. Placed in to service on 18th June 1960, the Bo-Bo's short career came to an end when withdrawn from Newton Abbot shed on 30th November 1968. Sadly, whilst the front of the engine was sharp, the rest image was a touch blurred. BILL POTTER/KRM

BELOW: We begin our journey along the branch with this view of No. 6415 heading past the goods yard bound for Dursley in June 1961. There is little sign of any traffic other than coal for the local merchant, some piled on the ground and some being unloaded directly from a steel mineral wagon. Whilst this long standing practice was a handy way of loading sacks of coal for delivery, it was also a grossly inefficient use of BR's wagon fleet, quite unlike today's policy of 'sweating the assets'! The goods shed, to a standard Midland Railway design, still survives and is Grade II listed. It post-dates the opening of the line and is likely to have been provided in the 1860s, possibly as a replacement for an earlier temporary shed. In the foreground is the weighbridge and attendant hut which stood near the entrance of the lengthy road leading in to the station. M.E.J. DEANE, COURTESY DR SIMON FOSBURY

THE DURSLEY BRANCH

LEFT: No. 6415 hurries towards Cam with the 8.25am train from Coaley on 22nd October 1959, the driver giving the photographer a wave as they head by. The train has just crossed Cam Viaduct (No. 1) near Draycott, which carried the line over the River Cam. It had been replaced by the pre-cast concrete structure seen here in 1948 after the original timber viaduct had become unsafe, the local ganger apparently refusing to take responsibility for it any longer. Intriguingly, the *Midland Bridge Register* notes the timber trestle structure as being *'filled up August, 1895'* but, as it crossed a farm access, footpath and the river, that cannot have been the case and, indeed, the 25 inch OS maps do not support that statement. In the background is a glimpse of Coaley Road crossing, which was protected by a ground frame and signals brought in to use on 29th March 1938. The road was later renamed Box Road but the plaque on the ground frame hut was not changed. B.J. ASHWORTH

BELOW: A lovely panoramic view over the lush agricultural land to the north of the line, which remains undeveloped and unspoilt – apart from the pylons! – today. No. 46526 heads over the River Cam viaduct bound for the junction with its two-coach train in May 1962. JOHN CHAMPION/COLOUR-RAIL

RIGHT: Viewed from the carriage window, the 5.25pm early evening train from Coaley enters Cam behind No. 1607 on 4th August 1961, the guard giving a wave to someone at the crossing. JOHN RYAN

BELOW: In bright but crisp early morning sunshine, No. 1630 produces a fine head of smoke and steam as it starts away from Cam with the 8.30am to Dursley on 10th October 1959. Although the station opened with the line on 17th September 1856, the building was a later addition, which explains why it bore no resemblance to those at Coaley and Dursley, the barge boards giving the clue as to its Midland origins. Presumably D&MJR finances did not stretch to the erection of a building here initially or perhaps a temporary wooden structure was provided. The building is thought to date from the 1860s and is likely to be contemporary with the goods shed at Coaley. Hunt & Winterbotham's Cam Mills private siding behind the platform did not run in to the goods shed and was to be removed fifteen days after this picture was taken. The vehicle standing there appears to be a lorry trailer. The goods shed was also a later addition; it does not feature on the 1881 25 inch OS but is present on the 1901 edition. Note the end of it was covered in a protective layer of black roofing felt. In the right background beyond the crossing, a steel mineral wagon and a box van occupy the station siding. B.J. ASHWORTH

Level crossing pictures are almost always fascinating, full of interest and intensely nostalgic, a reminder for many of us of the road/railway interface as it used to be. In the summer of 1962, No. 46527 straddles Station Road Crossing, Cam blocking it completely whilst paused at the station with a service for Coaley. The cars waiting patiently for the gates to be opened are standing on a bridge spanning the River Cam. At the back of the queue is a Ford 8hp Model 7Y, which was only produced from August 1937 for two years. The ENC 111 number indicates that its first registration was in Manchester circa April/May 1938. The van at the front of the queue looks as though it may be a circa 1952 Austin A40. Standing in this same spot today, little remains of the railway but the scene is otherwise very recognisable. The brick building behind No. 46527's tender was part of what at this date was a large bakery, and dated from around 1890. Shown as disused on the 1972 25 inch OS, the buildings have since been refurbished, the brickwork rendered and are agin in commercial use. The red brick bridge parapets and the wall on the right all still stand and the house visible through the smoke in the centre background still gazes down on to Station Road. ROY DENISON

The pedestrian entrance on to the station platform on Saturday 8th September 1962, the last day of the passenger service; official closure was on and from Monday 10th but there was no Sunday service. The 'PUBLIC NOTICE' on the board on the right announces the details of the withdrawal of the branch passenger service; there would be no more excursions by rail from Cam to Weston-super-Mare. In 1938, the LM&SR decided to improve the signalling on the line and as well as the aforementioned ground frame cabin at Coaley Road Crossing, another was provided here at Cam, along with an enormous lattice post bracket signal which carried just one arm. Cam Station Frame cabin had a 5-lever frame, which operated the Home signals either side of the crossing and also locked the gates, the latter being opened and closed by the station staff, which in the final years comprised just one man. The small building on the right was the porters office, which in later years was used only by the local pw gang. Also of note here are the stay wires required to hold the signal steady against any high winds, the gas lamp by the entrance gate and the ubiquitous 'YOU MAY TELEPHONE FROM HERE' blue enamelled sign half hidden by the noticeboard. NPC

THE DURSLEY BRANCH

RIGHT: A close-up of Cam Station Frame cabin on 8th September 1962, with a glimpse of the inside and the small 5-lever frame and instrument panel. It was taken out of use on 5th April 1964, crews thereafter being responsible for opening and closing the gates, for which trains had to come to a dead stop first anyway. The chimney indicates that the box was fitted with a small stove. NPC

BELOW: A view showing the full height of the lattice post bracket Up Home signal in 1962. The published histories of the branch mention two of the levers in the box as operating Distant signals, which seems a little unlikely and I have seen no views of the station which show any. The bracket does not appear to have ever hed a Distant arm. ROY DENISON

BELOW RIGHT: BR 'Standard' Class '3' 2-6-2T No. 82036 rattles over the level crossing with the RCTS Gloucestershire Rail Tour of 21st July 1963, that we saw previously on the Nailsworth and Stroud Branch. The train is waved through by the sole remaining member of the Cam station staff, who had secured the gates for its passage. NPC

ABOVE: A small group of local lads, who would all be in their mid to late sixties by now, watch No. 6415 arriving at Cam with a Down passenger service in June 1960. A coal wagon stands on the station siding beyond the crossing. In the 19th century, Mr Thomas, the local coal merchant, had owned wagons lettered with his name and the business traded up until the 1930s. The buildings of Steel & Sons Ltd's bakery can be seen again in the right background, complete with their nameboard above the window. As mentioned all these buildings survive today, still with their Roman tile roofs. In the ground frame cabin, the Cam porter-cum-signalman can just be made out, no doubt about to return the arm of the Down Home signal to danger. He will then unlock the gates and re-open them to road traffic before waving the train away to Dursley. A poster for trips to Weston-super-Mare can again be seen on the left.
M.E.J. DEANE, COURTESY DR SIMON FOSBURY

ABOVE: An overall view of the two-coach platform and buildings at Cam circa 1961, which is sadly slightly out of focus in the left foreground. The siding was clearly in regular use. Points to note include the gas lamp on the platform, the wooden station nameboard, with the name repeated on a smaller board on the goods shed and on the seat backs, and the colourful spray of flowers in front of the shed. This had doors opening on to the platform and to Hunt & Winterbotham's Cam Mills and may have been provided specifically for the firm's use. The station siding was taken out in April 1964. NPC

RIGHT: The sad scene at Cam on 30th June 1965, with all of the buildings having been demolished, although the nameboard still remained. No. 78001 heads towards Dursley, the fireman climbing back on the footplate having opened the gates. The train will shortly pause again for the guard to close them. BILL POTTER/KRM

Between Cam and Dursley the line ran parallel for a short distance to a road named simply Everlands and part way along a metal footbridge carried a footpath from Sandpits to St. George's church over the railway. Providing a useful vantage point, photographer John Champion took this classic view from the steps of the bridge of the branch passenger train heading to Dursley behind No. 46526 in May 1962 and passing the Fixed Distant signal for Cam. Much development has taken place in this area over the intervening years and much of the footpath no longer exists but, amazingly, the footbridge still stands, albeit out of use and overgrown, the section of the path that it carried now crossing the trackbed alongside it on the level. Surely the bridge merits conserving as a memento of a branch line that provided over a hundred years of service to its local community? Apart from tree growth where the line ran, this section of Everlands road has changed little since the picture was taken. JOHN CHAMPION/COLOUR-RAIL

Looking the opposite way from the steps up to the footbridge, pannier tank No. 6415 hurries a two-coach Up train back to the junction in June 1960. Even with the stop at Cam, the journey only took nine minutes, so with a good connection at Coaley, the trip to Gloucester might only take three quarters of an hour. It was to be the motor car ultimately that the train could not compete with. M.E.J. DEANE, COURTESY DR SIMON FOSBURY

Mark Warburton also found the footbridge a useful vantage point and took a very similar view to John Champion's of No. 45627 approaching on 3rd September 1962 with a single coach and box van. However, he then swung round to capture the 'going away' shot of the train as it ran alongside Everlands towards Quag Bridge, which spanned Church Road; a Ford Anglia can be seen turning towards Dursley having just passed through. Note the driver glancing back to have his photograph taken. To the left, on the north side of the line and the far side of Church Road, had once stood Bennett's Mill, a corn mill that was served by a private siding which had opened with the branch but was removed in 1909; the mill was demolished by 1920. MARK B. WARBURTON

BRITISH RAILWAY HISTORY IN COLOUR: 4B. GLOUCESTER MIDLAND LINES SOUTH – STONEHOUSE TO WESTERLEIGH 249

RIGHT: Bill Potter used the same viewpoint for this shot of No. 78001 heading through with the Dursley goods on 12th May 1965. The wooden building in the distance half hidden by the signal post was the local scout hut and it too remains today as the home of the 1st Cam Scout Group. The footbridge dated from 1955, being a BR replacement for a timber footbridge which had to be demolished when a boy fell through the rotten wooden decking. BR fortunately made a photographic record of the old bridge before it was demolished and its appearance can perhaps best be discerned from its local nickname of 'The Gallows', although this may have been a derivation of its official name as given in the *MR Gloucester District Bridge Register* as Gallops' Footbridge (No. 6).
BILL POTTER/KRM

LEFT: An echo of a much earlier age, as ex-Midland Railway Johnson Class '2F' No. 58165 steams carefully over the wooden span of Quag Bridge on 14th March 1958. The locomotive was built for the MR in Glasgow by Neilson, Reid & Co. Ltd in May 1876, so was only twenty years younger than the branch line it was traversing. Originally MR '1142' Class No. 1224, it became No. 2992 during the company's 1907 renumbering and then No. 58165 under BR. It left Barnwood shed in December 1958 and was withdrawn in September 1960. At some stage it was fitted with vacuum brakes and carriage warming equipment for hauling passenger trains. B.J. ASHWORTH

RIGHT: Pannier tank No. 6415 approaches Quag Bridge with a Down passenger service on 29th August 1959, as a competing Bristol Omnibus Co. service climbs up Everlands in the left background. To its right the iron footbridge can just be made out along with the Cam Distant signal. The two histories of the branch state that the official name for the span was 'Littleham' (Maggs) or 'Littlecombe' (Carpenter) Bridge and that Quag Bridge was how it was referred to by locals. However, the *MR Gloucester District Bridge Register* proves otherwise and that Quag Bridge (No. 7) was in fact its official name. The Littlecombe Valley is the name for the area to the north-east of Dursley town centre, which was largely occupied by Listers engineering works, although it does not appear on any OS maps of any period but it is now perpetuated in the name of a new residential development near the top end of Long Street, close to the site of the terminus. BILL POTTER/KRM

Yet another wonderfully nostalgic study, for which the photographer must have blessed his incredible good fortune. The driver of No. 46526 leans nonchalantly out of his cab to watch Bristol Omnibus Company single decker registration number 527 JHU about to squeeze beneath Quag Bridge en route to Gloucester with service No. 26 on 4th August 1962. The published histories make another claim for the bridge which the *MR Gloucester District Bridge Register* disproves – as seen here it did not date from the opening of the line but had been reconstructed in 1891, which makes it something of a surprise that a timber span was once again used. Carrying the line over Church Road, the site of the bridge was obliterated soon after closure when the road junction was enlarged but the houses in the background still remain. BILL POTTER/KRM

BRITISH RAILWAY HISTORY IN COLOUR: 4B. GLOUCESTER MIDLAND LINES SOUTH – STONEHOUSE TO WESTERLEIGH 251

No. 6415 takes water standing on the main line of the branch, which ran perilously close to Dursley engine shed, on 29th August 1959. The shed lay around a quarter of a mile on from Quag Bridge but was some way short of the terminus and was nowhere near as modern as it appears from this view. In a classic example of careful housekeeping, the building was bought in 1856 for a sum of £270, possibly through the local connections of the line's surveyor John T. Harrison; it would appear to have been an outbuilding of the nearby brewery which operated here at that date and was almost certainly originally used to house the contractor's engine when the line was being built. In red brick with a slated roof, it had an arched entrance with wooden doors but was rebuilt as seen here, with a square entrance and a concrete lintel, some time after 1936 and possibly in the early years of the BR era circa 1950. Overlooked in later years by a new Listers factory, it was a sub-shed to Gloucester Barnwood, coded 22B by BR and closed on the same day that the passenger service was withdrawn. BILL POTTER/KRM

No. 6415 eases away from the tank after filling up with water in June 1960. The Southern Region-style hut built from pre-fabricated concrete panels probably housed the pumping equipment for the water tank. This was pumped up from the nearby River Cam, which flowed just to the north (right) of the line and also supplied water, via a succession of leats and reservoirs, to the various mills ranged along the valley, as well as to the adjacent Dursley Steam Brewery. This latter is shown on the 25 inch OS maps of 1880 and 1903 but most of the buildings had been demolished by 1920. Bought from Messrs King & Worsey by Thomas William Elvy in 1899, a succession of poor financial decisions led to him being declared bankrupt in 1906. It is also rumoured that the ales produced by Elvy were poor. The brewery itself failed to sell at auction in 1907 and would appear never to have functioned again. The property in the background, possibly originally the brewery manager or owner's house (although Elvy did not live there), would appear to be the only building that survived being demolished but, along with everything else here, is no more today. A coal stage was also positioned here, just out of sight on the left. M.E.J. DEANE, COURTESY DR SIMON FOSBURY

No. 78001 takes water whilst standing on the running line alongside the disused engine shed on 30th June 1965. Clearly maintenance on the shed had ceased nearly three years previously and the roof was deteriorating quite noticeably. Access to the shed had been controlled by a ground frame comprising a single lever mounted on a wooden platform with a large nameboard reading Dursley Engine Shed Siding, which was closed when the siding was lifted on 27th July 1964. In the background, behind the water tank, is one of the gas holders of the Dursley Gas Company's works, which had opened in 1836 and was served by a private siding that had been lifted in 1961. Coal gas production had ceased in 1948, however, so the siding had probably seen little use afterwards, with the holders subsequently being used for storage. The original two gas holders were sited a couple of hundreds yards further west but only one of these remained by the date of this view, the holder seen here being built probably circa 1945. Nothing now remains of the works. BILL POTTER/KRM

Around 100 yards further east of the engine shed, a siding branched off to the north side of the line serving Listers works, access to it being controlled from a ground frame named Listers Siding and in this view, taken on the same day as the previous picture, No. 78001 appears to have just deposited two loaded coal wagons at the entrance to it. Brought in to use on 17th March 1930, it served the westwards extension of the works that paralleled the line to just past the engine shed but Cooke lists the ground frame as being taken out on 5th April 1964 and the rails do not look used so it is not quite clear what actually is happening. The locomotive would first have taken its train to Dursley, where it would have shunted the yard as required but then, having run round these two wagons, has brought them down the branch to here. The locomotive has then presumably gone to take water, as shown in the previous picture, before returning for the wagons but quite where they were bound for is not at all clear. On passing through the gated entrance to the works, the line had served two sidings to the east, with a kick-back line heading west to a loop siding running parallel to the running line, behind the fence on the right. BILL POTTER/KRM

RIGHT: Not the greatest of pictures taken during the visit of the of the RCTS Tour to the terminus on 21st July 1963 but included here because it shows Dursley Station ground frame, with its enormous nameboard that took up most of the front of the cabin. It was in the process of being recorded on *ciné* film – does any reader recognise the cameraman and has his film ever been issued on video or DVD? The ground frame was taken out of use on 25th June 1968, when operations for the final two years were reduced to using the goods yard sidings only. NPC

LEFT: From ground level, No. 78006 is seen running round its train at Dursley on 30th July 1965. Bill Potter's panoramic view on pages 258-59 was taken from up on the hillside, by the houses on the skyline above the tender, and I suspect that this slide was also originally one of his, which he must have swapped at some stage. G. PARRY COLLECTION/COLOUR-RAIL

BELOW: A few years earlier, on 1st March 1961, pannier tank No. 1630 was photographed from a similar spot, running round after arriving with a passenger service. This involved reversing out of the platform once all the passengers had got off and then uncoupling from the carriages, drawing forward and then using the loop to run round to the other end. The train would then shunt back in to the platform to await the next departure time, bunker-first, back to the junction. Note the Dursley Station ground frame cabin had only three sides, being open to the elements at this end. M.J. READE/COLOUR-RAIL

THE DURSLEY BRANCH

No. 46527 simmers gently after arriving at the terminus on 3rd September 1962. MARK B. WARBURTON

At the other end of the train, the guard and porter load a consignment of metal containers in to the box van. The acar behind the station building is a Riley '1.5', registration No. XDG 707 – Gloucester in late 1959. This was an upgraded, more luxurious and sporty version of the Wolseley 1500 from BMC. MARK B. WARBURTON

A fine view of the yard looking west from the end of the platform, with No. 46527 in the process of running round its train having first backed it out of the platform. The porter, having used the Train Staff and Key to unlock, set and then reset the point in the foreground operated by the Station ground frame, is now walking the length of the loop to the Goods Yard ground frame, to unlock and operate the point at the far end. On the left, Listers power station can be seen just beyond the timber sheds. The sidings were clearly in need of a visit by the weedkilling train. MARK B. WARBURTON

On 30th July 1965, Bill Potter returned to Dursley to capture this splendid panorama of BR 'Standard' Class '2' No. 78006 shunting the yard. The locomotive is standing on the siding straddled by the wooden goods shed that was provided in 1914, probably to cater for Listers ever expanding traffic which the existing shed, hidden here by the large tree, would have been too small to cope with. Just to the right of the tree can be seen the twin gabled roof of Listers power house, which was also rail served and accessed by the Goods Yard ground frame. The view from this point today has changed out of all recognition and of the infrastructure that forms the main focus of the picture – the railway and Listers distinctive factory building of circa 1908-09, with its extensive saw-toothed roof – nothing now remains. Part hidden in the trees on the left can be seen 'The Towers', the red-brick mansion built in the early 1890s for Robert Ashton Lister, the founder of R.A. Lister & Co., from where he could gaze down upon his empire. The octagonal tower at the north-west corner of the building is topped by a belvedere visible from most parts of the town. The building has recently been renovated as residential apartments for retired folk and renamed 'The Woodlands'. BILL POTTER/KRM

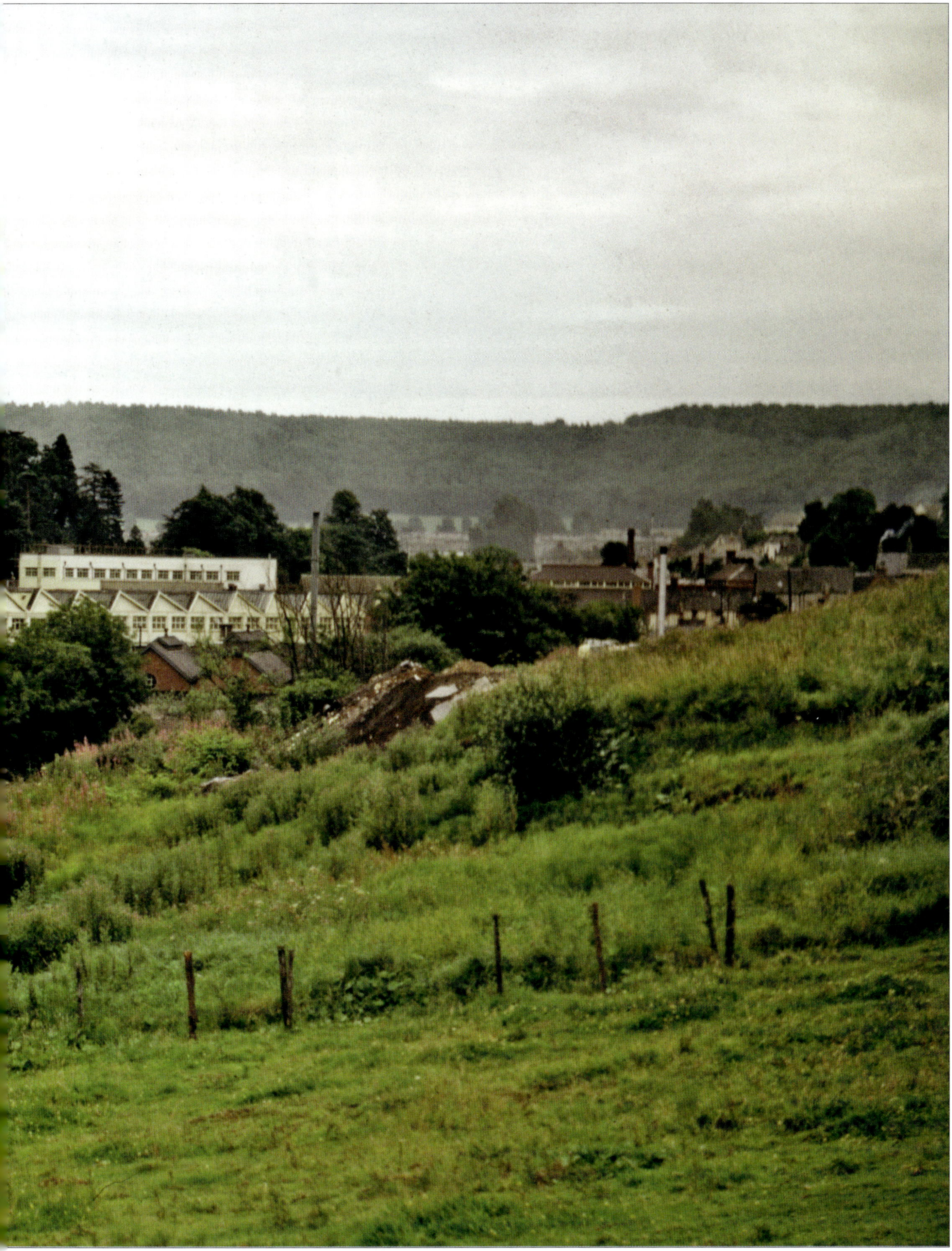

Having first run round its train, No. 78006 is seen shunting the wagons in to the middle siding in Dursley yard. I'm inclined to think that this is another slide originally taken by Bill Potter. The creosoted timber goods shed in the right distance was the one first provided here, later supplemented by the larger shed seen in the previous picture. The closed doors suggest that it may have been out of use by this date, as were the cattle pens behind the platform, served by the short siding coming off the end of the run round loop. Note what appears to be a section of a very old carriage body by the shed. COLOUR-RAIL

BRITISH RAILWAY HISTORY IN COLOUR: 4B. GLOUCESTER MIDLAND LINES SOUTH – STONEHOUSE TO WESTERLEIGH 261

LEFT: Almost every description of Dursley station that you read begins along the lines of '... *the terminus was on a very cramped site*' and this selection of views illustrates that fact very well. There was room only for a single line in front of the platform, so as mentioned, the run-round loop was alongside the goods yard. In point of fact this had not always been the case, the station as built originally having a very short loop opposite the platform, off which a siding ran to a saw mill. With the loop probably too short to be of much use as carriages got longer, the Midland significantly rearranged the track layout circa 1890 and Listers later built storage sheds, seen here on the left, on the land freed up. No. 1605 is seen reversing out prior to running round its train on 4th August 1961. JOHN RYAN

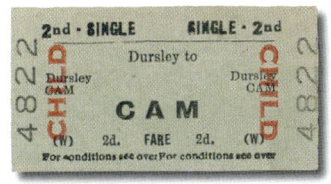

LEFT: A short while later, the crew of No. 1605 pose for the photographer as they wait for departure time to arrive for their next run to Coaley with the 7.05pm service. The locomotive's bunker is fully loaded with coal, suggesting that they had restocked from the coal stage alongside the water tank. As well as a few passengers, the train would also be carrying the evening mails from the town and surrounds, being loaded aboard from the bright red Royal Mail Morris Minor van parked on the platform. JOHN RYAN

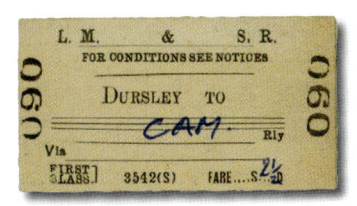

RIGHT. A few days later, on 12th August 1961, John Phillips paid a visit to Dursley, finding No. 1630 in charge of services and here waiting to make the return journey. From this angle it can be seen that the short platform – around three bogie carriages in length – was not just curved it was 'S' shaped and although from the pictures, showing the encroaching local industry, that might seem to make sense, it is actually quite odd when once considers that the station was built on a virgin site. Was this stylish shape an aesthetic detail by architect John Harrison perhaps? The fact that the livestick pens had not been used for some time would seem to be confirmed by the rake of container wagons that had been parked in the bay for at least a week. JOHN PHILLIPS/NPC

THE DURSLEY BRANCH

RIGHT: Seen from the buffer stops at the end of the line, three local lads – one holding the obligatory stick with which those of us who enjoyed rural childhoods could not be without – gaze upon No. 6415 standing at the terminus. The date of the picture is given as 1956 but is in fact a little later than that; when the two ex-Midland Johnson Class '1F' tank engines were retired in August that year it was Class '16XX' 0-6-0PTs that took over first. The date is post March 1958, when No. 6415 was first allocated to Horton Road and may even be a couple of years after that – we have seen the engine several times already on the branch in 1961. J.M. CHAMNEY/COLOUR-RAIL

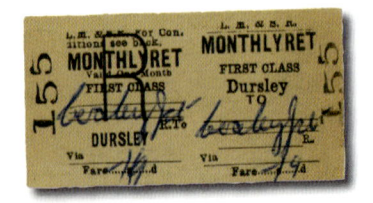

LEFT: No. 1632 waits at the terminus with the single coach forming the 5.56pm to Coaley a few days before closure in early September 1962. Listers works had expanded round the terminus to practically squeeze it out of sight of the town by the end and it is little surprise that the company quickly engulfed the site once BR finally closed it completely in 1970. No. 1632 was new from Swindon Works on 23rd January 1951, going to straight to Horton Road shed. It is recorded as being sent to Shrewsbury in May 1962 and then on to Croes Newydd, near Wrexham, in early July, so it seems a little surprising to see it back in Gloucestershire a couple of months later. However, Paul Strong was normally quite careful with his dates and I have no reason to belive that the information he appended to the slide is wrong. PAUL STRONG/NPC

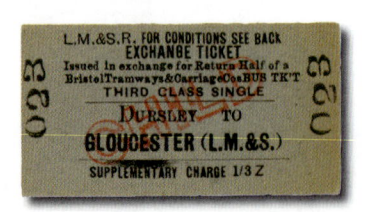

RIGHT: A view of the platform line without a train but with photographers swarming all around, giving a clue to the date, the picture being taken on the day of the RCTS Tour. The train was in the loop with the locomotive in the process of running round, which was facilitated by the removal of the buffet car at Coaley Junction, as the loop could only hold a maximum of five carriages. The hemmed in location made photography difficult, particularly with the early slow speed colour films, as the light rarely reached down to the running line. NPC

STONEHOUSE TO WESTERLEIGH   263

LEFT: With a very youthful looking fireman on the footplate, No. 6415 waits to depart from the terminus in June 1960.
M.E.J. DEANE, COURTESY DR SIMON FOSBURY

BELOW: A second visit to the branch in June 1962 saw No. 46526 in the platform at Dursley, with staff loading parcels in to the box van attached to the single coach for passengers.
M.E.J. DEANE, COURTESY DR SIMON FOSBURY

BOTTOM: The passenger service for the Dursley Branch, from the *Working Time Table of Passenger Trains, Gloucester District, 12th June to 10th September 1961.*

ABOVE: A passenger inside the coach watches the photographer with interest, as a couple of young enthusiasts seated on the platform bench discuss the finer merits of No. 46526. There seems to be an inordinate number of chalked instructions on the side of the box van, whilst the goods yard in the background looks busy with wagons and a brake van has been parked out of the way in the platform bay.
M.E.J. Deane, courtesy Dr Simon Fosbury

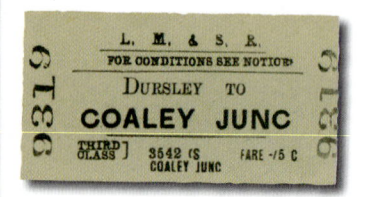

LEFT: The freight service for the Dursley Branch, from the *Working Time Table of Freight Trains, Gloucester District, 12th June to 10th September 1961*. There were three round trips a day and two on Saturdays, with an extra weekdays trip that ran only to Workman's Mill and back.

Time for a chat at Dursley on 30th June 1965, with the station platform being used to load vans that have been shunted in to place by No. 78001. The terminus was not signalled, so no signal box was ever provided, all points being operated by ground frames. Slightly confusingly, a photograph from an earlier period shows that the ground frame here, which operated the east end of the loop, was also named Dursley Station. It had to be unlocked by the train crew before the points could be changed and, in the foreground, it can be seen that the silver coloured Train Staff and Key has been inserted to facilitate this. On the left, there is a glimpse of the original goods shed and the weighbridge hut through the wooden fence at the rear of the livestock platform, whilst Listers factory buildings opposite the station housed their churn and woodware works. BILL POTTER/KRM

A closer view of No. 78001 and its train of box vans being loaded from the platform. BILL POTTER/KRM

A month later, on 30th July, No. 78006 was photographed shunting more box vans in to position to be loaded at the platform. The fact that all parts of the station were being used to load Listers goods suggests a considerable amount of traffic was being generated at this date. BILL POTTER/KRM

Bearing in mind the comment a little earlier about the difficulties of photographing the terminus, this delightful colour view of the station lit up by evening sunshine was a most fortuitous acquisition. It may again have been taken on the day of the RCTS Tour but there is a thick coating of rust on the rails and as we have seen, the platform was used for loading after closure to passengers up until 1965 at least, so it may well be circa 1966. The small building with the enormous chimney nearest the camera was the extension erected by the Midland in 1890, the additional room it contained being the office for the station master. Note the station name on a small board above the window. At the far end, the gents urinal is also likely to have been a later addition, again probably in 1890, accommodation in the original building having become very cramped. As built it matched Coaley in design, with a Brunellian style awning (which again probably extended all round the building prior to the 1890 alterations), diamond pattern chimneys, steeply pitched slate roof and Cotswold stone door and window surrounds. Note how the red brickwork of the front wall beneath the platform canopy had discoloured quite badly, in similar fashion to the platform face. NPC

268 — THE BRISTOL & GLOUCESTER LINE – COALEY JUNCTION TO BERKELEY ROAD

'Hall' Class No. 4973 *Sweeney Hall* heads south past Coaley Junction signal box. The engine was based at Cardiff Canton shed from March 1956 and was withdrawn from there in July 1962. The year is likely to be 1961, as there is an 88A shedplate on the smokebox door, Canton having changed from 86C earlier that year. The train was not recorded and the oblique angle is not helpful but the lamps mounted on the front buffer beam indicate that this is probably a parcels service to Bristol. New in January 1930, No. 4973 was coupled to a standard Collett 4,000 gallon tender for most of its career but at some date after August 1958, when it was photographed leaving Stratford-on-Avon still attached to that, it was swapped for the Hawksworth-designed, slab sided, 4,000 gallon tender it is seen paired with here. NPC

SECTION 9

THE BRISTOL & GLOUCESTER LINE
COALEY JUNCTION TO BERKELEY ROAD

'Jubilee' No. 45662 *Kempenfelt* heads south past Coaley Junction signal box on the same day. New in December 1934, it was a resident of Bristol Barrow Road shed for most of its BR career, transferring to Shrewsbury in autumn 1961, from where it was withdrawn in November 1962. NPC

As noted earlier, the Bristol & Gloucester main line comprised a series of junctions, so the next section of our journey is a short one indeed, just two miles from Coaley Junction to Berkeley Road, the route curving all the way from west to south. There were no other intermediate stations, no engineering features of note and four overbridges, with the A38 trunk road crossing the line twice; a fifth bridge has appeared since the end of steam, carrying the M5 Motorway over the railway about a quarter of a mile to the west of Coaley. Berkeley Road station opened with the line in July 1844, near a road junction but little else, the name giving a clue as to the fact that the town it purported to serve lay two miles away. Even today, the area around the station site comprises little more than the Prince of Wales Hotel, opened soon after the railway, and a few scattered houses.

In 1916, a huge ammunition dump was established in the Vale of Berkeley, in the fields to the east of Slimbridge. A branch ran from the main line sidings near Gossington, where transfer sidings were also established, to Shepherd's Patch on the Gloucester & Sharpness Canal, with sidings to the various storage sheds, and traffic in and out was probably quite intensive during the First World War. Closed in 1924, all of the track had been lifted by 1926 and there is little sign today that the dump and its railway ever existed.

RIGHT: The Coaley Junction to Berkeley Road section of the Br&GR line, as shown on the 1961 edition 1 inch OS. The M5 Motorway now crosses the line just to the west of the site of Coaley station, between the A4135 and A38 bridges.

Saltley-based 'Black 5' No. 45006 trundles slowly through the station with a Birmingham to Bristol freight on 22nd May 1963. Built at Crewe in April 1935, the locomotive transferred to Oxley in early April 1965 and then to Crewe South in March 1967, from where it was withdrawn in September that year. NPC

On the same day, BR 'Standard' Class '4' No. 75001 was seen heading north 'light engine' through Coaley. Built at Swindon in August 1951, the engine had been reallocated from Oxford to Bristol Barrow Road just a few weeks before the picture was taken. In September 1963 it transferred to Yeovil and went from there in to store in October 1964, withdrawal officially taking place in December. NPC

RIGHT: We now begin another run of views taken from the Coaley Junction signal box by signalman Gilroy Kerr. Here, in 1963, BR 'Standard' Class '5' No. 73019 calls with an Up local from Bristol Temple Meads to Gloucester Eastgate. Built at Derby Works in October 1951, the 4-6-0 spent most of its career relatively locally, with allocations successively from new to St. Philips Marsh, Bath Green Park, Barrow Road, Green Park again, Barnwood and then Horton Road, transferring away to Oxley at the beginning of November 1964. Its final posting, up north to Bolton in April 1966, ended when it was withdrawn in January 1967. Note the Royal Mail van on the left. GILROY KERR

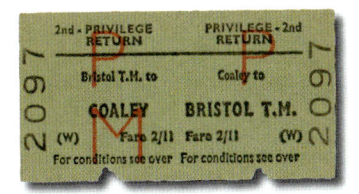

LEFT: Also in 1963, ex-LM&SR 'Crab' 2-6-0 No. 42707 was seen heading through and making steady progress with a lengthy Up goods train. New from Horwich Works in January 1927 as No. 13007, the engine became No. 2707 in the LM&SR renumbering scheme of 1934 and was given its BR number on 2nd October 1948. Based at Saltley at the date of the picture, No. 42707 was withdrawn from Birkenhead Mollington Street shed in September 1964. GILROY KERR

RIGHT: We saw ex-GWR 'Manor' Class 4-6-0 No. 7814 *Fringford Manor* in this appalling condition on the Gloucester to Hereford line in Volume 1 and here it is once more, passing the Up platform at Coaley with a short Sharpness to Gloucester goods, comprising a single Mexphalte tank and an empty steel mineral wagon, on 13th August 1965. New in Janaury 1939 and based at Horton Road since June 1964 – apart from a short two month stint at Didcot in mid-1965 – No. 7814 unsurprisingly had just four weeks left in traffic, the end coming on 10th September 1965. It was sold to Birds of Swansea for scrapping but was cut up at their Long Marston base, just north of Honeybourne. GILROY KERR

On 15th April 1965, No. 6956 *Mottram Hall* throws up an impressive but very sooty cloud of smoke as it storms through the station after recovering from a permanent way slack. New in March 1943, the 'Hall' was based at Horton Road at the date of this view, so this was probably a Bristol to Gloucester freight. Moving to Oxford just over two months later, it was withdrawn in December 1965. GILROY KERR

On 14th June 1965, Class '4F' No. 44264, which we saw a lot of on the Nailsworth & Stroud Branch in Volume 4A, heads past tender-first with the Sharpness to Gloucester pick-up goods, which on this occasion mainly comprised empty coal wagons. GILROY KERR

In the last year of steam on the Western Region of BR, even the handsome 'Britannia' Class 'Pacifics' were starting to look very neglected, as demonstrated here by No. 70053 *Moray Firth*, heading north with an Up Class '6' freight including a long rake of Class 'A' tank wagons on 19th June 1965. Historically, these express goods trains had colloquially been referred to on the LM&SR as a 'Maltese' freight, simply because they were indicated in the working time tables by a Maltese Cross against their timings, so Gilroy had presumably picked the term up from an older colleague. New from Crewe Works on 3rd September 1954, the 'Brit' had transferred from Holyhead to Oxley shed in the week before the picture was taken. Although in filthy condition here and minus its nameplates, withdrawal from Carlisle Kingmoor was not until early April 1967. GILROY KERR

RIGHT: Although not a good quality picture, colour views of green diesels on the Br&GR main line are sufficiently scarce to make this photograph of Sulzer Type '4' No. D17, passing Coaley in wintry conditions on 5th March 1965, worth including here. Hauling an Up Class '5' freight, the locomotive was based at Leeds Holbeck shed at this time. Redesignated as BR Class '45' No. 45024 under TOPS in April 1975, the 'Peak' was withdrawn in October 1980 and scrapped at Swindon. GILROY KERR

ABOVE: An unusual consist passing Coaley box on Friday 18th June 1965, as Class '8F' No. 48345 came through hauling 'Black Five' No. 45190 'dead engine', with a box van acting as a barrier vehicle and an ex-LM&SR brake van on the rear. No. 45190 was based at Derby at this date and still had plenty of service to give, being withdrawn from Heaton Mersey at the start of May 1968. New from Armstrong Whitworth in October 1935, it fared slightly better than the Shrewsbury-based 2-8-0, built at Horwich Works in March 1944, which was withdrawn in March 1968. GILROY KERR

LEFT: On Monday 16th August 1965, diesel-hydraulic No. D1019 *Western Challenger* passed through heading north with what the headcode indicates was a Class '6' freight. The 'B' was for Bristol District trains, so the 'Western' was probably heading for Gloucester. Entering service on 2nd May 1965, No. D1019 was a Laira engine, so was presumably covering this turn before heading back south to Plymouth. It was withdrawn from Laira depot on 6th May 1973, just four days after its tenth birthday and after being repainted in BR blue in December 1969. GILROY KERR

Coaley station from the signal box in 1964. The building faced north, into the 'Vee' of the junction. Built of red brick, with Cotswold stone door and window surrounds, a steeply pitched slate roof, red brick chimneys in a diamond pattern and a canopy that ran round three sides (and may have extended to the fourth over the forecourt entrance prior to BR's extension to the building), it was distinctly Brunellian in style, a reflection of its having been designed for the D&MJR by ex-Brunel assistant John T. Harrison. Note that the flower beds were still lovingly and beautifully tended, and also the slight difference in height between the branch and Down main platforms, with a distinct slope towards the latter. The scooter, which is an unusual one – either a Sun Wasp, Dayton Flamenco or Panther Princess, all used the same bodywork – was owned by Ernie Morris, one of the porters, who was also the man who tended the flower beds. He had an allotment nearby too and was apt to get quite cross whenever Gilroy and others were playing football and the ball was kicked on to it. GILROY KERR

Class '4F' No. 44146 hauls No. 53808 past the station *en route* to Barry scrapyard on 14th May 1964. Both were Bath Green Park engines, with the Class '7F' 2-8-0 having been withdrawn two months earlier, in March. Built for the S&DJR by Robert Stephenson & Co. Ltd in July 1925, it entered service as No. 88 but was renumbered by the LM&SR in 1930, becoming No. 9678. This was short-lived and it became No. 13808 in 1932, receiving its BR number in August 1949. Whilst the sight of it heading by here, on what everyone at the time would have considered as its final journey, may seem something of a sombre occasion, purchase for scrapping by the Woodham brothers at their Barry yard was actually hugely fortuitous and it was to be one of the first locomotives rescued from there for preservation. Now owned by the Somerset & Dorset Railway Trust based at Washford on the West Somerset Railway, it is currently operational and is turned out in BR black. Sister engine No. 53809 also made it in to preservation but the '4F' was not so lucky. A similar age to the '7F', being new in November 1925, it returned to Bath Green Park but was withdrawn in early October 1964 and scrapped the following year by Cashmores of Newport. GILROY KERR

Clearly burning some very poor coal and thus leaving a trail of filthy black smoke behind it, Leicester Midland shed's 'Black Five' No. 44659 scurries through Coaley with train No. 1M48, a Paignton to Leeds holiday express, on 5th September 1964. Clicking the shutter just in time, the locomotive has not obscured the ornate Up side waiting shelter. With its decorative bargeboards and diamond pattern windows, the structure differed in design from the station building, probably provided by the Midland in the early 1860s. MARK B. WARBURTON

Stanier '8F' No. 48109 heads north with a van train from Avonmouth on 22nd May 1963. New in February 1939, this was another of Saltley's massive roster, having transferred from Toton in May 1959. It was withdrawn in January 1966. M.J. READE/COLOUR-RAIL

'Peak' No. D95 coasts through the Down platform at Coaley with train No. 1V39, the 10.38am from Bradford to Paignton, on 21st July 1963, the driver clearly wondering about the crowd of enthusiasts on the platform. This is explained by the stock of the RCTS Gloucestershire Rail Tour of that date, just glimpsed in the branch platform in the right background. New from Crewe Works on 15th April 1961, the Sulzer Type '4' was based at Derby for the first seven years of its life, transferring to the Nottingham Division on 17th June 1968. Becoming Class '45' under TOPS, the locomotive was renumbered as No. 45054 in May 1975. It was withdrawn on 21st January 1985 and scrapped on site at Toton by Berry's of Leicester. The loss of locations such as this in the mid 1960s with the closure of all of the intermediate stations between Gloucester and Bristol means there is a dearth of good colour views of green era and early blue period diesels south of Standish Junction. COLOUR-RAIL

LEFT: Courtesy of the ex-Midland & South Western Junction Railway line which arrived at Cheltenham from Southampton, we were able to feature locomotives from all of the 'Big Four' pre-Nationalisation companies in the previous volume, as well as those of BR but I thought there was little chance of achieving that in these pages. And then these views of ex-Southern Railway 'West Country' 4-6-2 No. 34002 *Salisbury* came to light in the yard at Coaley in September 1967! New from Brighton Works in June 1945, the 'Spam Can', as they were nicknamed, had been withdrawn from Nine Elms shed in April 1967 and was on its way to Cashmore's of Newport for scrapping when it was dumped here, no doubt due to problems arising when it was being towed. The picture was taken on 13th September. BILL POTTER/KRM

ABOVE: No. 34002's presence here unsurprisingly proved an attraction and this second view, taken on 7th September, shows the other side of the engine. The chalked additions to the front end hark back to its SR days and its original number – 21C102, albeit mistakenly added here as 21C002. The engine was clearly reluctant to complete its journey; after departing Salisbury shed, it was first dumped at Bath from a convoy of scrap engines but then made its way here. It was later dragged to Horton Road, where enthusiasts apparently spruced it up somewhat but all to no avail and it finally arrived at Cashmore's Newport yard, where it was summarily scrapped. NPC

RIGHT: With the branch now being operated as a long siding serving Listers works, this was the sad scene at Coaley Junction on 22nd March 1969. The box looks smart but the armless signals give the clue to its status, having been closed on 14th October 1968, whilst rail-borne coal deliveries here had ceased on 28th June. M.H .YARDLEY/COLOUR-RAIL

RIGHT: Bill Potter snapped this view of the remains of Coaley Junction from a passing train but otherwise gave no details about it on the mount. It appears to have been taken from a goods train, which leads me to believe that the date is 4th November 1968, when the RCTS arranged for an extra brake van to be attached to the the 11.35am from Gloucester New Yard to Sharpness Docks, hauled by 'Hymek' No. D7033. Coaley Junction box had closed three weeks previously, on 14th October but a Wickham pw trolley can be seen in the branch run round loop. A new ground frame had been brought in to use on the day the box closed, as the branch was still open for traffic and a coal concentration depot had been opened in the yard here on 7th October 1966, which closed circa 1977. Jim Clemens was also on board this trip and his ciné film of it is available on DVD. BILL POTTER/KRM

LEFT: Another poor quality view but included because it provides a rare glimpse of the M5 Motorway bridge over the line under construction in the background. An unidentified blue-liveried 'Western' heads north past the remains of the station with a mixed freight, carrying train reporting No. 8B07, circa 1970; the section of the M5 from Junction 13 for Stroud to Junction 15 with the M4 at Bristol opened in December 1971. UNKNOWN

BELOW: Class '9F' No. 92105 rumbles through the stone arch of Dursley Road Bridge (No. 77), carrying the A4135 over the line, on 14th April 1964. Built at Crewe Works in September 1956, the 2-10-0 was based at Kettering at the date of this view, so is probably heading south with a trainload of ironstone. Note the engine had clearly been having priming problems, an issue with which many of the Northamptonshire-based '9F's suffered due to the hard water found in that area. No. 92105's very short career of just over ten years came to an end with withdrawal from Birkenhead Mollington Street shed in January 1967. The tubular steel post on the left held the Coaley Junction Up Home signal. DON MANN

From a position around 100 yards further south, smartly turned out 'Jubilee' No. 45675 *Hardy* is seen heading away from Coaley with a Birmingham to Bristol local circa 1962. The engine displays a 55A Leeds Holbeck plate on its smokebox door so was some way from what was its home for most of the BR era. New in December 1935, No. 45675 lasted in service until June 1967. NPC

Viewed from the A4135 bridge, 2-10-0 No. 92155 looks to be making brisk progress as it heads north with a train of coal empties on 22nd May 1963. Built at Crewe in November 1957, the engine spent its entire nine year career based at Saltley, apart from the final two months when it transferred up to Liverpool Speke Junction, from where it was withdrawn in November 1966. The wagons are thus likely to be heading back to the Warwickshire coalfield. NPC

RIGHT: Looking in the opposite direction from the previous picture, BR 'Standard' Class '5' No. 73091 passed by at the head of a Bristol to Gloucester local on 25th July 1964. Built at Derby Works in October 1955, the 4-6-0 went new to Patricroft shed, then to Shrewsbury in August 1958 before arriving at Barnwood in September 1961. It had recently transferred to Horton Road at the date of this view after closure of the ex-MR shed and was withdrawn from there in May 1965, after less than ten years in service.
TONY BOWLES/COURTESY THE RESTORATION & ARCHIVING TRUST/REF. ARC5500

LEFT: A little further south from the bridge in a view taken from the 'right' side of the fence (unlike that of *Hardy* above), No. 6879 *Overton Grange* drifts southwards with a summer express to the West Country probably from Birmingham Snow Hill on Wednesday 7th July 1965. The train reporting number is not decipherable but No. 6879, which was new in May 1939, was Tyseley-based from April 1960 until withdrawal in October 1965. DON MANN

BELOW: We saw the SLS's 'GWR Cavalcade' rail tour of 17th October 1965 passing Cheltenham Lansdown in *Volume 4: Gloucester Midland Lines Part 1: North* but here it is again, with 0-6-0PT No. 6435 piloting No. 7029 *Clun Castle*, about to pass Berkeley Road Jc signal box, as its nameboard titled it. A Midland Railway Type '3a' design opened on 29th July 1900, this is the best colour view seen of the box, which was closed on 14th October 1968 and converted to a ground frame. We shall see more of this tour later on at Yate. FRED BUTLER/KRM

'Royal Scot' No. 46162 *Queen's Westminster Rifleman* coasts in to Berkeley Road station with a Birmingham to Bristol 'stopper'. Built at Derby Works and new in to service in September 1930, the 4-6-0 transferred from Kentish Town to Saltley in June 1961, moving on then to Carlisle Upperby twelve months later, then to Carlisle Kingmoor was the 'Scot's final posting, from where it was withdrawn in May 1964. On the left, an unidentified ex-GWR 0-6-0PT is parked with a two-coach set forming the Sharpness Branch shuttle, which up until the autumn of the previous year had run across the River Severn to Lydney, the service having been curtailed following the October 1960 accident to the Severn Bridge (see *Vol. 2 Forest of Dean Lines and the Severn Bridge*). The Sharpness train would shortly advance forward to the Up branch platform, connecting with the Down 'stopper' to collect any passengers before departing. Apart from coal deliveries, the goods yard latterly seems to have been mostly used by the civil engineers. GERALD PEACOCK

A fine panorama of the north end of the station on 18th June 1961, with the yard on the right again largely occupied by engineers wagons. There is much in the picture to suggest that it was taken shortly before the following view, below and thus shows No. 92152 approaching and passing an ex-GWR 4-6-0 waiting in the Down lie-by loop with a mixed freight. The Up platform was extended northwards in 1876, when the Midland's Sharpness Branch opened. ROY DENISON

Moments later, Class '9F' No. 92152 whistles as it clanks through Berkeley Road on 18th June 1961 with a southbound train of Warwickshire coal. Built at Crewe in October 1957, the locomotive went new to Saltley shed and stayed there until late October 1966, when it moved to Birkenhead Mollington Street from where it was withdrawn in November 1967. Berkeley Road Jc signal box faced the junction for the Sharpness/Severn Bridge line and was a replacement for an earlier lofty wooden box on an immediately adjacent site. K. HORAN/COLOUR-RAIL

'Black Five' No. 45418 of Rugby shed eases a van train through Berkeley Road, passing No. 6943 *Farnley Hall* waiting in the Down lie-by with another southbound freight on 25th March 1961. The redundant rails in the right foreground are from the south end of the goods yard, which had been lifted two weeks earlier. The 'Hall' was based at Hereford at the date of this view but was transferred to Horton Road in early 1962, from where it was withdrawn in December 1963. NPC

The wide aperture of the stylish brick-built goods shed, seen here in 1963, betrayed its broad gauge origins. The track at this end – a trailing connection from the Up main that served a short loading bay and livestock pens, and the extension of the siding through the shed to a trailing connection with the Down main – had been removed as noted above. The two lines actually crossed each other and there was also a direct connection then between the loading bay siding and the line through the shed, the whole arrangement thus forming a scissors crossover. Goods traffic, latterly mostly deliveries of house coal, was finally withdrawn and the yard closed on 1st November 1966. The load of logs (telegraph poles?) on bogie bolsters in the background had been collected from Sharpness Docks. BILL POTTER/KRM

The footbridge provided a fine vantage point for views of the north end of the station, goods shed and junction, as here in September 1963. 'Black Five' No. 44528 rumbles southwards with a mixed goods. In an era when BR was renowned for doing odd things, mostly to force the closure of what they considered to be unremunerative lines, the destruction of the edges of station platforms was just another policy which only looks unusual with hindsight. The north end of the Up main line platform faced the goods shed, the Down platform being much shorter, so at some point around the first half of 1963 they dismantled the edge at this end. Given that maintenance of it would have been minimal and the inherant dangers that it would have presented – albeit it was fenced off in rudimentary fashion – it seems an odd policy indeed. Did it have something to do with the rateable value of the station? The neatly tended platform garden suggests that the staff would have been none to impressed with this untidy desecration either. DEREK CHAPLIN

Class '4F' No. 44466 enters with a Bristol-bound local on 12th October 1963. The junction between the main line and the Sharpness Branch was simplified from 2nd May 1965, when the connection from the Down main to the Down branch was taken out of use. The box closed on 14th October 1968 when it was converted to a ground frame. BLAKE PATTERSON/COURTESY THE RESTORATION & ARCHIVING TRUST/REF. BPUK1R33

On Saturday 14th March 1964, a typically damp spring day, 'Standard' Class '5' No. 73015 of Bristol Barrow Road shed arrives with a Gloucester to Bristol local. New from Derby Works in September 1951, the 4-6-0 was withdrawn from Bath Green Park shed in early August 1965, a month after being alloacted there. NPC

Berkeley Road goods yard from the station footbridge in late October 1964, with the Sharpness Branch locomotive – a '14XX' 0-4-2T – standing in front of the signal box whilst in the process or running round. In the yard, an ex-GWR 4-6-0 shunts the Gloucester engineers train in the far siding which, as we shall shortly see, was here in conjunction with the imminent closure of the branch to passenger trains. The local coal merchant can be seen standing on the bed of his lorry whilst loading coal in to sacks directly from one of the steel mineral wagons. A glimpse inside the shed would seem to indicate that it saw very little use for general goods traffic after removal of the trackwork at this end. Unfortunately, no colour view has yet been seen showing the layout of this end of the yard prior to its removal in March 1961, so I am unable to illustrate it here. JOHN STRANGE/NPC

The Sharpness train is seen parked just clear of the branch platform between services in an otherwise quiet moment at Berkeley Road on 18th July 1964. JOHN RYAN

The driver of 'Black Five' No. 45222 waits for the green flag from the guard before starting away with a northbound local on 4th August 1964. Built for the LM&SR by Armstrong, Whitworth in December 1935, the engine was based at Bescot at the date of this view. It was withdrawn from Newton Heath shed in February 1967. Note the British Road Services lorry visible in the goods yard through the shed arch. Station Footbridge (No. 72) was erected in 1883, the wrought iron lattice girders resting on cast iron columns having a span of 59ft. BLAKE PATTERSON/COURTESY THE RESTORATION & ARCHIVING TRUST/REF. BPUK0482

This view, from the end of the Down platform, gives a good indication of how tight the space was at this end of the goods shed and thus how cramped the pointwork would have been in the centre of this space, joining the goods shed road where the buffers stops are now positioned, whilst the direct connection between this road and the bay siding paralleled the loading platform wall. Coupled with the fact that the yard also had a direct connection at the north end, unlike at Charfield and Frocester a wagon turntable was therefore not required. On 28th September 1963, BR 'Standard' Class '5' No. 73028 was photographed making its scheduled stop here with the 12.45pm Bristol to Gloucester 'stopper'. New from Derby Works in December 1951, the engine was based at Barnwood at this date and was withdrawn in December 1966. Note the enamelled warning sign, the twin to the one illustrated in the Introduction on page VI, hanging beneath the footbridge on the right. R. PATTERSON/COLOUR-RAIL.

ABOVE AND RIGHT: Two views of Class '4F' No. 44045, which we have seen several times already, first arriving at Berkeley Road circa the autumn of 1963 with a Gloucester to Bristol local and then preparing to depart a few minutes later in the lower picture. Note the local engineering department handcart beneath the footbridge steps, above, a fascinating item of old railway equipment which we shall shortly study in detail. BOTH NPC

LEFT: Working hard, another '4F', No. 44131, powers through the station with a northbound train of coke empties on 18th August 1962. This end of the station was always more difficult for photography, particularly early colour film with its slow speeds. Hemmed in as it was on each side by low tree-lined embankments and with the A38 road bridge crossing over the south end of the platforms, the light was simply not good enough most of the time for colour pictures but this view was worth including as an example, because of the train itself and also because it provides a glimpse of the road bridge with its twin spans, the newer wrought iron girder span nearest and the original 1840 brick arch on the far side. An early LM&SR build, at Crewe Works in September 1925, No. 44131 had been based at Saltley for just over five months when the picture was taken but had transferred to Burton-on-Trent by the time it was withdrawn in November 1964. NPC

RIGHT: On 16th August 1962, Sulzer Type '4' No. D64 passes Berkeley Road with train No. 1V38, from Sheffield to Bristol Temple Meads. The 'Peak' was new from Crewe Works on 9th April 1962, so was only four months old when seen here. In June 1965 it was honoured by being one of a handful of the class given military names when it became *Coldstream Guardsman*. Redesignated as Class '45' under TOPS, it was renumbered in February 1975 as No. 45045 and was withdrawn on 8th May 1983, after sustaining collision damage in an accident at Saltley on 10th February. NPC

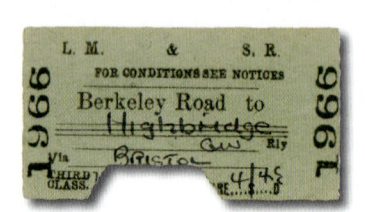

LEFT: On the same day, work stained 'Jubilee' No. 45685 *Barfleur* was photographed also heading south with a mixed freight for one of the Bristol yards. New in February 1936, the 'Jube' was a long term Bristol Barrow Road resident, so was heading back home but these duties would have been quite a come down from the express passenger work the engine was originally built for. Withdrawal took place in April 1964. NPC

RIGHT: The attractive Brunellian building on the Down platform, viewed from an evening Up train circa 1962. When the station first opened to passengers on 8th July 1844 it was named Dursley & Berkeley, although it was about two miles from both. It was a short-lived title, however, the name being changed to Berkeley Road on 1st June 1845. NPC

RIGHT: A small fortune in railwayana abandoned at Berkeley Road in February 1967. Sadly, to the best of my knowledge, none of the items seen here was rescued. What a centrepiece for any display the Berkeley Road Engineering Dept cart would have made today, whilst the LM&SR 'hawkseye' nameboards would also easily command a four figure sum each at auction. JOHN STRANGE/NPC

BELOW: On the same visit, John Strange also took this view of the other side of the goods shed, showing the unusual construction of the entrance doors here, the original open aspect having been closed and the nearer arch bricked up in the 1860s. Road vehicles had a choice of two doors to back through and butt up to the loading platform, which were divided by a timber panelled pillar and there was further such panelling across the top of the whole aperture. The arched stone windows and door surrounds were a stylish feature in a very functional building. JOHN STRANGE/NPC

LEFT: Although there was little left of the station when this view was taken on 25th September 1976, I have included it because it shows the north elevation of the goods shed, which has gone, and a glimpse of the stylish station master's house, which happily still survives as a private residence. The last of the sidings in the yard were removed in October 1978 and it is likely that the goods shed, having apparently not found any alternative commerical use, was demolished in the years following. The A38 road bridge in the distance has also been rebuilt since the picture was taken. The original single brick arch on the skew – Gloucester and Bristol Road Bridge No. 71 in the register and seen in the picture opposite – was supplemented by the additional girder span seen here when the A38 was dualled for a short length here circa 1973. However, the girder span has also been replaced in recent years by a new concrete span, although the original brick arch still remains in use by southbound traffic on the other side. The photographer's position seems a worry given the approaching Up train but this appears to be held at the signal just visible through the arch. D.L. DOTT/COLOUR-RAIL

A lovely study of the main building and the entrance road from the A38 to the station, which basks quietly in the warm sunshine of a fine summer's day on 18th June 1961. As at other Brunel-designed or influenced station buildings, the canopy had originally extended around the building but had been cut back to just the portion seen here apparently in the early years of the British Railways regime. The scar on the end of the building clearly shows where it had been removed from. An unusual feature is the chimney rising up from the front of the building, above the waiting room bay window. Passengers could only now change here for the branch as far as Sharpness, the closure of the Severn Bridge in October of the previous year meaning a piece of paper had been pasted over Lydney on the station nameboard. Whilst nothing remains from this view today of the station, the Prince of Wales Hotel on the horizon is still open and the shed to the right of the entrance, probably originally a stables and garage for the hotel, also still survives. ROY DENISON

SECTION 10
THE SHARPNESS BRANCH

A busy moment at Berkeley Road Junction in August 1960, with No. 1426 and the auto from Lydney Town in the process of 'turning round'; the driver in the end compartment has driven the train to this point, whilst the fireman is on his way to the signal box to exchange the token for the next trip across the Severn Bridge, two months before the accident which was to close it for ever. On the right a short pick-up freight waits in the Down lie-by for the express in the distance to pass. New in November 1933 and sub-shedded at Lydney at the date of this view, No. 1426 was withdrawn on 3rd April 1962. COLOUR-RAIL

In 1870, construction commenced of large new docks at Sharpness, superceding the original small basin. This allowed a new entrance to be built from the River Severn to the Gloucester & Berkeley Canal, through the new docks. However, construction was hampered by the lack of a rail connection, whilst the old docks had been unable to provide coaling facilities for ships. Although opposed by the GWR, the Midland and certain factions on the Forest of Dean side of the river, along with the canal company, had combined to investigate the feasibility of bridging the Severn at Sharpness, thereby providing a further outlet for Forest coal. On 18th July 1872, the Severn Bridge Railway Act was authorised, with capital of £225,000, to build a line from Lydney (Severn & Wye) to Sharpness, a distance of just over 4 miles. Just a week later, on 25th July, the Midland gained a separate Act authorising the construction of a second branch, 4 miles long, from their station at Berkeley Road on the Bristol to Gloucester main line to Sharpness, to connect with the Severn Bridge Railway.

The single track Midland branch from Berkeley Road traversed reasonably level countryside and involved little in the way of major engineering works, so construction proceeded briskly once commenced. The line opened for goods traffic on 2nd August 1875, to take advantage of trade through the docks. A full year later, on 1st August 1876, passenger services began to a temporary platform on the line to the docks.

Meanwhile, construction of the bridge across the Severn had begun in 1875 and was completed in September 1879, with the ceremonial first train running across it on 17th October. The line commenced at Otterspool Junction, Lydney and ran through the 506 yards Severn Bridge Tunnel in to Severn Bridge station, before crossing the river. The bridge totalled 4,162 feet in length, including the masonry approach arches either side and the swing section over the canal. From the eastern end of the bridge, the line curved south for about half a mile to reach its end-on junction with the MR's Sharpness Branch at Sharpness station. This section of railway was covered in detail in *Volume 2: Forest of Dean Lines and the Severn Bridge*. Two new platforms were provided at Berkeley Road and there was one intermediate station at Berkeley, which also had two platforms and a loop so trains could be crossed there. From Berkeley, the line dropped gently but consistently for about a mile down to Sharpness, where another two platform station was provided overlooking the docks and where the SBR made an end-on junction with the Midland branch.

From the opening of the bridge and by an Act of 21st July 1879, the Severn & Wye and the Severn Bridge Railway companies were amalgamated. The Severn & Wye & Severn Bridge Railway (S&W&SBR), as the new company was known, thus operated trains from Lydbrook and Coleford to Sharpness, with a connection too into the docks, where they had their own coal tip on the canal at the old dock. In 1885, a deep water tip was built in the new docks but the old tip continued to be used until the late 1950s. From Sharpness to

Providing a touch of variety to the Class '14XX' 0-4-2T motive power more commonly seen on these services, one of the smaller '16XX' pannier tanks, No. 1642, waits in the Up branch platform with the regular two coach shuttle across the bridge to Lydney Town on 15th August 1959. New from Swindon Works on 2nd April 1951, the engine went to Gloucester Horton Road where it was to spend the whole of its brief ten years and nine months career, being withdrawn in January 1962. The gate across the end of the Up platform was an unusual feature and note that the Down platform face was still intact at this date, although as the following picture shows, not for its entire length. TREVOR OWEN/COLOUR-RAIL

An interesting view showing No. 1454 and two coach train starting away for Sharpness alongside the remaining section of the Down branch platform. The view dates from autumn 1959, the locomotive having been transferred from store at Bristol Bath Road to Horton Road on 17th July. It was in Caerphilly Works from 26th October to 27th November but was withdrawn from Horton Road on 23rd December and cut up at Swindon in early September 1961. NPC

Berkeley Road remained the property of the Midland but, in reality, following the combining of the time tables for the two lines in *Bradshaw* in 1879, passenger services were operated throughout as one line.

Little changed until 1894 when, after another spate in severe financial straits, the effectively bankrupt S&W&SBR was taken over jointly by the GW and Midland railways, the former also paying the latter £62,475 for a half share of the Sharpness Branch. The joint venture was formulated by an Act of 17th August 1894 and the Severn & Wye Joint Railway (S&WJR), administered by the Great Western & Midland Railways Joint Committee, came into being. From Berkeley Road to Lydbrook Junction was now under joint ownership and this remained the situation through to the 1923 Grouping, when ownership then became vested jointly in the GW and London Midland & Scottish railways.

A feature of the whole of the S&WJR line was its joint signage, a few examples surviving until closure.

The only significant physical change following the 1894 joint takeover was the construction, by the GWR, of a south curve at Berkeley Road in 1908, to enable through running via the Severn Bridge when the Severn Tunnel was closed for maintenance. This left the Sharpness Branch at Berkeley Loop Junction, midway between Berkeley Road and Berkeley, and joined the main line south of Berkeley Road station at Berkeley Road South Junction. Sadly no colour views of the curve or its junctions have been seen to date.

In 1948, the 'Joint Line' finally disappeared, along with the GWR and the LM&SR, with the Nationalisation of the railway system. Under British Railways, weight testing of the Severn Bridge was carried out, in order that it could be used by heavier locomotives

THE SHARPNESS BRANCH

ABOVE: A pair of enthusiasts chat with the train crew on 4th June 1960, whilst No. 1431 simmers gently between services. Behind the engine, the face of the Down platform had now been removed. BILL POTTER/KRM

An undated view of the branch platforms prior to the closure of the Severn Bridge and again featuring No. 1431. New in July 1934 and transferred to Horton Road in February 1960, this was to be No. 1431's final posting. Sub-shedded at Lydney, it was put in to store there on 5th July 1960, which leaves us with little more than a five month window in which the photograph could have been taken. Officially withdrawn in April 1961, the engine was cut up at Swindon in the August. COLOUR-RAIL

The Up branch platform bench seems to have seen more use from footplate crew than from pasengers in later years, as here with the driver of Class '57XX' pannier tank No. 8717, seen enjoying some warm sunshine between shuttles in the summer of 1961. The engine was built for the GWR in March 1931 by Beyer, Peacock Ltd at their Gorton Works, some two hundred of the class being built by outside firms in 1929-31 as part of a Government initiative to alleviate the trade depression then prevalent. The tank engine was a long time resident of Horton Road shed, spending most of its career in Gloucester after being sent there from new, only finally transferring away in January 1962, to Abercynon, from where it was withdrawn in early July 1964. GERALD PEACOCK

and thus be even more useful as a diversionary route for the Severn Tunnel. It was decided to strengthen the diagonals, so that Western Region locomotives up to 'Castle' Class (route availability red) could be used over it on a regular basis. However, this work was only partly completed when, on the night of 25th October 1960, two petroleum barges collided with the bridge in thick fog bringing down two of the spans. After several years of prevarication, the decision was finally taken to demolish it, work commencing in 1967 and taking three years.

The disaster had immediately ended the Lydney Town-Sharpness passenger service, Lydney Town station officially closing to passengers as from 26th October. With the publication of the Beeching Report in 1963, the death knell was sounded for the remaining service on the Berkeley Road-Sharpness stub and the branch subsequently closed to passengers on and from Monday 2nd November 1964, the last trains actually running on Saturday 31st October. However, the docks continued to be rail served whilst the establishment in the early 1960s of a loading facility for the nuclear power stations at Berkeley and Oldbury in the old yard at Berkeley station further ensured the survival of the Sharpness Branch. Although both power stations are now closed, nuclear trains continue to serve the loading facility in the old goods yard at Berkeley as decommissioning continues, work which is scheduled to carry on for many years yet. In the meantime, following one preservation attempt which failed in 2012, since 2015 the Vale of Berkeley Railway has been actively working with Network Rail and Direct Rail Services Ltd, who operate the nuclear flask trains, towards opening up the line as a heritage railway.

Class '54XX' No. 5420 waits at the Up Branch to Main signal in the background, for the train signalled on the Up main line, from which this undated view was taken, to pass by. It is post closure of the bridge, as the locomotive was only transferred from Banbury to Horton Road in November 1961, so the date will be sometime between then and withdrawal in October 1963. Lydney shed continued to provide the locomotive and stock for part of the day for the first two years after the Severn Bridge was closed, to cover the school run. The nearest secondary education school for Sharpness children was Lydney Grammar, so trains ran via Gloucester until July 1962, to allow Sharpness school children to complete their exam courses, and this might be a school train heading back to Lydney. As we shall see in due course, No. 5420's final rail journey was, rather fittingly, to be hauled dead from Gloucester and along the branch to Sharpness in the early spring of 1964, having been bought by Cooper's Metals for scrapping. NPC

RIGHT: Whilst rural branch lines could in no way be construed as fertile locations for 'spotters', a surprising range of engines appeared on the Sharpness Branch over the years. Here, No. 6437, in BR lined green passenger livery, is seen shortly after arrival with an Up service in April 1963. Built at Swindon in April 1937, No. 6437 spent most of its career in the South Wales valleys, going new to Pontypool Road before transferring to Aberdare. Its final posting, to Horton Road, was in May 1960 and it had only a few weeks left in service when photographed here, being withdrawn in July 1963. Notwe that the Down branch platform now had the whole of its face removed. A BR 'Standard' 4-6-0 heads south in the background, whilst Hengaston Farm and its imposing main house, which sits on the far side of the A38 road, can be seen in the distance. J.L. CHAMPION/COLOUR-RAIL

LEFT: With the branch curving away to the junction in the right background, an unidentified '14XX' 0-4-2T stands at Berkeley Road after arrival with a single coach auto working from Sharpness on a damp and dismal Saturday, 14th March 1964. Loadings were generally sparse following closure of the Severn Bridge, only the morning and evening school and workmens/commuter trains, and the Saturday services used by shoppers, being loaded to any degree. J.R. NEWMAN/COLOUR-RAIL

RIGHT: Some four months later, on 4th July, classmate No. 1445, was photographed in the same spot but with the engine facing towards Gloucester, as it still was a month later when seen by Blake Patterson, in the lower picture on page 304. As the engines had to work the shuttle backwards in one direction, Barnwood and, subsequently, Horton Road paid little heed to which way the engines were facing when dispatched off shed. MARK B. WARBURTON

BERKELEY ROAD JUNCTION. WORKING OF UP BRANCH TRAINS
The person conveying the Token from the Driver of an Up Branch train to the Signalman must first ascertain that the train, complete with tail lamp attached, has arrived on the loop line clear of the Single line and so advise the Signalman. See Table D.2.

TABLE D2 LINES WORKED UNDER ELECTRIC TOKEN OR ONE ENGINE IN STEAM ARRANGEMENTS

(HANDLING OF TOKEN OR STAFF)

The following is a list of places where persons other than the Signalmen are authorised to receive or deliver the Token or Staff:—

Section of Line	Token or Staff Station	Person authorised to receive or deliver Token or Staff
Berkeley Road Jn. to Berkeley Loop Jn. or Sharpness South	Berkeley Road Jn.	Fireman in the case of a light engine or passenger train without guard. Guard in the case of a freight train, or passenger train with guard.

Another of Ben Ashworth's fine studies, as the crew of No. 6437 while away the time between trips on 17th May 1963, whilst the engine gently lets off steam and a solitary passenger sits in one of the carriage compartments. *B.J. Ashworth*

INSET TOP: Instructions for one engine in steam working of Up Branch trains, from the *Sectional Appendix to the Working Time Table, Gloucester Traffic District, Oct. 1960.*

THE SHARPNESS BRANCH

LEFT: A brief glimspe of the RCTS Gloucestershire Rail Tour paused at Berkeley Road behind No. 82036 before heading down the Sharpness Branch on 21st July 1963. This was fairly early in the tour, with only the visit to Avonmouth Docks accomplished by this stage but with the time having passed 2.00pm, nearly 30 minutes had already been lost and, as already noted, things were only going to get worse. NPC

RIGHT: A poor quality view but included because it is a rare record of further motive power on the branch, in the form of BR 'Standard' Class '2' 2-6-0 No. 78006, which we have previously seen much of on the Dursley Branch. The engine would not have been fitted for auto working, so would have had to run round the carriage at each end of the trip and it must have been a rare day indeed that Gloucester could not supply a '14XX' or a pannier tank to cover the duty. The slide is unfortunately not dated but is summertime, probably in 1963 or 1964. NPC

BELOW: The Berkeley Road to Lydney Town service, from the *Working Time Table of Passenger Trains, Gloucester District, 10th September 1962 to 16th June 1963*. The Sharpness to Lydney section is noted as 'Suspended' with the bridge closed. NPC

A lovely panoramic view of the Sharpness Branch platform and the attractive wooden building in September 1963, with No. 1455 resting after bringing in its single coach auto train. The station building behind, largely built of wood but with brick chimneys, was separate from the main buildings, having been provided when the branch opened to passengers in 1876. The triangular platform extension on which it sat was built at the same time. The footbridge was also a later addition, provided in 1883 when it was realised that the foot crossings between platforms were no longer adequate or safe. Although situated effectively in the middle of nowhere, the passenger service to Sharpness and across the Severn Bridge to Lydney ensured that the station remained quite busy up until 1960. DEREK CHAPLIN

No. 1474 alongside the Up branch platform after arrival from Sharpness with a late afternoon service on 12th October 1963. This engine was officially the last of the class to be built, one of a batch of five originally numbered 4870 to 4874 completed in April 1936. Restored to service after being in store at Slough and sent to Barnwood shed on 26th August 1963, No. 1474's reprieve lasted until withdrawal from Horton Road on 28th September 1964. BLAKE PATTERSON/COURTESY THE RESTORATION & ARCHIVING TRUST/REF. BPUK1R31

Classmate No. 1445 was facing the opposite way when photographed in the same spot on 4th August 1964. Another of the class which was put back in service after seventeen months in store but in this case from Didcot, the engine again went to Barnwood, which had responsibility for the Sharpness Branch, arriving in December 1963, subsequently being withdrawn from Horton Road on 1st September 1964 BLAKE PATTERSON/COURTESY THE RESTORATION & ARCHIVING TRUST/REF. BPUK0468

With vegetation starting to encroach in all directions as the end neared and the station flowerbeds growing wild, No. 1445 poses in late afternoon sunshine on Saturday 1st August 1964, as the crew make ready to depart with the 5.00pm train to Sharpness. JOHN DAGLEY-MORRIS

Again looking south at Berkeley Road, on 22nd August 1964, No. 1472 waits in the branch platform whilst the driver chats with a passenger. Note that there was a Gents toilets at this end of the wooden station building, which was provided in 1876. BILL POTTER/KRM

A 1963 study of the main line facing elevation of the branch platform building, a commodious and stylish structure built mostly of wood, with a slated hipped roof and brick chimneys serving three fireplaces. The south end of the building had a Ladies Room to match the Gents at the other end. Quite separate from the other station buildings here at Berkeley Road, the Up platform was extended to form a 'Vee' with the Down branch platform to accommodate it. BILL POTTER/KRM

In glorious late afternoon sunshine on 10th October 1964, No. 1444 waits with auto trailer No. W244W forming the 4.55pm service to Sharpness, which would carry workers and commuters returning home from Gloucester. Note the rake of ballast hoppers in the yard in the background. JOHN STRANGE/NPC

LEFT: An undated view incorporating the 'hawkseye' station nameboard held between two stout posts. The dismantled signal and the neglected garden combine to suggest that this is a late October 1964 picture with closure imminent. No. 1453 is also one of the '14XX' class that we have not yet encountered on this service and we will not see it again, suggesting it was an unusual visitor here. New in to service on 23rd July 1935, it arrived at Gloucester for the first time in July 1962 and was one of the last five of the class withdrawn from Horton Road on 9th November 1964, a week after all auto working officially ceased on the Western Region of BR with the cessation of the Chalford and Sharpness services. NPC

RIGHT AND BELOW: On 16th October 1964, the Gloucester Barnwood engineers train was seen at Berkeley Road when returning from dealing with a minor derailment in the docks/BR exchange sidings at Oldminster. Our old friend No. 44123 was in charge of the train, a motley collection that comprised a tool van with sagging clerestory roof (right – possibly a panelled over Royal Mail carriage of circa 1907 vintage that had been withdrawn from regular service circa 1951), a box van and another ancient Midland bogie coach of unknown origin. In the picture below the train is seen about to head back to Gloucester in late evening sunshine. Note, too, with closure imminent the dismantled items lying around in these pictures, such as the 'hawkseye' nameboards and the signal seen above (and lying in the same spot in the background of the picture below). As we have seen, many of these items seem to have been put in to store here for a few years but the signal would have been removed to Gloucester. BOTH JOHN STRANGE/NPC

ABOVE: This 4th July 1964 view is clearly posed, with No. 1445's footplate crew and the train guard all looking out at the photographer. Taken on the Up branch line between the end of the Up platform and the three-arch Bridge No. 2, carrying Breadstone, a lane leading to Halmore and Purton, it would appear that the crew may have reversed the train a few yards back to this point for the picture to be taken. MARK B. WARBURTON

BELOW: A distant view of the station in late October 1964, from the lane crossing over the bridge seen above. JOHN STRANGE/NPC

A fine view from Bridge No. 2 on 19th May 1964, with No. 1472 propelling the Sharpness auto away from the station and about to pass beneath. The driver is controlling the train from the driving compartment at this end of the carriage, a mechanical system allowing him to operate the footplate regulator, whilst a valve in the brake pipe also permitted control of the automatic vacuum brake. The fireman, meanwhile, remained on the footplate keeping the firebox fed and steam up. The driver, fireman and guard were able to communicate with each other by means of an electric bell, whilst a cord enabled the driver to still operate the locomotive whistle, although the warning bell seen above the driving compartment windows provided a more effective warning. Fred Butler/KRM

Although presenting a scene of semi dereliction in January 1967, I have included this view and at full page size for the detail it gives of the station building, which is only fully visible from this angle as a result of the demolition of the Up side platform and waiting rooms. The Down branch platform had also gone, along with the wooden building that served Sharpness and Lydney Town trains. As already mentioned, Brunel's original canopy had been dramatically reduced in size by BR but this view indicates that it had not extended around the south end of the building. There is a partial view of the lofty station masters house behind and another view of the garage/stables that probably served the Prince of Wales Hotel; both these buildings survive today. Note the rakes of Shell Mex/BP 40-ton glw, vacuum braked bitumen tanks in the goods yard; the reason for their presence is not known but these wagons seem to have regularly worked along the Sharpness Branch at this time, possibly in connection with the construction of the M5 Motorway, the Severn Bridge and/or Berkeley nuclear power station. The signal box can be glimpsed in the left distance, still fully operational at this date, reduction to ground frame status being applied in October 1968. JOHN STRANGE/NPC

The raised arm of the Up Home signal gives the clue that this is actually an auto working arriving from Sharpness, with No. 6415 propelling its two-coach train beneath Bridge No. 2 in August 1961. The A38 runs parallel to the branch for a short distance on top of the low embankment on the right. As we have seen, No. 6415 was also a regular on the Dursley Branch at this time. M.E.J. DEANE, COURTESY DR SIMON FOSBURY

From a vantage point at the side the A38, classmate No. 6412 heads in the opposite direction with a train for Sharpness in late October 1964 – I do not know the exact dates of John Strange's visits (I'm certain he made more than one) to photograph the branch shortly before the passenger service finished because he did not mark his slides. Built at Swindon in November 1934, No. 6412 only arrived at Horton Road in the August of 1964 and was withdrawn in early November as the auto services came to an end. Bridge No. 2 can be seen again in the right background. JOHN STRANGE/NPC

The mount of this slide is simply marked 'Sharpness Branch' so the location is not certain but I am fairly sure that it is a short way along the line from the previous picture, looking west towards Sharpness, the photographer having walked out in to the fields a hundred yards or so from the A38. The only clue to the date was not helpful either, the mount being stamped 'Jan 65', three months after withdrawal of the passenger service, but again I'm fairly sure that the picture was taken in October 1964, on a Saturday during the last couple of weeks of operation. An unidentified 0-4-2T propels a two-coach auto towards Berkeley Road, in a view which, despite the lack of definite information, provides an emotive record of the Sharpness Branch service in its last days. The variety of '14XX' locomotives seen on the branch in its last few years and on the Chalford auto service (as we shall see in the next volume), is explained by Horton Road being sent many of the surviving members of the class in the hope that, as the last shed providing motive power for auto trains, they would find a use for them. The week after both services ceased to run, a forlorn line of stored 0-4-2Ts could be seen outside Horton Road shed, awaiting their ultimate fate. JOHN STRANGE/NPC

LEFT: No. 1444 heads towards Berkeley Road on 25th July 1964. The train has just passed over what I think is Bridge No. 6, an occupation arch with brick abutments of blue engineering brick and a span made up of wrought iron internal girders and cast iron external ones, at 1 mile 40.5 chains from the junction.
TONY BOWLES/COURTESY THE RESTORATION & ARCHIVING TRUST/ REF. ARC05544

ABOVE: In September 1963, with sileage making underway in the left background and the south Cotswold escarpment forming a backdrop, No. 1455 departs Berkeley past the nuclear plant loading gantry. This had been erected in the yard, the goods shed having been demolished a year or so previously. The two-mile run to Berkeley Road was through the pleasant scenery of Berkeley Vale which, as can be seen from the terrain, had been an easy section of line for the railway's builders. The permanent way hut just in front of the locomotive was converted from the brick base of Berkeley signal box, closed on 26th July 1931 following singling of the line between Sharpness and Berkeley Road. As in the lower picture on page 311, the auto trailer, with a single window at the driving compartment end, is one of the 1955 conversions from a Brake Third coach. DEREK CHAPLIN

RIGHT: No. 1433 arrives at Berkeley with a two-coach train bound for Lydney Town in the summer of 1960. This would have been another unusual sighting, as the engine was actually based at Cheltenham, from 18th February 1960 up until it was put in to store at Gloucester on 13th September; official withdrawal took place on 17th February 1961.
M.E.J. DEANE, COURTESY DR SIMON FOSBURY

THE SHARPNESS BRANCH

BERKELEY

The points connecting the Siding with the Main Line are worked from a Ground Frame released by the Electric Staff for the Berkeley Road—Sharpness South Section or by the Electric Staff for the Berkeley Loop Junction—Sharpness South Section.

Few photographers seem to have bothered with freight services on the branch during the steam era, so this is a rare and interesting picture indeed. The yard at Berkeley seems to have been closed to general goods traffic quite early, with most of the sidings being removed in June 1958 and the shed seemingly then used by a local road transport company. Only the back road siding was left in place and all this was as a result of the plan to construct a new nuclear power station on the Severn estuary, a mile to the west of Berkeley, in 1956. Materials for the construction were brought in by rail and unloaded here using the new gantry crane provided especially for this and still *in situ* today. On 8th September 1964, '4F' No. 4404S had worked down to Sharpness with the brake van and an item of nuclear plant on a bogie well wagon, collected the rake of bogie bolsters loaded with logs landed at the docks and returned to halt here at Berkeley. The locomotive will now uncouple the brake van and well wagon from the rest of the train and drop the latter in to the nuclear plant siding, where a small reception committee awaits its arrival. Coupling back to its train, the locomotive will then head back to Gloucester. Waiting to receive the load is a circa 1962 Scammell 'Highwayman' articulated tractor unit or 'Ballast Tractor', which would be Gardner diesel powered. In the middle is a circa 1961 BMC FFK 5- or 7-ton payload truck, powered by the 5.1 litre BMC diesel engine, which could be badged Morris or Austin, both of course in the British Motor Corporation. On the right is an Austin A40 'Farina' of similar vintage, the name denoting the Italian styling house which produced the design for BMC. FRED BUTLER/KRM

INSET ABOVE: Details for working the nuclear siding points, from the *Sectional Appendix to the Working Time Table, Gloucester Traffic District, Oct. 1960*.

RIGHT: Berkeley nuclear power station as seen from across the River Severn, on the mud flats alongside Lydney docks circa 1964. The bow of one of the sailing ship hulls that were hulked here in the 1950s protrudes in to the picture in the left foreground; some of these were illustrated in *Vol. 2: Forest of Dean Lines and the Severn Bridge* but very little remains of any of them now. The power station, which was equipped with two Magnox reactors producing 276 Mw in total, began generation in 1962. Reactor No. 2 was shut down in October 1988 and No. 1 in March 1989, and Berkeley became the first nuclear power station in the UK to be decommissioned. Although the site operated safely for twenty-seven years, the huge cost of establishing a new plant and the controversial nature of nuclear power has to date prevented any future plans for a new facility from making progress.
ANNE BEAUFOY

RIGHT: Berkeley flask loading gantry and siding on 25th September 1976, with a couple of Flatrol MJ nuclear flask bogie wagons waiting to be collected. Decommissioning of both Berkeley and Oldbury nuclear power stations continues at the time of writing and will do so for many years yet, with the sites not due to be cleared until 2070 at the earliest. In addition, Berkeley power station has become the designated storage site for the waste from Oldbury. The nuclear waste trains are operated by Direct Rail Services, a wholly owned subsidiary of the Nuclear Decommissioning Authority. With no run-round facility here, nuclear waste trains on the branch travel first to Sharpness, where a loop has been retained, before heading back the mile and a half to Berkeley and reversing the wagons into the loading compound. Proposals by the Vale of Berkeley Railway for running heritage trains on the line and possible a commuter service too thus have to take these trains in to account. D.L. DOTT/COLOUR-RAIL

LEFT: A fascinating juxtaposition of the old and the then new at Berkeley in August 1963. This Great Western & Midland Railways trespass notice, a reminder of the line's Joint status from 1894 up until Nationalisation of the railways in 1948, contrasts sharply with the nuclear flask unloading gantry in the background. ALAN JARVIS

No. 6437 arrives at Berkeley station with a two-coach train for Sharpness circa 1962. The goods yard had an interesting if somewhat complicated layout, which included five possible loops. There were two sidings at the back or south side of the site and a long siding running through the goods shed to terminate at the loading dock just visible behind the lamp post, which also ran to a short shunting neck at the Berkeley Road end. As a result of all the loops, goods trains could access all points of the yard from either end and either direction, although prior to 1931, when the loop was removed, Up trains would have had to set back along the Down line first. The goods shed remained in what appears to be road transport use after closure of the yard and was still extant in October 1963, as will shortly be seen, but had been demolished by the time of Fred Butler's photograph in September 1964. Published plans of the station make no reference to the large wooden shed on the right, or its purpose; it was probably dismantled at the same time as the goods shed. JOHN STRANGE/NPC

ABOVE AND RIGHT: Berkeley station and forecourt from the road entrance on 18th June 1961. Although closer than Berkeley Road, the station was still over half a mile from Berkeley town centre and house building along Station Road never made it all the way out. These were the original station buildings and the design, particularly the overhanging roof, was typically Brunellian. It remained standing for many years after closure but was demolished in the early 1980s. The Vale of Berkeley Railway have plans to rebuild it as near as possible to how it was, so the close up of one of the windows, right, should prove useful. ABOVE: ROY DENISON; RIGHT: NPC

As elsewhere on the network, the platform at Berkeley was shortened in later years, the unused west end being fenced off and the face taken down. A two coach length was all that was required, as seen here with the driver of No. 8717 looking back for the 'right away' signal from the guard, with a train for Lydney Town in the summer of 1960. GERALD PEACOCK

Auto-fitted No. 5420 pauses at Berkeley with a Lydney Town working, again in the summer of 1960. As an official resident of Gloucester Horton Road, the engine wears an 85B shedplate on its smokebox door but it was sub-shedded at Lydney for working these services. GERALD PEACOCK

ABOVE: A minute or two after the picture on page 316, No. 6437 stands at the platform as a friend of the photographer poses with his foot on the carriage step. Both would join the train to travel down to Sharpness. JOHN STRANGE/NPC

BELOW: No. 1474 calls at Berkeley *en route* to Berkeley Road, with a single coach train again formed of one of the BR 1955 Brake Third/auto trailer conversions, on 12th October 1963. BLAKE PATTERSON/COURTESY THE RESTORATION & ARCHIVING TRUST/REF. BPUK1R27

RIGHT: A couple of local schoolboys chat to the driver of No. 1444 as a third friend prepares to take a photograph at Berkeley in October 1964, a burst of interest no doubt prompted by the imminent cessation of the passenger service. With a low late afternoon autumn sun, the train is in the shadow of the station building but beyond the end of the platform, the line is brightly lit as it curves away over Station Road Bridge and down the bank to Sharpness. NPC

ABOVE: No. 1472 arrives at Berkeley on 22nd August 1964. This angle of the building nicely shows the overhanging eaves, which only serves to emphasize what a shame it is that it was eventually demolished. Note the 'hawkseye' nameplate on the platform face of the building at either end, which were probably removed from wooden running in boards and fixed here when the platform was shortened. BR(WR) benches had also replaced the original Midland ones. A couple of schoolboys wait to catch the train back home, one of them clearly more interested in Bill Potter and his camera than the arriving train. BILL POTTER/KRM

LEFT: Bill moved to stand on the old loading dock to take this second picture a short while later, with No. 1472 easing away to Berkeley Road. Note that there was a second surving GW&MR cast iron sign here at this date, on the opposite side of the line just off the end of the old Up platform. Have either of them survived I wonder? BILL POTTER/KRM

BRITISH RAILWAY HISTORY IN COLOUR: 4B. GLOUCESTER MIDLAND LINES SOUTH – STONEHOUSE TO WESTERLEIGH

A simple quick stroll across the line to the disused Up platform produced this superb panorama of the station building, with a Sharpness-bound auto propelled by No. 1472 waiting for any prospective passengers to board on 22nd August 1964, the driver in his compartment watching the photographer with interest. Note the covered waiting area in the centre between the two projecting wings of the building, which was semi-glazed at the front and may also have had a glazed roof. Behind on the right is just a glimpse of the roof and chimneys of the station masters house, which happily does still remain today, although most of the site is now occupied by light industrial units. BILL POTTER/KRM

THE SHARPNESS BRANCH

RIGHT: A distant view of No. 1443 arriving with the 5.45pm train from Sharpness on 18th July 1964, primarily included here because it nicely illustrates the summit of the branch as it crosses Station Road Bridge. JOHN RYAN

BELOW: No. 1445 heads over the three-arch Bridge No. 8 spanning Station Road as it approaches Berkeley station on 1st August 1964. The bridge is built mostly of blue engineering brick but with red brick parapets, and stone quoins and parapet toppings. It is of a most unusual design, having two arches on opposing skews, one over the road and the other over a stream which then passes under the road on the diagonal. To join these opposing arches together, there is a central filled arch on the north side, which being triangular in plan tapers to an abutment on the south side. With a clearance of only 13ft, the road arch is painted with yellow and black hazard warning stripes both sides, although lorries now use the B4066 Berkeley bypass since it was built in the late 1980s. This completely new stretch of road parallels the branch all the way down to Oldminster. JOHN DAGLEY-MORRIS

BELOW: Silhouetted against a late afternoon bright autumn sky, an unidentified '14XX' tops the bank from Sharpness with a single coach auto service bound for Berkeley Road in October 1963. The train is just about to pass over Station Road Bridge. JOHN STRANGE/NPC

North British Type '2' diesel-hydraulic No. D6320 heads out of the dock sidings towards Sharpness South Junction with a train of Shell Mex/BP 40-ton VB bitumen tank wagons on 8th September 1967. Oldminster Foot Bridge (No. 15) carried a footpath named Severn Way, which linked Oldminster Road and the B4066 road in to the docks; the footpath still exists but now crosses the track on the level, the footbridge having been dismantled. Built in 1905, it comprised three girder spans of unequal length (48ft 9¼ins + 54ft 7½ins + 44ft 9ins) mounted on four brick piers, with steps either end and lit by oil lamps. Sharpness South Junction was where the line to the docks split away from the line to Sharpness station, the Severn Bridge and Lydney. Prior to the opening of this route in 1879, the original temporary Sharpness station, opened on 1st August 1876 and closed on 16th October 1879, had been sited on the line to the docks just beyond the footbridge. The signal box controlling the junction was first named Docks Junction, then Oldminster Junction before finally becoming Sharpness South Junction; the first box, which had stood on the left here facing the junction, was replaced by the GWR in January 1914 by a new box sited in the 'Vee' of the junction, just in front of the footbridge, which was closed on 9th May 1965. Behind the photographer on the left side of the line a short siding had run to a locomotive turntable installed in January 1898, which was removed in the late 1950s. New in to service on 23rd March 1960, No. D6320 had been named *Lister* in January 1967 and reallocated from Newton Abbott to Bristol Bath Road in June; it was withdrawn on 22nd May 1971 and cut up at Swindon Works. BILL POTTER/KRM

LEFT: A Bristol-based Gloucester Cross-Country unit of Class '119' (in its standard formation of DMBC/TSLRB/DMS) stands at the end of the South Dock Branch on 22nd March 1969. This Branch Line Society organised Gloucestershire Railtour had been advertised to depart Bristol Temple Meads at 9.30am and return at 7.00pm. It first traversed the Severn Tunnel to visit the branches to Sudbrook, Caerwent, Parkend and Llanthony Docks on the way to Gloucester. Calls were then made at High Orchard Sidings and Hempsted Sidings, before the DMU travelled via Eastgate to Cheltenham and then returned south via the Avoiding Line. The Dursley Branch was then traversed prior to reaching Sharpness, the last call before returning to Temple Meads. What a day! NPC

ABOVE: With the dock workers houses on Bridge Road forming a backdrop and a ganger cutting the long dry grass with a scythe in the foreground, No. 1445 departs Sharpness station for Berkeley Road on 5th August 1964. BILL POTTER/KRM

LEFT: On leaving the station, the line began a gentle climb that steepened after passing Sharpness South Junction. Looking the opposite way to the picture above, on 26th March 1964, No. 1474 is heading towards the remains of the disused Oldminster Sidings, marked by the buffer stops just beyond the locomotive, which were lifted two months after this photograph was taken. The photographer was standing on the site of Sharpness South signal box, a Midland cabin opened with the S&W&SBR's Sharpness station in 1879 and closed in 1903 when the GWR opened the new Sharpness Station Signal Box behind the Down platform. To the right is the bed of a second track between South Junction and the station that had been lifted in 1956. TREVOR OWEN

No. 6415 arrives at Sharpness with the branch shuttle in August 1964. M.E.J. Deane, courtesy Dr Simon Fosbury

The station's semi-rural setting belied its position in between the small town, which lay off to the right of this view, and the docks, to the left. Taken a few moments prior to the bottom picture opposite, No. 1474 prepares to leave on its journey back to Berkeley Road. The station remained neat and cared for, the staff having plenty of time to tidy up and tend the gardens between trains, the service by this date comprising only six return workings a day. Trevor Owen

No. 1474 takes water at Sharpness on 12th October 1963. A siding had run behind the disused Down platform but it had come in from the other end and ran behind the signal box, so could not be accessed from the platform; it was lifted when the line was singled in 1956. BLAKE PATTERSON/COURTESY THE RESTORATION & ARCHIVING TRUST/REF. BPUK1R19

The station's picturesque setting attracted plenty of photographers. Here, No. 1455 lets off steam as it waits for departure time in September 1963. DEREK CHAPLIN

LEFT: In the gentler, slower steam age, station gardens were always a delight and even during the years of the BR era when many were being run down prior to closure, staff sought to keep their environs looking their best. On 4th July 1964, No. 1445 quietly simmers behind a colourful bed of flowers, the whole scene bathed in warm sunshine.

BELOW: Clearly there was still some time to go before the next departure and all was quiet and peaceful for this view along the Up platform. The station was opened jointly by the Midland and Severn & Wye railway companies and thus the design of the building, a handsome, solid structure in red brick, was not redolent of other Midland stations of the period.
BOTH MARK B. WARBURTON

RIGHT: Standards were maintained right up until the end, as indicated by this view of No. 6412, waiting to head back to Berkeley Road with a late afternoon service in October 1964, days before final closure. The signal box, which was built in 1903 and had stood just the other side of the corrugated lamp hut, was a standard GW brick-built cabin with hipped roof but was unique in having the small waiting shelter on the Down platform built out from the front of it. The box is illustrated on page 328 of *Volume 2 Forest of Dean Lines and the Severn Bridge*. JOHN STRANGE/NPC

No. 1474 stands in the station with its single auto trailer on 12th October 1963, as the crew enjoy a chat sitting in the sunshine on the platform bench. The gents urinal and WC were at this end, whilst the rear wall was blank, access to the building being from the platform only. The only weather protection afforded to passengers was by the roof projecting forward a little and at both ends, vaguely Brunellian in style but fairly ineffective. After closure, the building stood empty for three years before being demolished in 1967. Note the row of BR fire buckets hung on the wall and the 4-wheeled platform trolley stored clear of the platform beneath. The platform lamps were gas lit, the supply coming from the gas works by the canal. BLAKE PATERSON/COURTESY THE RESTORATION & ARCHIVING TRUST/REF. BPUK1R20

No. 1445, here waiting patiently for departure time at Sharpness on 5th August 1964, appeared to have been having priming porblems. When the line between Sharpness South Junction and the station was singled in 1956, no loop was left in to serve the Down platform which was closed. This was another odd economy given that the line over the Severn Bridge was used as a diversionary route when the Severn Tunnel was closed for maintenance, whilst BR were looking to pass its use for heavier and more frequent trains by strengthening the bridge. Removal of the double track section thus left no crossing point between Berkeley Road and Lydney, a section of railway that it would have taken 20-25 minutes to traverse, restricting its capacity quite considerably. However, BR were also able then to effect another economy by closing Sharpness Station Signal Box, on 27th October 1957. Bill Potter/KRM

As we shall see, footplate crews sometimes moved their train away from the platform completely between services, 'parking' west of the station near to North Dock Branch Junction; the branch to North Dock can be seen crossing from right to left through the arch of the bridge, as No. 1472 trundles back in to the platform on 22nd August 1964. To the right of the train the bridgeplate for Bridge No. 16 can be seen near the base of the arch. The terrace of seven houses in the left background, built circa 1895 and known as Sunnybrook, still stand today. After a period when they were abandoned and derelict, they were converted as a smallholding in the early 2000s, called Sunnybrook Farm and part established on the railway formation; the west end is in residential use, with the rest used as farm buildings. The brick hut with the flat corrugated roof was built circa 1900 possibly as a pump house as there was a second GWR conical water tower (hidden behind the bridge pier – see next picture) provided here. BILL POTTER/KRM

BRITISH RAILWAY HISTORY IN COLOUR: 4B. GLOUCESTER MIDLAND LINES SOUTH – STONEHOUSE TO WESTERLEIGH

ABOVE: No. 1474 pulls back into the station on 12th October 1963; the resting point was usually just beyond the Up Fixed Distant signal seen above the carriage roof. Bridge No. 16, which still stands today, carried the road that ran across the high level swing bridge but is now only used as access to Sunnybrook Farm; between there and the swing bridge the road is now only used as a footpath. Built mostly of red brick but with blue brick strings at road level and stone parapet copings, the bridge comprises two semi-elliptical arches of 34ft 4ins. As can be seen, the gas main from Sharpness gas works was carried on cast iron stanchions across its east face. The North Dock Branch can be seen again in the background and also the water tower referred to in the previous caption. Note, too, the wire-fronted lock-up store on the right at the end of the Up platform.

BLAKE PATTERSON/COURTESY THE RESTORATION & ARCHIVING TRUST/REF. BPUK1R22

BERKELEY ROAD JUNCTION TO MIERY STOCK SIDINGS
WORKING OF PASSENGER TRAINS WITHOUT GUARDS BETWEEN LYDNEY TOWN AND BERKELEY ROAD

Auto coaches, fitted for control from one end only, are used for the local passenger train service between Lydney Town and Berkeley Road. Not more than one coach may be propelled by the engine and all other vehicles must be attached to the rear of the train.

The trains are worked without guards provided the formation is restricted to three vehicles and all the vehicles are fitted with the continuous brake complete. In the event of any train exceeding three vehicles, a guard must be provided.

The following instructions will apply to trains worked without guards:—

In the event of an accident or failure, the train must be considered as coming within the category of a light engine.

Should a train be stopped by accident, failure, obstruction or other cause, the Driver and Fireman must carry out the provisions of Rules 178, 179, 180, 181.

At stations where the trains commence their journey, and at intermediate stations where staff are on duty, the responsibility usually attaching to the Guard must be carried out by the person starting the train.

Should a train arrive at a station, and there be no station staff on duty, the Fireman must attend to the opening and closing of the doors, and give the signal to the Driver to start.

The Station Master, or other authorised person must see that the tail lamp is in position (and burning properly when necessary) before the train leaves the starting point. Should a vehicle be attached or detached from the train at an intermediate station, the Station Master or person in charge at that station must see that the tail lamp is transferred to the last vehicle of the train before it leaves the station.

In order to ensure the safe custody of letter mails, etc., the brake compartments of each set of coaches in the working will be provided with special locks and keys. A supply of keys will be issued to each Station Master for the use of the staff at his station.

ABOVE: Instructions regarding the working of auto trains between Berkeley Road and Lydney Town, taken from the *Sectional Appendix to the Working Time Table, Gloucester Traffic District, Oct. 1960* – the month the Severn Bridge disaster occurred. The opening intruction stating only one coach was to be propelled was clearly not adhered to from the photographic evidence and guards were not required.

RIGHT: Speed restrictions on the Berkeley Road to Lydney Town route, from the *Working Time Table of Passenger Trains, Gloucester District, 10th September 1962 to 16th June 1963.*

BERKELEY ROAD AND LYDNEY TOWN

Berkeley Road Junction	Main line to Branch (Through Junction). All Down and Up Trains	20
Berkeley Road Junction	Through Branch Platforms to Junction with Single line. All Down and Up trains	40
Berkeley Road Junction	Junction from Double to Single Line. All Down and Up trains	15
Berkeley Road to Sharpness (Single Line)	All Down and Up trains	40
Berkeley Loop	Berkeley Road South Junction to Berkeley Loop Junction. All Down and Up trains	15*
Berkeley Loop Junction	To and from the Loop Line	15
Sharpness South : 3m. 38ch. to 3m. 42ch. and 3m. 69ch. to 3m. 73ch.	All Down and Up trains entering or leaving Loop	15
Severn Bridge	No engine or train must cross the iron portion of the Severn Bridge in less than 3 minutes	
Severn Bridge Station	Entering or leaving Loops	15
	All Down and Up trains	15
Severn Bridge to Otters Pool Junction	All Down and Up trains	25
Lydney Junction	Otters Pool Junction to South Wales Main Line	15
	South Wales Main Line to Otters Pool Junction	15
Lydney Junction	Otters Pool Junction to Lydney Engine Shed Box. All Down and Up trains	10
Lydney Town	Junction from Double to Single Line	15
Lydney Town	Up Line to Up Goods Line	10
	Trains passing over the Goods Line must not exceed a speed of 10 m.p.h.	

*—Permanent Speed Restriction indicator provided.

THE SHARPNESS BRANCH

A fine view of the GWR conical pattern water tower at the end of the Up platform, with No. 1409 at the platform on 28th September 1963. This is our first encounter with No. 1409, which was new in October 1932 and that had spent most of its career from the summer of 1942 allocated to Gloucester but sub-shedded at Lydney. Based at Barnwood for the final months of its working life, it was withdrawn just over a fortnight after this picture was taken, on 14th October. Sold to Coopers Metals for scrap, it returned to Sharpness in early 1964 for cutting up. R. PATTERSON/COLOUR-RAIL

A second view from Oldminster Road, with No. 1445 again on 5th August 1964, looking across the old goods yard to the damaged Severn Bridge in the background. The wooden shed was the goods office but had been out of use since the limited amount of goods traffic here ceased when the sidings were lifted in 1956. It looks, however, as though it may subsequently have been converted for use as a residence. BILL POTTER/KRM

The Severn Bridge & Railway Hotel was opened at the same time as the station, in 1879. Here gazing down on No. 6437 in the summer of 1964, it is a rather fine building in red brick with stone window and door surrounds that has sadly fallen on hard times since the loss of the railway. Closing in the early 1980s, it became a care home for many years but is now in use as offices. Note the blue brick base of the demolished signal box in the right foreground. JOHN STRANGE/NPC

With the old line across the river to Lydney curving away through the bridge arch, No. 5420 stands at ease having just brought in an auto service from Berkeley Road, probably in the summer of 1963. The pannier tank was withdrawn from Barnwood shed in October of that year. GERALD PEACOCK

A delightful view of the station in October 1964, with the station master's floral handiwork to the fore. No. 1444, which had spent most of 1963 in store at Gloucester, was clearly in need of a polish, a thick layer of dirt obscuring the lined green livery applied in January 1958, but the maroon liveried auto trailer was gleaming and everything else looked spick and span, the station being kept neat and tidy to the end. The smart paintwork on the headless gas lamp post could have been an indication of the station's impending closure. BR had a habit at this period of such seemingly wasteful expenditure but loading a branch line's running costs – by whatever method – and thereby increasing its losses helped in the case for closure. It got to the stage that railwaymen and enthusiasts alike dreaded the sight of the paint brushes coming out. DEREK CHAPLIN

A view of the station from across the old goods yard, with No. 6437 and auto trailer at the platform on 17th May 1963. There was seemingly little call for goods facilities here at Sharpness, with no goods shed ever being provided, the yard comprising just two sidings running in from the west end of the station at North Dock Branch Junction. One ended alongside a loading bay on which stood the cattle pens seen in the foreground, whilst the other ran behind the Down platform and signal box, and was probably used for house coal deliveries. Livestock deliveries here were a regular traffic up to the 1950s, with various local butchers over the decades supplying fresh meat to ships discharging at Sharpness Docks. Note the Midland-style diagonal fencing around the station and bordering Oldminster Road above. A bus can be seen on the road, providing a local service connecting with the trains, what we would refer to today as an 'integrated transport system' – what a novel idea! B.J. ASHWORTH

THE SHARPNESS BRANCH

The sun did not always shine at Sharpness! No. 1474 is enveloped in its own steam, struggling to rise above the damp drizzle that lent the station a depressing air on 21st March 1964. DON MANN

But it was shining again for this view from a similar vantage point on 4th July 1964, which also shows that the old cattle pens had been dismantled in the fifteen weeks since the previous picture was taken. MARK B. WARBURTON

RIGHT: Even more historic than the joint GW and Midland notices at Berkeley were these Severn & Wye & Severn Bridge Railway and Severn & Wye Joint Railway cast iron signs near the old goods yard entrance. Still *in situ* in October 1964, both would be considered highly collectable nowadays but did either survive? JOHN STRANGE/NPC

ABOVE: Atop Bridge No. 16 would have seemed an obvious viewpoint for photographing the station but generally seems not to have been favoured by the photographers recording the last years of the branch. However, a sadly unrecorded 'photter' took this fine panorama from the bridge on 7th June 1962, with No. 6437 at the platfrom at the head of a two coach auto working. The giant Severn Ports warehouse dominates the right background and a couple of long rakes of wagons can be seen in some of the dock company sidings in the centre, beyond the water tower. The long siding running behind the platform had ended by the low mound visible above the far nameboard. The flat roofed extension at this end of the building is thought to have been a porters store. Earlier views of the station show that it was open to the elements, the roof being a BR addition in the early 1950s. COLOUR-RAIL

LEFT: Just over two years later, shortly before closure in October 1964, the same engine and two-coach combination feature in this similar view taken from the bridge by John Strange. Little had changed in the interim. JOHN STRANGE/NPC

Right: An 0-4-2 tank taking water from the tower at the end of the Up platform in 1964. The tower does not feature in a circa 1910 view of the station, so was probably a post-First World War addition. NPC

Below: No. 6412 and trailer are turned to gold by the low autumn sun in this October 1964 view. Note the bus again waiting on Oldminster Road. John Strange/NPC

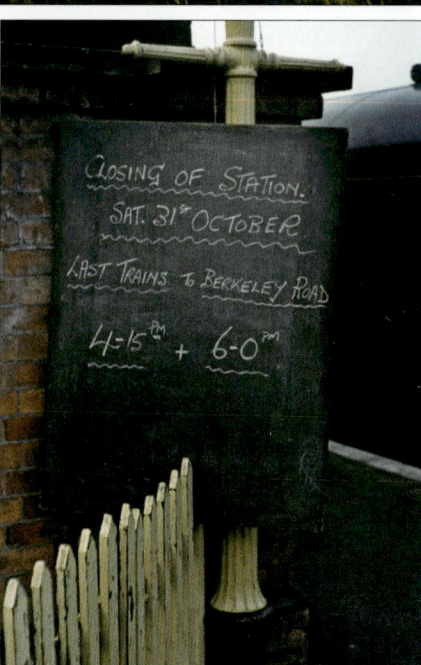

Bottom Left: This Midland Railway fireguard, seen on the disused platform in February 1967 shortly before the building was demolished, had been a fixture of the station waiting room. John Strange/NPC

Bottom Right: The end, 31st October 1964. NPC

LEFT: Not too many bothered with shots like this, showing the interior of the auto trailer whilst it was waiting at Sharpness on 4th August 1964. There are several of these vehicles in preservation but this is a rare colour view of the inside of trailer No. W244W in service. One of a batch of twenty-five built by BR at Swindon in 1954 to Diagram A43, these were the last GWR style trailers constructed. They were 63ft 0¾ins long, 8ft 11ins wide and with a wheelbase of 52ft 6ins on standard 9ft GWR pressed steel bogies. Seating was 70 + 4, with the seats being contemporary with those then being fitted in the first DMUs. It was intended that all would be given bird names but in the event, only the first two ever received them. No. W244W was turned out in plain maroon livery and spent most of its career in the West Country, arriving at Gloucester by March 1964. It was condemned at an unknown date but probably not long after all of the Gloucester auto diagrams ceased at the start of November 1964. BLAKE PATTERSON/COURTESY THE RESTORATION & ARCHIVING TRUST/REF. BPUK0476

RIGHT: It is not clear why footplate crews sometimes moved the auto trains a short distance to the west of the station between services, rather than waiting in the platform, unless it was simply to discourage prospective passengers from arriving too early and boarding when there was a long wait until the next departure. However, it does give us a chance to study North Dock Branch Junction, which had been out of use since the Severn Bridge disaster in October 1960, the line to which can be seen curving away in the distance. On the same damp day as the picture on page 336, No. 1474 stands by the Up Fixed Distant signal whilst waiting for the next departure. The North Dock Branch served the coal tips, trains loaded with Forest of Dean coal being able to reach them directly via the High Level swing bridge. The loop siding in the background to the left of the line to the Severn Bridge was a headshunt for the branch. DON MANN

BELOW: No. 1445 stands at the same spot on 5th August 1964. The junction had at one time been controlled by Sharpness North signal box but this was closed in 1904. The small hut visible in the left distance housed the North Ground Frame, which was brought in to use on 23rd October 1957 after the station sidings were lifted. BILL POTTER/KRM

The Severn Bridge and the line on to Lydney was covered in detail in Volume 2, *Forest of Dean Lines and the Severn Bridge*, but having reached Sharpness and afforded myself the luxury of additional pages courtesy of splitting this volume in two, it gave me the ideal opportunity to present a couple of superb views that have turned up since. With the photographer standing on top of the hill through which the 506-yards long Severn Bridge Tunnel burrowed, an ex-GWR 'Mogul' 2-6-0 passes by on the Severn Tunnel Junction to Gloucester main line with a train of vans on 20th June 1964. The damaged bridge with its two missing spans strides across the River Severn in the background. Until the tragic accident of the night of 25th October 1960, the line from Berkeley Road had connected Sharpness with Lydney and carried Forest of Dean coal over the river to be shipped from the docks at Sharpness. Opened to traffic in 1879, the line was operated by the Severn & Wye & Severn Bridge Railway until jointly taken over by the Midland and GWR companies in 1894. TREVOR OWEN/NPC

A fine study of Severn Bridge station, slumbering in bright sunshine on 12th August 1962. Nearly two years after the accident, the rails through the platforms are rusty and the station buildings await the return of trains. Sadly, apart from the two 'Severn Boar' rail tours, run within a fortnight of each other in June 1964, no trains were ever to call here again. The wooden station buildings matched those found elsewhere on the Severn & Wye system, being supplied by the Gloucester Railway Carriage & Wagon Company, whilst the signal box was a standard Midland cabin which opened on 12th November 1911, replacing the much taller wooden box which had been provided here originally. In the left background, the line curves round in a cutting which led to the rather discordantly named Severn Bridge Tunnel. Note the tablet catching apparatus in the left foreground and the occupation underbridge (No. 18, stone-built, 12 foot span) just beyond the station. ROY DENISON

The Floating Dock at Sharpness on a bright sunny day in October 1964, with the coastal trader *Alderd L* of Steendam in-bound. This 384 tons gross Dutch-owned vessel was built in 1955 by G.J.v.d. Werffs Schps of Westerbroek and at the date of this view was much engaged sailing to Cork in Ireland to collect cargoes of chocolate crumb, which was also made at the Cadburys factory alongside the Gloucester & Sharpness Canal at Frampton on Severn, where she thus may well have been bound. Traffic inwards in more recent years included gypsum coming in for a plasterboard factory adjacent to the docks (an employment enterprise project which has since foundered) and scrap metal, and the docks continue to be busy with shipping today. The deep water coal tip on the left fell out of use after the Second World War and had been decommissioned for nearly a decade when seen here, the tipping apparatus on the end of it having been dismantled. Note the grey painted box van in front of the warehouse on the right, which appears to be lettered M? I L – was this an internal user vehicle? The tall grain silo remains today but all of the warehouses and sheds to its right have gone, the warehouse to its left being the only one of traditional design still standing. DEREK CHAPLIN

SECTION 11

SHARPNESS DOCKS AND RAILWAY, AND COOPER'S METALS SCRAPYARD

The British Waterways tug *Primrose* moored up near the entrance lock in 1966. Built by Robert Cock & Sons at Appledore in 1906 for the Sharpness New Docks & Gloucester & Birmingham Navigation Company and fitted with a steam engine by Sissons of Gloucester, she came in to BW ownership upon Nationalisation of the waterways in 1948. Re-equipped with a Ruston oil engine in 1960, she was sold to the inimitable Captain Peter Herbert of Bude in 1981. She went to the Laxey Towing Co. Ltd in the Isle of Man in 1985 and to Tyne Towing Ltd in 1989, then changed hands twice more before very sadly being broken up at New Holland in 2014. Behind *Primrose* is the tanker barge *Wheldale H* of Hull, one of the large fleet of vessels built, owned and operated by John Harker Ltd of Knottingley and a sister to the *Arkendale H* and *Wastdale H*, which had collided with and brought down two spans of the Severn Bridge six years earlier. NORMAN ANDREWS/NPC

The Gloucester & Berkeley Canal had its original entrance at Sharpness Point, with gates from the River Severn leading to an outer tidal basin and then a lock to access the canal itself. The canal had been constructed southwards from Gloucester but had extended only five miles to Hardwicke by the time money ran out in 1799. It was not until 1817 that building work was recommenced and the canal was finally officially opened throughout on 26th April 1827. As the new traffic route gradually became more successful, by the 1860s the company were finally able to pay off the debts incurred in completing it forty years earlier but other problems were about to force further great expenditure.

The greatest problem with the rapid growth in trade were the restrictions imposed by the small tidal dock at the entrance and the width of the lock in to the canal. With ever larger sailing vessels starting to arrive, the lock was simply not big enough for them to pass through, so they were forced to discharge their cargoes into lighters in the tidal basin. This inevitably led to delays, with ships moored near the Bristol Avon for five days on average – and occasionally much longer – whilst waiting for access to the canal. Accordingly, the canal company's engineer, W.B. Clegram, drew up plans for a new entrance half a mile downstream at a place known as Holly Hazel Pill, with a tidal basin, a lock double the size of the original one and a huge new floating dock. With the company's finances in a healthy state, Clegram's plans, which he had costed at £162,000 including a dry dock, were approved by the shareholders and an Act was obtained in 1870 to raise the additional capital required.

Construction work had begun by early 1871, the contract having been awarded to George Wythes, an experienced contractor who had recently completed a dock extension at Millwall. Decades on from building the original entrance and dock, excavation of the new dock was greatly aided by steam-power, with railway lines laid along the bed to carry away the spoil, cranes for lifting the giant stone blocks used to build the dock walls and portable engines pumping water out of the workings. An army of navvies were also employed in the construction, most housed in rows of huts made of turf with felt covered boards for the roofs. The company also built Dock Row at this time (now part of Dock Road), four pairs of semi-detached houses for key dock workers, which was to be the precursor of numerous other terraces spread around

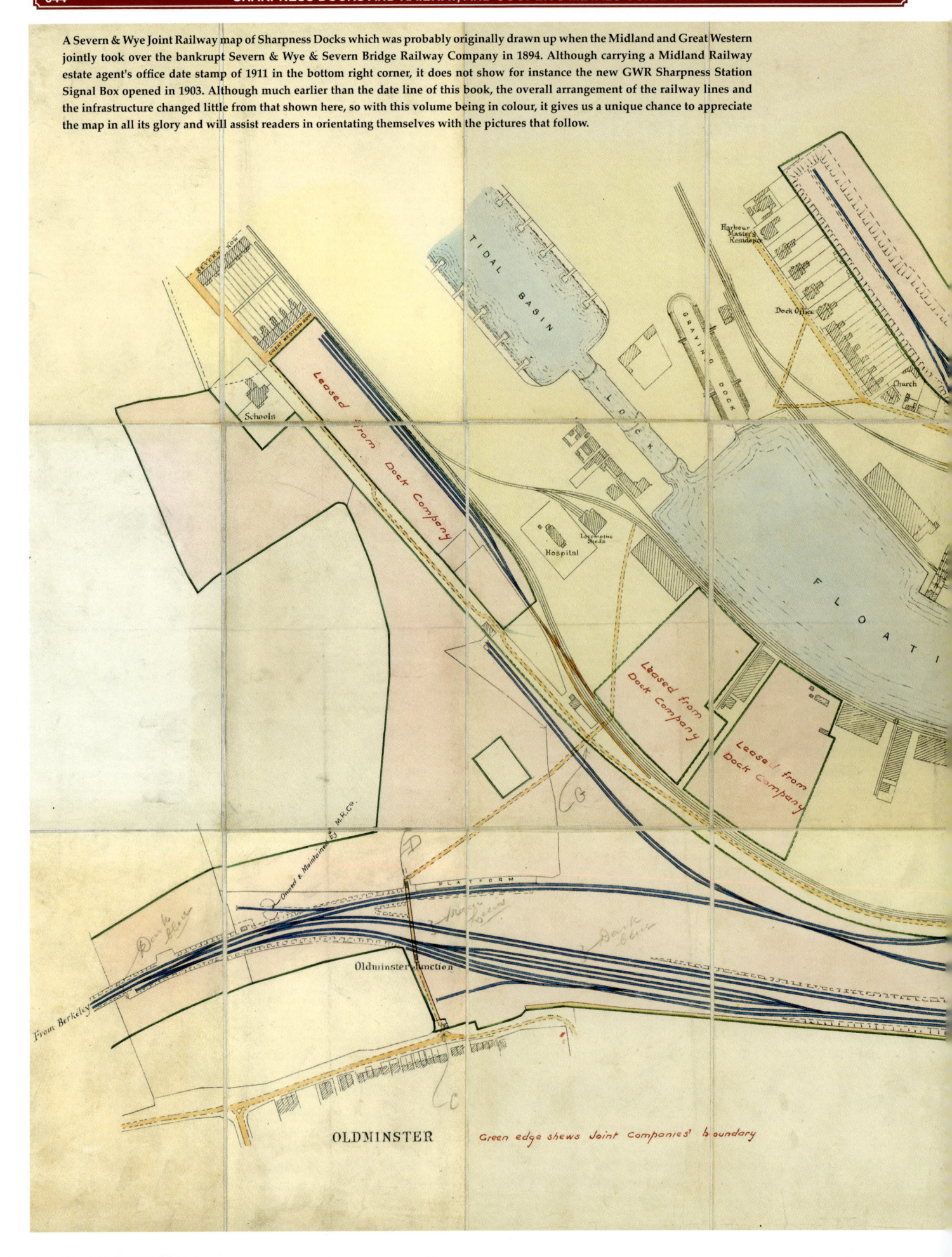

SHARPNESS DOCKS AND RAILWAY, AND COOPER'S METALS SCRAPYARD

A Severn & Wye Joint Railway map of Sharpness Docks which was probably originally drawn up when the Midland and Great Western jointly took over the bankrupt Severn & Wye & Severn Bridge Railway Company in 1894. Although carrying a Midland Railway estate agent's office date stamp of 1911 in the bottom right corner, it does not show for instance the new GWR Sharpness Station Signal Box opened in 1903. Although much earlier than the date line of this book, the overall arrangement of the railway lines and the infrastructure changed little from that shown here, so with this volume being in colour, it gives us a unique chance to appreciate the map in all its glory and will assist readers in orientating themselves with the pictures that follow.

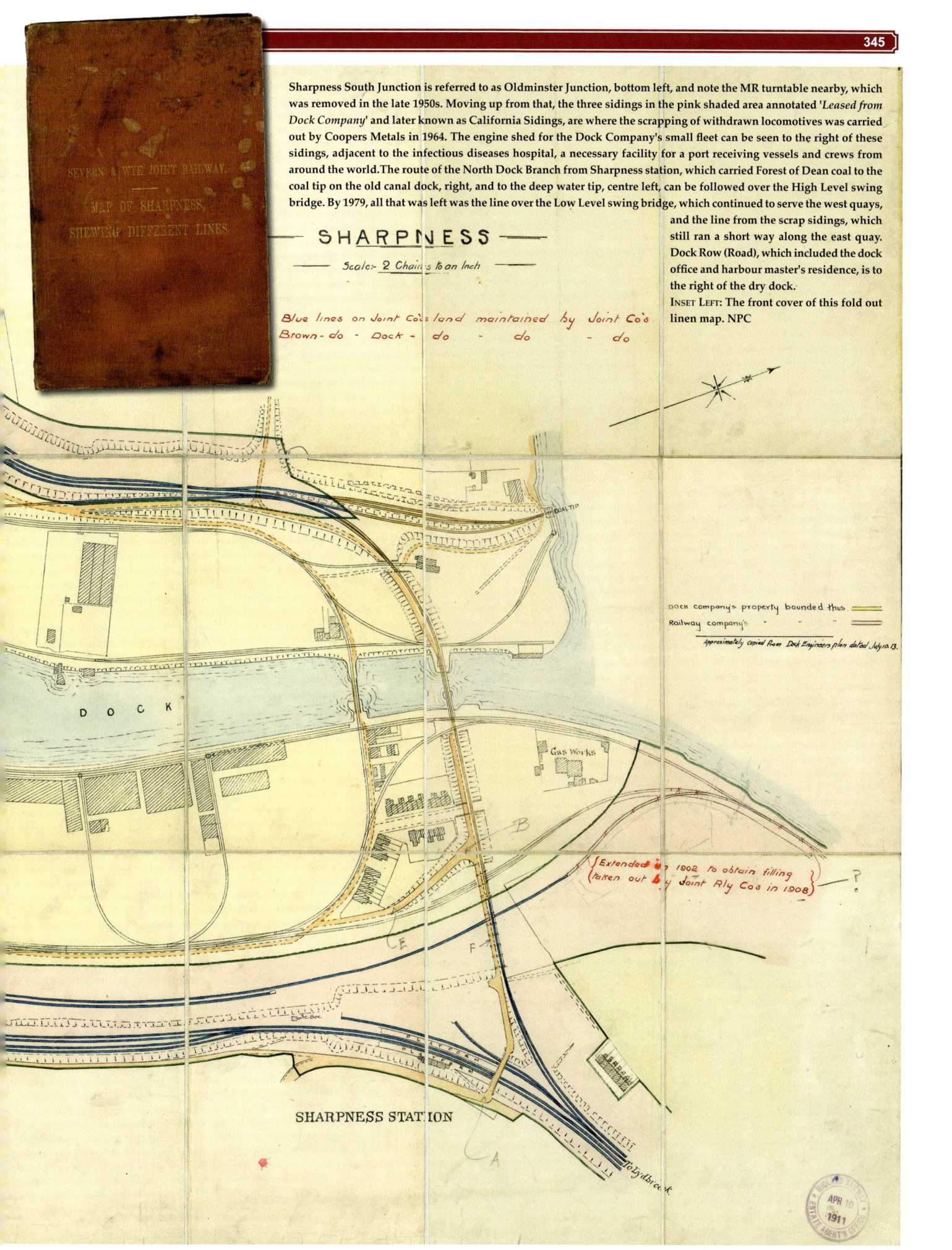

Sharpness South Junction is referred to as Oldminster Junction, bottom left, and note the MR turntable nearby, which was removed in the late 1950s. Moving up from that, the three sidings in the pink shaded area annotated '*Leased from Dock Company*' and later known as California Sidings, are where the scrapping of withdrawn locomotives was carried out by Coopers Metals in 1964. The engine shed for the Dock Company's small fleet can be seen to the right of these sidings, adjacent to the infectious diseases hospital, a necessary facility for a port receiving vessels and crews from around the world. The route of the North Dock Branch from Sharpness station, which carried Forest of Dean coal to the coal tip on the old canal dock, right, and to the deep water tip, centre left, can be followed over the High Level swing bridge. By 1979, all that was left was the line over the Low Level swing bridge, which continued to serve the west quays, and the line from the scrap sidings, which still ran a short way along the east quay. Dock Row (Road), which included the dock office and harbour master's residence, is to the right of the dry dock.

INSET LEFT: The front cover of this fold out linen map. NPC

Three of the dock company's steam fleet of 0-4-0 saddle tanks, *S.D. No. 3*, *S.D. No. 5* (both built by the Avonside Engine Co.) and *S.D. No. 6* (a Peckett), passed in to British Waterways ownership in 1948 but only one was still in operation by 1961. Here, on 3rd March, *S.D. No. 3* (AE Works No. 1446, delivered new to Sharpness in 1902) is seen in steam, the only colour view I have seen showing it so, on the dock railway lines bordering the east side of the estate. The houses in the background are on Oldminster Road and are all still recognisable today, with Oldminster Sidings just visible running along in front. M.E.J. Deane, courtesy Dr Simon Fosbury

the site of the new dock, whilst the community grew to include shops serving ships crews as well as dock workers and their families, a post office, a tin chapel, three hotels and even an infectious diseases hospital.

The new dock was formally opened on 25th November 1874 and, as already noted, led directly to the construction of a Midland Railway branch from Berkeley Road, opened to goods traffic in 1875 and passengers a year later, followed by the opening of the line over the Severn Bridge from Lydney in 1879, allowing Forest of Dean coal, which had hitherto been shipped out coastwise from the harbour at Lydney and the tiny dock at Bullo Pill, access to a deep water port. A coal tip was built on the old canal arm, which was supplemented by a deep water tip on the west side of the Floating Dock in 1886; both were served by the North Dock Branch which left the Lydney to Berkeley Road line just before Sharpness station and ran across the High Level swing bridge.

The main commodities handled at Sharpness were grain, timber and, from the mid-1920s, petroleum, with the vast bulk of the cargoes being inwards. However, as these long established trades faded away through the 1960s, leading to the closure and eventual demolition of some of the big warehouses, British Waterways began looking for new flows, which started to include outward traffic such as scrap metal and containers. A new grain silo was built in the 1970s and new cranes were also installed. Since 2012, the port has fallen under the remit of the Canal & River Trust, formed to take over all of state-owned BW's responsibilities but all quayside activities are run by Sharpness Dock Limited. The dry dock also remains operational and is run by Sharpness Shipyard & Drydock Ltd. However, many of the dock workers houses around the dockyards were demolished in the early 1990s.

Rail access to the new dock was comprehensive, with a line also running across the Low Level swing bridge to serve the quays on the west side. Meanwhile, lines running the length of the east side could be accessed from both ends. From circa 1882, when they took over working the North Dock Branch, the dock company began operating what grew to be a small stud of steam locomotives. In 1961, the first diesel shunter arrived, supplemented by a second in 1963, with the last of the steam engines, *SD No. 3*, then placed in storage. They also had their own fleet of internal user wagons, including 5-plank opens and at least two long wheelbase box vans.

Sadly, despite a number of initiatives and although the docks remain busy with ships coming in, rail traffic to and from Sharpness ceased circa 1989, although the line still runs to Oldminster and is still operational, the loop there being used by the nuclear waste trains to Berkeley to run round. A fair amount of the dock railway system still remains in place, albeit mostly buried under grass or new concrete. To date, no new flows have been identified that would merit reopening the line in to the docks, public pressure in the early 2000s preventing the construction of a waste incinerator at Sharpness that would have been rail served; it was built near Gloucester instead and has no rail connection.

However, the Vale of Berkeley Railway have established a base in the old diesel locomotive shed near the Dry Dock, on the west side of the Floating Dock, where they are currently restoring several locomotives and items of rolling stock, whilst making plans and raising funds to reopen the branch as a heritage and, possibly, commuter line. Although not intending to bring back freight traffic to and from the docks, might this yet prove a catalyst for that to happen?

Having been retained as a back-up engine in case of failure of the first diesel shunter delivered to Sharpness in 1961, S.D. No. 3 was probably taken out of use following the delivery of the second diesel in 1963. The steam locomotive shed was on the east side at the south end of the Floating Dock – so was just out of sight to the right here – and the 0-4-0ST had been dragged out to be photographed on the occasion of a society visit (GRS7) in 1964. This is the first of several studies of the engine all believed to have been taken on that occasion but only one of them is definitively dated, so it is possible that this may have happened more than once. Note that the cabside plates had already been removed and the 'For Sale' notice chalked there instead – did that relate to the plate or to the engine? The buildings in the background have all gone. NPC

The only one of these pictures to be properly dated is this view, recorded as being taken on 24th May 1964, with the engine posing against a backdrop of dock cranes. IRS *Handbook J, Industrial Locomotives of Central Southern England* (1981), states that *S.D. No. 3* was scrapped on site by Small & Lewis (Metals) Ltd of Gloucester circa May 1964 but these views would suggest the date of scrapping was later. NPC

An undated view but almost certainly taken on the same occasion, looking north with the deep water coal tip behind. BILL POTTER/KRM

INSET RIGHT: One of the cabside plates from *S.D. No. 3*. In unrestored 'off engine' condition, it was originally purchased by a member of the Gloucestershire Railway Society and can be seen on their stall at Dowty Ashchurch in the picture on page 46 of *Volume 3 Gloucester Midland Lines Part 1: North*; it is now in my safe keeping. NPC

The sun is shining here but the engine is in the same position, so this is again almost certainly on the same day. Note the British Waterways roundel on the tankside. NPC

A final look at Sharpness Docks *S.D. No. 3* in a slide that the photographer dated as October 1964, which would push the locomotive's scraspping date back even further. It is posed outside the engine shed, the entrance to which is just visible on the right, in a view looking north. The entrance lock lay behind the houses in the left background; none of the buildings seen here remain today. DEREK CHAPLIN

ABOVE: The High Level swing bridge being swung in January 1967 to allow a ship to pass through. It carried the North Dock Branch of the S&W&SBR, the route of which ran just to the left of the road heading up to and over Bridge No. 16 in the centre right distance. All Forest coal which was shipped out via Sharpness was brought in over this bridge, the operation of which was controlled from ground frames at either end. As can be seen, the rails were boarded in, so it could be used by road vehicles as well and also pedestrians. Today, the rails have gone and the surface is tarmacadamed. The Sharpness Railway & Severn Bridge Hotel, which is seen again on top of the rise in the right background, was one of three hotels here (the others being the Sharpness Hotel and the Pier View Hotel), none of which still operate today. Timber was an important trade here, the storage shed on the left being one of many around the docks. JOHN STRANGE/NPC

LEFT: A view of the high level bridge in 1979, looking north-west from the quayside. There is currently no commercial traffic along the canal to Gloucester but the bridge is still swung occasionally, particularly for masted sailing ships making their way up to the annual Gloucester Tall Ships Festival. The rails just glimpsed in the left foreground ran to a timber stacking area alongside the junction between the canal and the old dock, which we shall see shortly. AUTHOR

BRITISH RAILWAY HISTORY IN COLOUR: 4B. GLOUCESTER MIDLAND LINES SOUTH – STONEHOUSE TO WESTERLEIGH

SHARPNESS

Oldminster Sidings

The position of the Signal (worked by Guards and Shunters from a Ground Frame) regulating the running of trains and engines on the Up Goods Siding fixed near the connections with the Sidings alongside the Up Goods Siding and the Goods Siding at Sharpness South Box is normally at "Clear".

The Signal must be placed to "Danger" to protect shunting operations between the Sidings and the Down Goods Sidings or between the Up and Down Goods Sidings.

Truck Weighbridge Machine

Engines must not be allowed to pass over the truck weighbridge machine at Sharpness Station when the machine is in gear. No train or engine must pass over the truck weighbridge at a greater speed than 3 miles an hour.

North Dock Branch

A Ground Frame works the connection between the Single line and the North Dock Branch and is released by key on the Electric Token.

Only one engine may be allowed on the West side of the Docks at one and the same time, and when a train or engine has passed on to the North Docks Branch, no other train or engine may be allowed to go on to the Branch until the one from the West side has returned and the North Docks Branch is clear.

SWING BRIDGE. A fixed signal is provided at each end of the Viaduct to regulate the running of trains and engines over the Bridge; and catch points are provided to prevent any train or engine entering upon the Viaduct when the Bridge is open and the signals are at "Danger". The signals and catch points are worked from the Ground Frames from which the Swing Bridge and the level crossing gates are controlled.

The catch points must always be kept in the throw-off position and the signals at "Danger", except when it is necessary for a train or engine to pass, and before either of the signals is taken off, care must be taken to ascertain that the catch points are in the proper position, that the Swing Bridge is locked, and the line is clear, and that the level crossing gates are closed against the highway.

The Bridgeman will be responsible for working the bridge, points and signals, and for attending to the level crossing gates during the time he is on duty.

When the Bridgeman is not on duty, however, and a train is required to pass over the swing bridge, the Coal Tip Foreman or Shunter in charge of the work will be held responsible for working the points and signals, locking the bridge gates, etc.

Shunting at Sharpness Docks

It is important that Drivers shunting at Sharpness or running round the Docks should proceed cautiously, keep their engines under control, and be prepared to stop short of any obstruction; the following instructions for regulating shunting at Sharpness must be strictly carried out:—

East Side.—Traffic may be exchanged between the Docks Sidings and the Commission's Sidings by either shunting engine but a proper understanding must first be reached by the two Foremen concerned before the shunt is made. A Stop lamp indicator is provided applicable to Down movements from Sharpness South to the Docks Sidings. The Commission's engines must not pass this stop lamp indicator until instructed by the Foreman.

West Side.—Neither the Commission's engine nor the Docks engine may pass the stop board marking the boundary between the Docks Sidings unless accompanied by and in charge of the Foreman or Shunter on to whose Sidings the movement is to be made.

Vehicles with a wheel base exceeding 20 feet are prohibited in Sharpness Docks.

ABOVE: From the Sectional Appendix to the Working Time Table, Gloucester Traffic District, Oct. 1960.
BELOW: From the Working Time Table, Gloucester District, 10th September 1962 to 16th June 1963.

K150

ENGINE RESTRICTIONS—continued

BERKELEY ROAD AND SHARPNESS

In addition to types of engines authorised to work over this Section, as shown below, 78XX Class engines may work between Berkeley Road Junction and Sharpness South via Berkeley Loop or via Berkeley Road Junction, also over Sharpness North and South Dock Branches, subject to the following restrictions:—

(1) Not to use Crossover Road between Sharpness Branch Platforms at Berkeley Road Station.
(2) Canal (4¼ m.p. and 4⅜ m.p.)
(3) On Sharpness North Dock Branch may work up to but not over Swing Bridge No. 3 over Gloucester and Berkeley Canal (4¼ m.p. and 4⅜ m.p.)
(4) On Sharpness South Dock Branch may work up to but not beyond gate.
(5) Turntable at Sharpness not to be utilised.

The following restrictions also apply:
36XX, 37XX, 46XX, 57XX, 67XX, 77XX, 87XX, 96XX, 97XX, and 56XX Classes are prohibited over Sharpness North Docks.
2251 Class (2200 to 2298 and 3200 to 3219) may work over the Sharpness North Docks Branch up to, but not over, the first connection beyond Swing Bridge No. 3, 44 m.p.
Ex L.M.S. engines working over the Gloucester to Bristol Section may work between Berkeley Road and Sharpness South without restriction.

2-8-0 Engines of the 28XX and 38XX Classes may work between Berkeley Road and Sharpness North and South Dock Branches, subject to the observance of service restrictions:

Berkeley Road Junction to Sharpness South (Down Advanced Starting Signal)	Running Lines.
Sharpness South	Siding.
South Docks Branch (South Junction to Docks Gates)	Up and Down Lines.
Berkeley Loop (Berkeley Road South Junction to Berkeley Loop Junction)	Up and Down Lines.
Crossovers at Berkeley Road, Sharpness and on Docks Branch	—PROHIBITED.

Note.—All Lines, Sidings, Crossovers, etc., other than those specified—PROHIBITED.

B.R. Standard Class 3, 78XXX engines must not work over these sections except that Crossover Roads between Sharpness Branch platforms at Berkeley Road Station must not be used.

ABOVE AND BELOW: These ground frame cabins, positioned on the west side of the North Dock at either end of the High Level swing bridge, were also photographed in January 1967. They were brought in to use over the weekend of 6th–7th November 1904 but had been taken out by 1979. Happily, both cast iron nameplates survive and can now be seen in the Dean Forest Railway's museum at Norchard. BOTH JOHN STRANGE/NPC

SHARPNESS DOCKS AND RAILWAY, AND COOPER'S METALS SCRAPYARD

LEFT: This rake of ancient internal user wagons was photographed on 4th June 1967. Although the docks had been under the ownership of first the British Transport Commission and then British Waterways since Nationalisation in 1948, the wagons were still lettered 'SD' for Sharpness Docks, denoting their ownership by the Sharpness New Docks & Gloucester & Birmingham Navigation Company. A few of them survived in use until the mid 1960s and possibly slightly later. From the picture, it would appear that the livery was all over lead grey with white lettering; some had black strapping, solebars and buffer beams. Behind the wagons are the concrete arches that carried the lines to the deep water coal tip; the line at a higher level was for loaded wagons, whilst empties could run back by gravity on the lower line. BILL POTTER/KRM

RIGHT: SD wagon No. 16, seen here in June 1966, looks to be in an all over lead grey livery. There is also a cast 'MR' on the axleboxes, so it would appear that they were a standard design of 5-plank, 9ft wheelbase open wagon of 1880s or 1890s vintage, purchased second-hand from the Midland Railway. JOHN STRANGE/NPC

BELOW: Another rake of SD wagons in June 1966, looking from the higher level of the North Docks Branch, south-east across storage sheds V1, V2 and V3. These have since been demolished and replaced by a block of much larger modern industrial units. JOHN STRANGE/NPC

ABOVE: A January 1967 view of the rails of the North Dock Branch curving around from the High Level swing bridge. Note the protecting signal which was controlled from Sharpness Swing Bridge West Ground Frame, the cabin of which can be seen to the right. Beyond the signal is the swing section of the Severn Bridge, which was left permanently open after the disaster. Demolition of the bridge would begin later in the year. JOHN STRANGE/NPC

BELOW: Trains over the Low Level swing bridge were controlled by this hand operated semaphore signal, seen here in 1979 looking west. Its design and operation owed more to maritime practice and it replaced an earlier slotted post signal with twin arms. AUTHOR

BELOW: A row of standard gauge timber trolleys out of use in 1966, on the siding behind the north timber yard; laid in circa 1890, it had originally included a loop as well and ended just beneath the old coal tip. NORMAN ANDREWS/NPC

Looking south along the old barge arm and dock in June 1966, with the Training Ship *Vindicatrix* in the centre distance and the old Severn & Wye coal tip on the left. Provided when the Severn Bridge Railway opened in 1879, it enabled coal loading of vessels here. Built almost entirely of wood, it continued in use after the larger deep water tip opened in the new docks in 1886 and even after the accident to the Severn Bridge in 1960 – until February 1965 it was used to load coal delivered by rail from Forest pits, in to barges for delivery to the Cadbury works along the canal at Frampton on Severn. It was similar in design to the coal tips to be found across the South Wales coal ports in the 19th century, its situation on a backwater at Sharpness enabling its survival into the second half of the 20th century. It was demolished in 1971. The water tower in the left background was part of the *Vindicatrix* Sea Training Camp which housed the trainee merchant seamen. JOHN STRANGE/NPC

A side view of the coal tip, with the Severn Bridge in the background, in summer 1966. Wagons were gravity worked to and from the tip, a double track loop siding being provided for loadeds being tipped here, with a single empties road then dropping away at a lower level. NORMAN ANDREWS/NPC

A portrait view of the tip looking north on 22nd August 1964, with the canal turning east into the main docks behind, past the gas holder. BILL POTTER/KRM

ABOVE: The first diesel locomotive replacement for the steam engines was No. DL1, an 0-4-0 which arrived new from Ruston & Hornsby in 1961 (Works No. 463150). On 26th May 1970, with paintwork still gleaming, the engine is seen posed on the low level line at the north end of the dock site, with the high level line just visible in the background. DL1 remained in use until the cessation of rail traffic at the docks in the late 1980s.

BELOW: A rear view of the second diesel, No. DL2, on the line over the Low Level swing bridge on 27th July 1971. Note that the bridge was protected by lifting barriers for road vehicles, as well as the semaphore signal for rail traffic. BOTH BILL POTTER/KRM

No. DL2 was an 0-6-0 built by Bagnall's of Stafford in 1962 (Works No. 3151). However, when new it had first gone on demonstration at BP's oil refinery on the Isle of Grain in Kent, arriving at Sharpness in 1963; along with No. DL1, it remained here until the dock rail system was taken out of use in the late 1980s. Behind, in a classic post-war dock scene still being recreated here at Sharpness on 27th July 1971, the bagged cargo of the Cork-registered coaster *G.R. Velie* – a regular visitor to Sharpness – is being craned out of the vessel's hold into internal user wagons for transporting to the warehouses on the opposite side of the dock. Note the Severn Ports Warehousing Co. Ltd lettering on the warehouse; this concern had ceased operations in the early 1930s but its business was subsequently resurrected by a consortium of other companies led by the Bristol corn merchants Henry Hosegood & Sons Ltd. *G.R. Velie* was Dutch-built in 1958 and named *Carnissesingel* until 1966, her name being changed after purchase by Marine Transport Services Ltd of Cork. Sold on again in 1974, she was renamed *Solway Firth*, then becoming *Dynamic* (1975), *Frida* (1976) and lastly *Tarek* in 1978, in which guise she is thought to have been lost after being limpet mined at anchor off Tyre on 27th April 1979. BILL POTTER/KRM

LEFT: On 19th January 1983, the docks rail system was used for the onward transportation of a consignment of steel coil delivered by sea to Sharpness. No. DL2 is first seen on the quay alongside the MV *Dego* which had brought in the cargo of steel coils, one of which can be seen being craned off the ship. Built in 1964 at Groningen in Holland as *Diana*, her name was changed to *Tourmaline* after being sold to French owners in 1966. Bought by Dego Marine Ltd in 1982, she was renamed *Dego* and registered at Limassol, Cyprus. Newtime Marine Ltd were her next owners in 1984, who changed the name to *Deco* but retained her Limassol registration. On 12th July 1985, during a voyage from Sables d'Olonne to Warrenpoint in Northern Ireland with a cargo of barley, she stranded only two miles after leaving port and sank two days later. The picture is unfortunately not quite sharp but is a record of what was one of the last cargoes unloaded here on to rail wagons for onward despatch.

RIGHT AND BELOW: The sequence of photographs presented over these two pages show the route taken, with apparently two trips being required, one using covered steel coil carrying bogie wagons (which I think was the first trip) and one of 4-wheeled flat wagons and tarpaulins. These had to be alternatively propelled and hauled over the much reduced dock railway system to reach the quayside where the ship was moored. With loading of the bogie coil carriers complete, No. DL2 is first seen coming off the line from the quay (right), before then reversing back past the site of California Sidings (below), where Cooper's Metals had scrapped withdrawn steam locomotives nearly two decades earlier.

BRITISH RAILWAY HISTORY IN COLOUR: 4B. GLOUCESTER MIDLAND LINES SOUTH – STONEHOUSE TO WESTERLEIGH   359

ABOVE LEFT AND RIGHT: These final two views of the trip with the loaded bogie wagons show No. DL2 first reversing alongside Bridge Road, before then heading across it to deliver the train on to the BR siding.

ABOVE: With driver Colin Becket at the controls, No. DL2 poses whilst reversing the 4-wheeled flat wagons past the site of the steam locomotive shed on to the quayside. The lofty 6,000 ton capacity grain silo in the background was built by a Dutch firm in the 1970s, during a period when then owners British Waterways made a concerted effort to attract new traffic to the docks, and it remains in use today.

RIGHT: A different angle of the crossing of Bridge Road, as No. DL2 heads over with the loaded 4-wheeled flats.

These slides were taken by DEREK MARKEY, a remarkable man who had worked on the railway as a signalman at Coaley Junction and Berkeley Road. Having seen *Vol. 1 West Gloucester & Wye Valley Lines*, he thought that these rare pictures of one of the Sharpness industrial shunters at work may be of interest in a future part of the series, so very generously gave them to Paul Woollard in 2013 for scanning. Sadly, Derek has since died but I have presented all seven of the pictures here, even though a couple of them are not sharp, as a tribute to his foresight in taking them and his generosity in handing them to Paul so they could be used.

SHARPNESS DOCKS AND RAILWAY, AND COOPER'S METALS SCRAPYARD

Birmingham & Midland Canal Carrying Co. Ltd narrowboats at Sharpness in May 1967, whilst on a trial run to load 75 tons of Polish redwood and deliver it to the Avon Timber Co. at Warwick. This must have been a rather roundabout trip, travelling back loaded via the canal to Gloucester, the River Severn to Worcester and then on the Worcester & Birmingham Canal to meet the Grand Union Canal in Birmingham and head down to Warwick. Two pairs of boats made the trip, being, from the right, *Anson*, *Ash* and *Linda*, with the one hard against the dockside probably *Argon*. All are superb examples of traditional canal boat art, with decorative shaded lettering, painted panels and beautifully painted cans but this was the mark of a carrying company which had only been set up two years previously by a small group of Inland Waterways Association enthusiasts in an attempt to revive traditional canal transport. Insolvency was staved off in the late 1970s, the company carrying on until 2000, when a new concern, Birmingham Canal Boat Services Ltd was set up. *Anson*, now a trip boat, and the butty *Ash* continue in use with this new concern. The British waterways tug *Severn Iris* is moored to the far quay, next to the Low Level swing bridge. Built at Falmouth in 1905, she was rescued from imminent breaking in 1985 and is now converted as a houseboat in Cumbria, although is not seaworthy. Early OS maps refer to the Low Level bridge as a drawbridge, possibly because it swung from one end, rather than in the centre as did the High Level bridge. NORMAN ANDREWS/NPC

The timeline for this series of books is generally 1955-1975 but occasionally we stray outside of that for a good reason, such as here. This is a rare colour view of a very rare occurrence, when a DEMU traversed the dock railway with a rail tour on 12th October 1985. This joint Southern Electric Group/RCTS 'Avon & Somerset Rail Tour', using 'Hastings' Class '202' DEMU six car set No. 1017, started out from Watford Junction at 7.24am and travelled via Westbury and Taunton to Bristol TM. The branches to Portishead, Severn Beach, Tytherington Quarry and Sharpness Docks were then visited, before a return home to Watford via Gloucester and Swindon, arriving around midnight. The time here at Sharpness was approximately 6.20pm, hence dusk was falling and the tour was about 15 minutes down on schedule. I have no details but I doubt that the train crossed the bridge. All of the dock housing seen here has gone.
DEREK MARKEY/PAUL WOOLLARD COLLECTION

As these pictures show, the timber and grain trades were still the mainstay of the docks at Sharpness in the 1960s, although that was soon to change. Grain unloaded at Sharpness included wheat, barley, oats and maize, mostly loose in ships' holds, although some did arrive bagged. The unloading of loose grain was facilitated by the use of floating pneumatic elevators, of which at one time there were three, *Leitrim*, *Dunkirk* and *GWR No. 1 Cardiff*, the three together having a combined discharge capacity of 300 tons per hour. With big ships, all three would be used to speed up the process, with pipes running from the ship's hold directly in to the Severn Ports Warehousing Company's grain warehouse. *Leitrim* could even steam out in to the Severn to unload a ship too heavily laden to get over the lock cill in to the dock. I have been unable to find out anything in regards to *Cardiff*, seen here in 1966, but the *GWR No. 1* on the nameplate clearly indicates that it was originally a railway owned vessel. *Leitrim* was converted from an Irish Sea packet steamer and was here at Sharpness in 1900; *GWR No. 1 Cardiff* looks to date from a slightly later period and was probably purpose built, quite possibly for use at Cardiff Docks originally. If anyone has more information on this vessel I would love to hear from them. In the background, the coaster *Wroclaw* is unloading timber. NORMAN ANDREWS/NPC

LEFT: Seen in the background of the previous picture, the Polish Steamship Company's *Wroclaw* is moored to the west quay in 1966, unloading a cargo of Polish redwood, some of which the B&MCC narrowboats in the foreground were waiting to load, as already noted. Built at Flensburg in 1935 and named *Otto Alfred Muller*, on 17th August 1944, the ship was set on fire and and sunk in the port of Szczecin by an Allied air raid. Raised by Polish services in 1947, she was rebuilt by the Gdynia shipyard and entered service in June 1951 as *Wroclaw*. On the night of 4th June 1968, while on voyage from Gdansk to Helsinki, she went on the rocks off the coast of the island of Saarema in the Baltic Sea and sank. NORMAN ANDREWS/NPC

LEFT: The nearly new coaster *Hanne R*, built at Fredrikshavn in 1965 and of 1,248 grt, alongside the east quay and rail-mounted crane No. CE8 in 1966. The vessel was shortly to be renamed *Hanne Dancoast*, reflecting the name of the Danish shipping company whose dc logo features on the bow, appearing again at Sharpness in 1976. She changed her name numerous times after 1982, finally trading as *Captain Moustafa* until March 2009, after which her registry was closed. NORMAN ANDREWS/NPC

ABOVE: Some of the cranes and loading hoppers on the west quay in January 1978, looking north towards the two swing bridges. NPC

RIGHT: The coaster *Gertrud Bratt*, owned by the Swedish shipping company of Adolph Bratt, riding high in the Floating Dock after having her cargo of timber unloaded on to the west quay circa 1962. Note the SD open wagons alongside, whilst much of the timber has been loaded on to standard gauge trolleys such as that seen a little earlier. *Gertrud Bratt* was built in March 1957 and renamed *Carmen* in 1967 after being sold to Chilean owners. On 12th October 1977, the ship ran aground and was wrecked on the island of Santa Maria, in the Azores. NPC

LEFT: A view from the High Level swing bridge in 1979, with three large ships in port, the nearest being the coaster *Kiekeberg* of Hamburg unloading on the left. Built and registered in Hamburg in 1977 and of 1,689 grt, *Kiekeberg* traded regularly to British ports, changing name to *Nordcarrier* in 1989. However, since early 2009 she has been based in the West Indies and is now named *Laguna*. Today, this scene has changed considerably, with only the nearer two cranes on the left still remaining and just one of the long line on the right. Beyond the Severn Ports warehouse and the 1930s grain silo on the left, none of the buildings remain but a new cement terminal has been constructed here. AUTHOR

RIGHT: With the low level bridge swung clear and the barrier in place across the road, the coastal tanker *Borman*, owned by Bowker & King and registered at the Port of London, heads into the Floating Dock, having made a delivery to the petroleum storage depot at Quedgeley, near Gloucester, in 1979. This trade ceased with the closure of the depot in 1985 and there is no commercial traffic on the canal to Gloucester today. On the right are storage sheds filled with timber. For many years, this section of the dock was undeveloped, little more than a field referred to by dockers as the 'green bank', which by tradition became the area where timber was unloaded and stacked. The quay wall was finally completed up as far as the low level bridge in 1941 and the timber sheds were erected shortly after. For a number of years, between the two world wars, Sharpness had the third largest trade in imported timber in the UK. AUTHOR

Another of the John Harker fleet, the petroleum barge *Kerrydale H*, undergoing maintenance in the dry dock in 1966. This was an important feature of the new docks when they opened in 1874, with visiting ships regularly requiring repairs particularly in the age when sail still reined supreme. The Dock Company leased the dry dock to the Cardiff Channel Dry Docks & Pontoon Co. Ltd from around 1900 but when they gave up the lease in 1929, a local man, Ivor Langford, was encouraged to take over instead, taking on some of the Cardiff Co's workers. In 1946, John Harker Ltd established a yard here under a separate company, Sharpness Shipyard Ltd, presumably using this dry dock, and four craft were built; *Huntdale H* in 1950, *Wastdale H* and *Wyesdale H* in 1951 and *Waterdale H* in 1953; *Wastdale H* was one of the two craft lost in the Severn Bridge disaster. The 380-ton *Kerrydale H* was built by Harkers in 1961 at their shipyard on the Aire & Calder Navigation at Knottingley. A pipeline carrying fuel oil from Quedgeley to Worcester was brought in to operation in 1969, which spelt the end of the heavy river traffic. The twelve tankers used on the Quedgeley-Gloucester-Worcester runs were down to just four by the end of 1969 and Harkers withdrew from carrying on the Severn in 1975. Harkers shipyards at Knottingley, Gloucester and Sharpness were transferred to a new company in 1968, trading as John Harker (Shipyards) Ltd but the one at Gloucester was soon closed. The Sharpness yard was sold in November 1986 but the dry dock is still in full operation today, now under the auspices of Sharpness Shipyard & Drydock Ltd, so remains an integral part of the docks. NORMAN ANDREWS/NPC

ABOVE: A laden Shell/BP petroleum barge turns in to the old canal arm presumably to lay up for a while whilst a John Harker barge heads up the canal towards the Severn Bridge, bound for Quedgeley in January 1967. Neither barge's name is quite readable but the nearer tanker's name starts 'BP'. Run for many years as a joint operation, Shell and BP split their fleets in the mid 1970s. In the foreground is part of the timber stacking yard that occupied this corner of the docks. JOHN STRANGE/NPC

BELOW: A similar view but taken in October 1967, with the swing section of the Severn Bridge, now swung across the canal as scrapping of the river spans was underway. Note the timber trolleys stacked high with planks at the end of the siding. On the right is the holder of Sharpness gas works, which had ceased production and closed down circa 1955 but the holder was retained for storage. It was dismantled circa 1970. JOHN STRANGE/NPC

SHARPNESS DOCKS AND RAILWAY, AND COOPER'S METALS SCRAPYARD

From 1939 to to 1967, the National Sea Training School was based at Sharpness in the hulk of an old sailing ship named *Vindicatrix*. Built originally in 1883 as the *Arranmore*, the vessel had led a particularly eventful life up to her arrival alongside the towpath on the old arm of the canal leading to the first entrance lock. Wrecked off the coast of South Africa in 1903, she was later salved and towed to Holland where she was repaired, sold to German owners in 1910 and renamed *Waltrute*. After conversion to a mission ship in 1913, she was commandeered by the German Navy in WW1 and based at Heligoland as a submarine depot ship. After the war, a further role awaited her following surrender to the British Navy, as a prison ship for German prisoners of war at Leith. Wrecked again, she was once more salved and, in 1925, towed to London's West India Dock for conversion as a seaman's hostel. It was at this time she gained the name *Vindicatrix* and was berthed off Gravesend. Her penultimate move was to Sharpness where she arrived on 1st September 1939, the day the Second World War broke out. A generation of merchant seamen learned their craft aboard her, over 70,000 lads ('Vindi boys') being trained in all aspects of seamanship.

ABOVE AND LEFT: Two views of *Vindicatrix* at her berth in the old Barge Arm, the original entrance to the Gloucester & Berkeley Canal. In the picture above, taken in January 1967, the old harbour master's house can be seen in the right distance. The view left, taken circa 1964, is looking the opposite way, from the entrance lock, with the Severn & Wye coal tip visible in the background. BOTH NPC

BELOW LEFT AND RIGHT: On 12th January 1967, *Vindacatrix* made her final voyage to a breakers yard at Newport. British Waterways' tugs *Primrose*, *Resolute* and *Annie* helped manoeuvre the ship away from her mooring, through the High Level swing bridge and out in to the main dock. Two larger tugs, *Pengarth* and *Falgarth*, then took over for the short trip across the Severn estuary and in to the Bristol Channel. She was scrapped almost immediately, with the result that a last-ditch attempt to save her and take her to America was just too late. With her demise, eighty-four years of incredible maritime history was lost but, to this day, she retains a special place in the hearts of thousands of retired merchant seamen. BOTH NPC

COOPER'S METALS, SHARPNESS

Alfred Cooper, who was born in Swindon in 1906, inherited a small locally-based animal feed and scrap metal business in 1926, which expanded rapidly after the Second World War, the company eventually having twenty-six depots spread across the country. One of these was at Sharpness, where Coopers set up a base in the redundant California Sidings, which they leased from British Waterways, to scrap withdrawn steam locomotives. A total of twenty-five engines, all ex-GWR types, are thought to have been scrapped here, whilst local labour problems are recorded as being the reason four other locomotives delivered to Sharpness for dismantling were later re-sold on to Cashmore's of Newport. Alfred Cooper retired in 1978 and in 1994 the company merged with the Sheppard Group to form European Metal Recycling, under which name and on an adjacent site the company still operates at Sharpness.

ABOVE: With echoes of the Woodham brothers yard at Barry but without the same happy outcome, spare siding capacity adjacent to the South Dock was utilised by Coopers Metals for the scrapping of withdrawn locomotives, as shown in this general view of early August 1964. PAUL STRONG/NPC

BELOW: A long row of ex-GWR engines minus their tenders at California Sidings in late summer/early autumn 1964, with the front of 'County' Class No. 1027 *County of Stafford* in the foreground and No. 5954 *Faendre Hall* just beyond. MICHAEL HALE

ABOVE: On 28th March 1965, 'Castle' Class engines Nos 7037 *Swindon*, 7009 *Athelney Castle* and 7015 *Carn Brea Castle* head 'Hall' No. 5986 *Arbury Hall* (still with its tender) on one of the sidings. With work having come to a halt, these four engines, along with 2-8-0 No. 4701, were resold to Cashmore's to be taken down to their Newport yard but No. 7015 was apparently then dismantled here before that move took place. The others did all make the move a few weeks after this picture was taken and were scrapped at Newport. NPC

LEFT: The photographer did not record the numbers of any of the locomotives seen here but the slide mount is date stamped May 1964, so they would have been some of the first to arrive at the site and we can put identities to some of them. Second in line is No. 2245, the only '22XX' Class 0-6-0 that was cut up here, whilst the three 'Mogul' 2-6-0s beyond would be Nos 6319 and 6365, with No. 9313 in the middle with its side window cab. In the foreground is probably No. 5978 *Bodinnick Hall*, which was the first 'Hall' to arrive here, some weeks before a further six classmates. The view is looking west to the terrace of houses on Great Western Road. The line on the right, which can still be seen on GoogleEarth, led to the quayside. JOHN STRANGE/NPC

One of the first locomotives delivered to Sharpness for cutting was Castle Class No. 5071 *Spitfire*, which is seen here at California Sidings on 21st March 1964. New in July 1938 and originally named *Clifford Castle*, renaming after the iconic fighter plane took place in September 1940. The engine had two allocations to Gloucester Horton Road, between April 1958 and February 1962, when it transferred to Bristol St. Philip's Marsh, from where it was withdrawn in October 1963. DON MANN

A general view of the site on the same day, with a couple of ex-GWR pannier tanks at the end of the siding and *Spitfire* just visible beyond. The two 0-6-0PTs are Nos 5420 and No. 3633, the only pannier tanks scrapped here, whilst the two pairs of driving wheels in the foreground are from '14XX' No. 1409. One of the '58XX' Class 0-4-2 tanks was also scrapped here, No. 5810, but possibly some time earlier, as Peto has it sold as scrap to Cooper's Metals on 9th July 1959 and cut up at Sharpness. DON MANN

Class '54XX' 0-6-0PT No. 5420 on 21st March 1964. DON MANN

Class '28XX' 2-8-0 No. 2872 on 12th July 1964. NPC

Class '42XX' 2-8-2T No. 5262 also seen on 21st March 1964. DON MANN

'Castle' No. 7037 *Swindon*, seen here on 30th August 1964, was eventually scrapped at Newport. NPC

A fine study of the front end of 'County' Class 4-6-0 No. 1006 *County of Cornwall* on 5th June 1964. DON MANN

Class '47XX' 2-8-0 No. 4701, also on 30th August 1964 and also later moved to Newport for scrapping. NPC

Again on 30th August 1964, 'Castle' No. 7015 *Carn Brea Castle* was also sold to Cashmore's for scrapping at Newport but was then dealt with here before it could be moved. NPC

SHARPNESS DOCKS AND RAILWAY, AND COOPER'S METALS SCRAPYARD

RIGHT: By 11th April 1964, three weeks after Don Mann's photograph a couple of pages ago, *Spitfire* was in a sorry state. All that was left of the tender were the three pairs of wheels, whilst the boiler barrel, tubes, firebox cover and top half of the cab had also all gone. BILL POTTER/KRM

BELOW: A mobile crane was in use when Bill returned in July 1964 to check on progress A close look at the wheel visible suggests that it may have had the capacity to run on rails as well as road. In the foreground is one of the massive cylinder block from one of the scrapped tender engines. BILL POTTER/KRM

TABLE OF LOCOMOTIVES SCRAPPED AT SHARPNESS		
CLASS	WHEEL ARR.	NOS
'County'	4-6-0	1006, 1027
'14XX'	0-4-2T	1409
'22XX'	0-6-0	2245
'28XX'	2-8-0	2842, 2872
'57XX'	0-6-0PT	3633
'Castle'	4-6-0	4087, 5040, 5050, 5071, 7015*
'Hall'	4-6-0	4924, 4996, 5905, 5935, 5943, 5954, 5978
'42XX'	2-8-2T	5262
'54XX'	0-6-0PT	5420
'58XX'	0-4-2T	5810
'43XX'	2-6-0	6319, 6365, 9313

*Sold to Cashmores of Newport but then scrapped here. Also delivered here were 'Castle' Class Nos 7037 and 7009, 'Hall' No. 5986 and '47XX' No. 4701 but they were then resold to Cashmores and had moved to Newport for scrapping by July 1964.

RIGHT: On 3rd June 1965, '57XX' 0-6-0PT No. 3633 gazes on the partially stripped remains of No. 5420 as it awaits a similar fate. The terrace of houses in the background, rather inappropriately named Great Western Road given that this was Midland territory, was built in 1876 for workmen at the new dock opened in 1874. It must have been quite surreal for the residents to see all these ex-GWR engines being scrapped just in front of their houses but the year and a half that this took was to be followed by years of steel mineral wagons being scrapped here, right up until the early 1980s. BILL POTTER/KRM

SECTION 12

THE BRISTOL & GLOUCESTER LINE
BERKELEY ROAD TO YATE

Looking from the end of the Down platform, beneath the A38 road bridge, ex-Midland 'Compound' Class '2P' No. 40426 is pictured arriving at Berkeley Road in the summer of 1956 with a Bristol to Birmingham 'stopper'. This is a relatively well known view, albeit one of huge interest being a few years earlier than most colour pictures, when these 4-4-0s still had charge of local trains on the line and BR's attractive carmine and cream colour scheme still looked its best. Taken by the famous Birmingham-based railway enthusiast Patrick B. Whitehouse, a preservation pioneer, photographer and joint presenter of BBC TV's 1957-63 *Railway Roundabout* series, I was fortunate to acquire the original slide from a well known internet auction site. Built at Derby Works in September 1896, this late Victorian era old lady was thus approaching her sixtieth birthday at the time of this view and was based at Bristol Barrow Road shed for most of the 1950s, up until her withdrawal in October 1957. She ran as No. 426 for most of her life, being renumbered by BR in September 1950. PATRICK B. WHITEHOUSE/NPC

After leaving Berkeley Road, the main line continued the long curve from west to south that it had been on as it passed through the station, for around another mile. It then heads south for about three quarters of a mile, before executing a lazy 'S' as it swings gently to the south-east to approach Charfield station. Whilst this section of track looks relatively level, the gradient diagram (overleaf) shows it to be on a gentle climb through the station and all the way to Berkeley Loop South Junction, when there was a short dip for southbound trains, before the line resumed an easy but steady climb all the way up Wickwar Bank to a summit just to the south of Yate.

Berkeley Loop South Junction was a north facing junction, opened by the GWR on 9th March 1908, which allowed trains to travel via the Severn Bridge, when the Severn Tunnel was closed for maintenance, without the need to reverse at Berkeley Road. It also gave direct access to Sharpness Docks from the south. Berkeley Loop South Junction signal box was an MR cabin but the loop itself, which formed the southern part of a triangle, was GWR property and the western end

of it was controlled by a GWR box, named Berkeley Loop Junction Signal Box. The loop was used mainly for freight, much of it at night, with no regular scheduled passenger service traversing it. However, some passenger trains were diverted over it when the Severn Tunnel was closed, although locomotive weight restrictions on the Severn Bridge precluded many of these, along with the occasional special. It would undoubtedly have seen more regular use if work to strengthen the bridge to carry heavier locomotives had been completed before it was closed after the October 1960 disaster. The loop continued to be used for freight traffic between Sharpness Docks and points south but this was limited and it was closed completely on 27th January 1963, the line being removed in June the same year. With both ends of it a little isolated, it was much under-photographed and no colour views have been seen to date of the line or its two signal boxes.

There were lengthy lie-by sidings on both the Up and Down sides of the line on the approach to Charfield, which both originally required goods trains to reverse in to them but, with the increase in war-time

LEFT: Something a bit different at Berkeley Road on 11th August 1964, where this Hunslet Engine Company 0-4-0T was to be found parked on a low loader trailer in a lay-by on the A38. Works No. 1684 of 1931, it was built new for Hall & Co. Ltd's Coulsdon Quarry, as their No. 6. Returned to Hunslet on 2nd February 1953, it was resold to the NCB for use at their Graigola Fuel Works at the King's Dock, Swansea, on 21st September 1960. From there it passed to the Phoenix Briquetting Plant at Port Talbot in January 1963. In 1964, it was transferred to the NCB's Norton Hill Colliery at Radstock, the IRS recording this as after May 1964, so this view now gives a more accurate date. In March 1966, it was sent to Kilmersdon Colliery, the last working pit in the Somerset Coalfield, from where it was bought by the GWR 1338 Locomotive Fund in 1968, moving to the Somerset Railway Museum at Bleadon & Uphill station in October 1971. It is currently back close to its birthplace at the Middleton Railway in Leeds, awaiting restoration. NPC

RIGHT: No. 7012 *Barry Castle* passes the Berkeley Road Up Home signal with train No. 1M37, the 11.20am from Newquay to Wolverhampton on 1st August 1964. Note that the Down Starter and its repeater arm higher up were on the same post for sighting purposes, the line being on a curve away from the station. The 'Castle' was a BR-build, completed at Swindon Works in August 1948 and sent new to Landore shed at Swansea. Moving to Carmarthen in 1959, it then went to Old Oak Common before a two year stint at Wolverhampton Stafford Road, finally moving over to Oxley shed in September 1963. Unsurprisingly given its filthy condition here, it was just over three months away from withdrawal, in November 1964.
JOHN DAGLEY-MORRIS

traffic, they were converted to loops in 1942. Incidentally, the appalling 1928 Charfield crash was caused when an early morning Down mail train passed through red signals and hit a goods train reversing in to the Down lie-by siding, the impact throwing the mail train off the track and in to the path of an empty Up goods working. The wreckage piled up beneath the Wootton Road bridge and escaping carriage gas was set alight by hot coals. Sixteen souls perished in the accident, including two children apparently travelling on their own who have never been identified.

A siding was laid in from the Down lie-by in 1921 to serve a newly opened brickworks, on the east side of the line. It was removed in 1961, although the brickworks remained in operation until the summer of 1969. The two loops are still in existence at the time of writing and may be required if a station is reopened at Charfield.

After passing through Charfield station, which in design and layout had much in common with Frocester and Yate, the line curved southwards again towards Wickwar. Another sweeping curve to a south-westerly direction took the line through Wickwar station (with a station building constrained by the narrow site), then quickly passing Wickwar Brewery and goods yard before entering a short cutting and plunging in to Wickwar Tunnel. Just short of a mile in length, the tunnel represented the largest engineering feature on the whole of the Br&GR route.

The line leaves the south portal and traverses another steep but loner cutting before emerging out in to open countryside at Hall End, where it begins a long gentle curve back the other way to head south towards Yate. Just to the north of the station, at Yate Main Line Junction, the Thornbury Branch curves away from the Up side to the west. Although it is nearly seventy years since the branch passenger service was withdrawn, the line remains open for stone traffic to Tytherington Quarry, having recently been reopened again after four years out of use. Meanwhile, whilst the stations at Charfield and Wickwar were closed in 1965 under the Beeching Report and remain so, Yate, which was closed at the same time, was re-opened by British Rail in 1989, albeit as a completely new build with staggered platforms either side of the A432 road bridge. The goods shed here does still survive, however, now in commerical use, whilst at Wickwar only the station master's house remains. At Charfield, however, the station master's house, the Brunel-style main station building and the water tower all remain. A feasibility study into a new station here led to an announcement in June 2019 of seven new stations for the greater Bristol area MetroWest network, including Charfield.

BRITISH RAILWAY HISTORY IN COLOUR: 4B. GLOUCESTER MIDLAND LINES SOUTH – STONEHOUSE TO WESTERLEIGH

LEFT: From a slightly higher position, at road level, 'Black Five' No. 44805 approaches the same signal with an Up freight on 16th August 1962. This is our third sighting of No. 44805, which we saw twice previously heading passenger trains south through Tuffley Junction. Berkeley South Junction, where the GWR spur of 1908 met the main line, allowing trains from Sharpness to head directly towards Bristol and opened up the Severn Bridge as a diversionary route away from the Severn Tunnel, lay in the far distance, at the point where the line curves out of sight to the left. NPC

RIGHT: 'Jubilee' No. 45725 *Repulse* passes Crossways, just to the south of Berkeley Road, with the southbound 'Pines Express' on 24th June 1961. The photographer was standing on the bridge carrying the lane named Crossways, which the MR bridge register refers to as Bristol & Gloucester line Mayo's Bridge (No. 68). New in September 1936, *Repulse* was based at Sheffield Millhouses shed at this date, transferring to Canklow six months later on the first day of 1962. It came back to Sheffield but to Darnall shed in June 1962, from where it was withdrawn at the end of the year. NPC

BELOW: Looking in the opposite direction on the same day, 'Royal Scot' No. 46118 *Royal Welch Fusilier* heads north with what could be an afternoon Bristol to York train – the third digit of the reporting number is not clear but it could be 1N84. The 'Scot' had transferred from Nottingham to Saltley just days before. NPC

THE BRISTOL & GLOUCESTER LINE – BERKELEY ROAD TO YATE

ABOVE: Still at Crossways on 24th June 1961, aptly named No. 6904 *Charfield Hall* speeds north with an eleven coach holiday express carrying Western Region reporting No. H25, the Saturdays only 2.05pm from Weston-super-Mare to Birmingham Snow Hill. A war-time build at Swindon Works in July 1940, the 'Hall' was based at Stourbridge Junction at the time of this view but moved to Banbury three months later, being withdrawn from there in January 1965. The site of the platelayers hut is now occupied by a GSM-R mast, one of around 2,500 now across the railway network providing digital communication between signallers and drivers. NPC

RIGHT: Another 'Jubilee', No. 45608 *Gibralter*, which we have seen before north of Standish Junction, heads by with train No. 1N86, the 8.05am from Newquay to Newcastle, which was due past here at approximately 2.35pm. An on time arrival at its destination was time tabled for just after 10pm, a fourteen hour journey! NPC

BELOW: A BR gradient diagram for the main line between Berkeley Road and Bristol TM. NPC

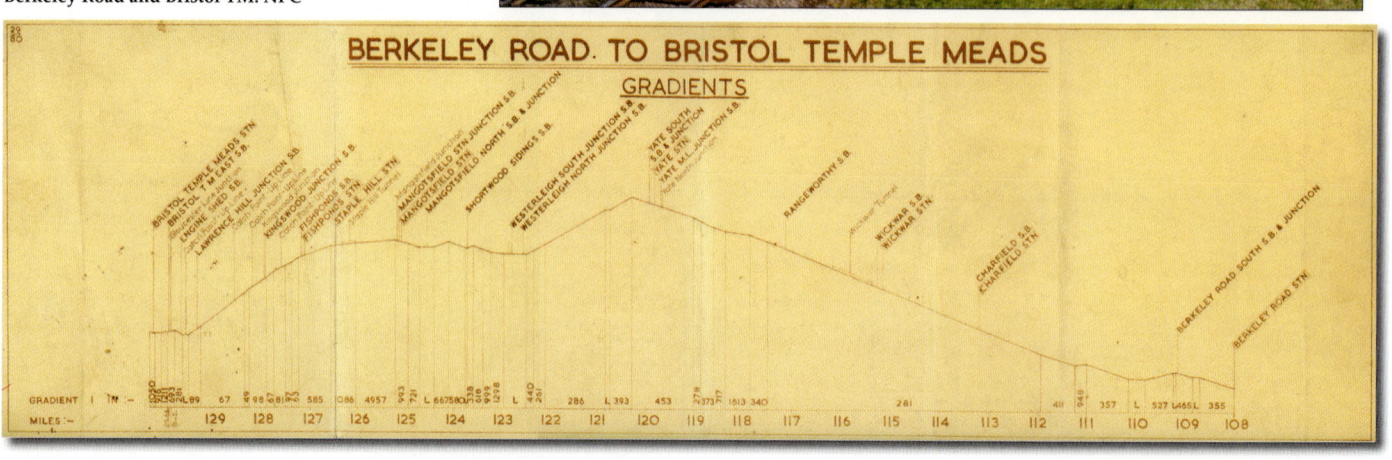

Still on the same day but a little further south, BR 'Standard' Class '5' No. 73015, which we saw a while ago at Berkeley Road, was photographed heading south with a ten-coach Birmingham to Bristol train. Taken from Lower Wick Bridge (No. 64), this shows a view which has much changed today. In the distance is Fitzhardings Bridge (No. 65), a farm occupation bridge which is no longer in existence, whilst the M5 Motorway near Michaelwood Services now crosses over the line just beyond the platelayers hut. NPC

The same location but over a year later, on 17th October 1965, as 'Black Five' No. 44919 of Wolverhampton Oxley shed heads south with a loaded coal train. Not only have we seen this engine before but with this same train, passing Standish Junction around 20 minutes earlier assuming it was not held anywhere. We shall shortly see it again too, passing Charfield after being held in the Up lie-by loop for a time. NPC

Our unknown photographer of 24th June 1961 clearly spent a very enjoyable day recording trains passing along this section of the Br&GR main line on a busy summer Saturday. Yet another 'Jubilee' was captured, Leeds Holbeck-based No. 45639 *Raleigh* with a southbound holiday relief. New in December 1934, the engine was withdrawn in September 1963 but of more interest here is the rare view of Charfield brickworks, on the Down side of the line. The Phormium Cavity Block Company Ltd was set up at Charfield in 1928 to mass produce a system of cavity blocks and the first kiln was fired in September 1929. In 1932, the works was purchased by the Great Western Brick & Tile Co., who in turn sold it to G.H. Downing & Co. in 1933-34. Downings went on to become the largest clay tile manufacturer in the country and possibly the world at this time. Sited on the Down side of the railway, just north of Charfield station, a siding was laid from the Down lie-by to deliver coal and to despatch products. The clay pit lay on the west side of the railway at Underhill Wood and was connected to the works by an aerial ropeway. Hot air drying was introduced in the late 1950s and the steam boiler removed, the increase in output meaning that the ropeway could no longer cope. Clay was delivered instead by road although the ropeway was kept in reserve but had clearly been removed by the date of this picture. The Private Siding Agreement was terminated on 14th September 1960 and it was lifted on 12th November 1961. The last kiln was fired in June 1969 but the arch of one chamber collapsed during firing and it remained with its load of bricks until the site was cleared. The works did not justify the investment required to replace the plant but Downings continued to remove bricks until July 1973. The site was bought by Bryant Homes Ltd and cleared in spring 1979, with houses now built on it. NPC

Watched by two young boys, one of whom is clearly not at all sure that he likes noisy, hissing steam trains passing by, 'Castle' Class No. 5056 *Earl of Powis* heads through the brick arch of Wotton Road bridge (No. 57) and in to Charfield station with train No. 1V54, a Wolverhampton to Kingswear summer Saturday holiday express, on 10th August 1964. New in to service from Swindon Works on 28th June 1936 as *Ogmore Castle*, No. 5056 was renamed in September 1937, during a period when the GWR transferred all of the Earl names previously allotted to Class '32XX' 4-4-0s to 'Castle' Class engines, reputedly because these much smaller locomotives were not considered grand enough on which to bestow the names of such noble personages. Based at Wolverhampton Oxley shed, having recently been reallocated from Hereford, No. 5056 would be withdrawn three months after this picture was taken. On the right is the goods shed and the feed store; the latter, a standard building found at stations all over the system and made of pre-fabricated concrete sections, was a BR addition, possibly in December 1956 when they remodelled the goods yard, taking out the wagon turntable. A footbridge built adjacent to this side of the road bridge is a fairly recent addition. MARK B. WARBURTON

RIGHT: Charfield goods shed in 1960. It was built to the same basic design as all the others on the Br&GR line, although the sheds at Berkeley Road and Wickwar had flying buttresses, whilst the shed at Frocester was the only one built of stone. As built, the end arches on the road side of the building were open, as was the main loading entrance facing the road. The arches in the shed here at Charfield were bricked up in 1847, with doors presumably being fitted to the loading bay at the same time; no doubt being so open to the elements had proved to be not ideal. The office extension hiding the bricked up arch at this end was added some time after 1930. The shed has survived closure and is now in commercial use, albeit is now partially covered in metal cladding and has an extension jutting out to the right, the goods yard having become a small industrial estate. COLOUR-RAIL

LEFT: Clearly burning some very poor quality coal, BR 'Standard' Class '5' No. 73137 leaves a trail of soot and clag in its wake as it heads past Charfield goods yard in 1959. New from Derby Works in November 1956, the 4-6-0 went new to Holyhead but then moved back to the Midlands in 1958, ending up back at Derby in early January 1959, where it was based at the date of this view. It lasted in service until June 1967, when it was withdrawn from Patricroft shed. Note the pre-fab building in the background with the BR delivery lorry parked in front, presumably an office and mess-room for the drivers. The black car is a circa 1937 Rover 12hp, whilst the BR 'blood & custard' lorry is probably a Thornycroft 3- or 5-tonner. They were made in Basingstoke and BR once relied heavily upon the make. COLOUR-RAIL

RIGHT: The Up platform was an ideal vantage point for photographing southbound trains, as we shall see. Here, on 27th June 1964, Saltley-based Class '9F' No. 92137 was captured making stately progress towards Bristol with a mixed goods train from Birmingham. New in to service from Crewe Works on 31st July 1957, the 2-10-0 had just three allocations, moving to Croes Newydd shed at Wrexham in early August 1966 and then on to Carlisle Kingmoor four months later. It was withdrawn from there in September 1967, a working life of just over ten years. Note the brickworks chimney in the background, above the roof of the goods shed. JOHN GRAINGER

BRITISH RAILWAY HISTORY IN COLOUR: 4B. GLOUCESTER MIDLAND LINES SOUTH – STONEHOUSE TO WESTERLEIGH 379

An overall view of the station from the B4058 Wootton Road bridge in July 1965, as 'Black Five' No. 45050 heads north through the station with train No. 1M37, which was probably a Bristol to the Potteries working – the locomotive, which was built for the LM&SR by Vulcan Foundry in November 1935, was based at Stoke-on-Trent at the date of this view. No. 45050 was to finish its career there, being withdrawn in early August 1967. It can be seen from this angle that the feed store here was a double block, agricultural traffic being the mainstay of the goods yard during its lifetime. MICHAEL MENSING/COLOUR-RAIL.

The main building was on the Down side and is seen here from a passing Bristol to Gloucester local circa 1962. Note the nameboard stating 'CHARFIELD FOR WOTTON UNDER EDGE'; this Cotswold market town about two miles to the east was never reached by a railway, so Charfield was its nearest station. Like other stations along the line, the canopy had originally extended right round the building but had been cut back as seen here most likely by BR around 1950. Note the end of the light grey box van in the left foreground, which is also seen in the picture above. With 'COND' painted on the side, it was presumably parked here for use as additional storage. NPC

An overall view of the main buildings at Charfield, which were all on the Down side. The signal box, a Midland Type '2a', dated from 18th April 1909 and was a replacement for two earlier boxes, North and South, that had been provided in 1897 on the Up side of the line. They in turn had replaced the first box here, opened circa 1875 when the lie-by sidings were laid in and sited on the Down side between the road bridge and the goods shed. The station master's house was built 1847 and the substantial water tower and tank were added around the same time, to improve the water supply here. The house was constructed of stone but the other buildings are in brick. Brunel, in the construction of the Br&GR, used local materials for the bridges and buildings, those here at Charfield all being of hand-made bricks locally referred to as 'Wotton brick', possibly from a brickfield at Hack Hill, just to the south of Wotton-under-Edge. In the right background, the Railway Tavern – still open for business today – can be seen facing on to Station Road and the entrance to the station. The signal box was closed on 16th May 1971 and was reportedly removed for preservation in the Forest of Dean but if that is correct, its current whereabouts are unknown. Rather amazingly and very happily, all of the other buildings seen here still remain; the platform is no more but the station building still faces the tracks, the station master's house is a private residence and the water tower and tank still stand, although as far as I can ascertain none of them are listed in any way. It is unclear if the plan to re-open a station here would use this site and include refurbishment of the buildings – it would be nice! COLOUR-RAIL

We return to 24th June 1961 again for this fine shot of the Down 'The Devonian' coasting through Charfield behind 'Royal Scot' No. 46123 *Royal Irish Fusilier*. Built by the North British Locomotive Co. in Glasgow and new in to service at the end of October 1927, the 4-6-0 had been based at Kentish Town shed in north London until a few weeks before this picture was taken but had then been transferred to Saltley. Moving north to Carlisle Upperby in June 1962, it was withdrawn from there four months later at the end of October. The siding running behind the Down platform and loading dock at this end of the station had clearly not seen any recent use. There were livestock pens on the loading dock, out of sight here to the right of the 10-ton capacity crane. Incidentally, the large collection of slides which these views are part of came to me via a general auctioneers in the Bristol area. They did not come with any provenance so I cannot credit the original photographer, although I am fairly certain that he lived in Keynsham. Many more will appear in this and future volumes, and they form an invaluable colour record of the railway around north Bristol and south Gloucestershire in the very early 1960s. NPC

The first of four more views from a similar spot just off the south end of the Up platform. The first two were taken on the same cold crisp day, Sunday 24th February during the bitter winter of 1963. Whilst many photographers did not bother getting their cameras out in the winter months, those who did could often be rewarded with excellent results, such as here. Producing a fine head of steam tinged with just a little smoke, Class '8F' No. 48393 slogs southwards with a heavy loaded coal train. With the 2-8-0 based at Nottingham at this date, it is probably safe to assume that this is Nottinghamshire coal bound for Bristol. The fact that the engine is working so hard suggests that the train may just have come out of the Down lie-by siding. Built at Horwich Works in April 1945, the 2-8-0 was one of the last survivors when withdrawn from Rose Grove shed at the very end of steam in August 1968. NPC

No. 92070 also looks to be making hard work of another heavy loaded coal train, so again may well have come out of the Down lie-by siding, just the other side of the road bridge. These saw a lot of use in steam days, as slow going southbound freights were looped prior to attacking the long climb up Wickwar Bank all the way to Yate, waiting for a suitable gap between faster passenger trains. No. 92070 had been built at Crewe Works in January 1956 and was based at Westhouses shed near Alfreton at the date of this picture, so this could well be a train of Derbyshire coal. The 2-10-0 was withdrawn in November 1967. NPC

Moving forward over two and a half years to Thursday 17th October 1965 and showing more of the varied motive power which, even at this late date, could still be seen on a busy main line during the steam age, ex-WD 2-8-0 No. 90385 heads south with another trainload of coal. A North British Locomotive build for the the War Department and new in to service in January 1944 as No. 78590, the engine was allocated to Wakefield shed when seen here, so this could well be Yorkshire coal loaded in these wagons. The 'Dub-Dee' and its train was to be captured on film again a short while after this, when passing Rangeworthy, north of Yate, by the well known and now sadly departed railway photographer Michael Mensing. NPC

On the same day, 'Black Five' No. 44919 was photographed crossing over from the Up road to the Down line again with a coal train. This would suggest that the train was held in the Up lie-by loop, which could only be reached by a Down train reversing in to it using this crossover. It may well have followed the 'Dub-Dee' seen above out on to the main line, once that train had cleared the section to Wickwar. Stretching the bounds of co-incidence, this is now the third time we have seen this same train. Indeed, it is possible given that it looks to have been 'looped' here that this picture and the one of it passing Lower Wick Bridge (page 375) were both taken by the same photographer, who had travelled a mile or two south to this location and overtaken it on the way. The car in the right background is a pre-1957 Ford Anglia 100E. NPC

THE BRISTOL & GLOUCESTER LINE – BERKELEY ROAD TO YATE

Although taken after closure of the station, these two views show it at an interesting time, with the track layout being altered over the weekend of 18th-19th October 1969. The trailing crossover seen in the pictures overleaf was taken out in October 1968 but then new trailing and facing crossovers were put in twelve months later. This first view, almost certainly taken on the Saturday, shows the new trailing crossover being laid in, with two Down trains being held beyond the bridge, one on the main line and one in the lie-by. The track gang have just moved clear and the flagman has given the signal for the first one to pass by the works at slow speed. Although the box was still open at this time, a new ground frame was also put in to operate both crossovers, the new works being brought in to use on Monday 20th October. The fenced off station building on the right remains much the same today and note the bricked up rail arch in the goods shed. NPC

A view from the Down side with the tail of an Up train seen disappearing in the distance. A hopper wagon loaded with ballast for the works in progress can just been seen through the bridge arch, in the spur at the south end of the Up lie-bye. Both lie-byes had spurs at each end but all four were removed in the early 1970s. The facing crossover was laid in just here, between the goods yard and the new relay building on the left, which is still in existence. Both lie-byes also remain in use today but the crossovers have been removed. The bridge and this end of the lie-bys are the scene of the 1928 Charfield railway accident. NPC

RIGHT: Little Bristol Lane, which parallels the railway for around half a mile on the Down side, was another useful vantage point from which to observe and photograph passing Up trains. On 24th June 1961, No. 5024 *Carew Castle* was not having to work hard as it drifted north down the bank from Wickwar with train No. H22, the Saturdays only 10.35am service from Paignton to Wolverhampton. New in to service at Plymouth Laira shed on Monday 28th April 1934, the 'Castle' spent most of its working life in the West Country, being based at Newton Abbot at the date of this view. It was withdrawn from there on Monday 21st May 1962. NPC

RIGHT: On 20th August 1962, 'Black Five' No. 48669 was photographed passing the same spot with a northbound train of coal empties probably bound for somewhere in the Warwickshire coalfield. The 4-6-0 was a wartime build at Brighton Works and was based at Saltley at the date of this view, which had been its home shed throughout the BR period, apart from a two month stay at Bourneville in early 1953. Moving on to Croes Newydd in the autumn of 1966, it was withdrawn from Heaton Mersey shed at the beginning of November 1967. Note the low bridge warning sign that had appeared in the fourteen months since the previous picture was taken. The circa 1954 Austin A40 10cwt van on the right is a design that was derived from the contemporary A40 'Somerset' car but the van had its own simple pressed-steel grille. NPC

LEFT: 'Black Five' No. 44825 eases down the gradient with a twelve-coach summer Saturday working from Paignton to Bradford on 1st August 1964. The train number is not readable but is likely to be 1N37. New in December 1944, the locomotive was based at Burton-on-Trent when seen here but was at Carlisle Kingmoor when it was withdrawn at the start of October 1967. The bridge warning sign refers to an arch through the low embankment, the parapet of which is just visible beneath the fourth coach. Charfield Subway (No. 56) in the register, it comprised brick abutments with a wrought iron span and was built in 1890 for a short road linking Little Bristol Lane with Station Road. The span has been replaced but the link is still in use today. The car on the right is a Ford Anglia or Popular 100E model, probably the latter which ran from 1959-62. MARK B. WARBURTON

Also on 1st August 1964, No. 7024 *Powis Castle* was photographed heading north with a Kingswear to Wolverhampton holiday express. A BR build, at Swindon Works in July 1949, the 'Castle' was allocated to Wolverhampton Oxley shed, from where it was withdrawn in early February 1965. Nearest on the right is a Ford Anglia 105E deluxe, 997cc, in Lagoon Blue. Behind could be another 105E but a base trim model as evidenced by the painted rear-lamp surround. MARK B. WARBURTON

From a little further south but with the brickworks chimney still just visible in the left background, 'Black Five' No. 44919 was photographed heading away from a stop at Charfield with an all stations Gloucester to Bristol local. No. 44919 looks smart in the attractive red and white lined black livery in which some of these fine looking engines were turned out by BR in the 1950s, in contrast to the careworn state in which we have seen it several times already on a 1965 coal working. Behind the train is a glimpse of the coal yard at Charfield, a pair of loop sidings on the Down side of the line. NPC

'Royal Scot' No. 46157 *The Royal Artilleryman* hammers up the bank towards Wickwar with the Down 'The Pines Express' in the summer of 1962. Starting out from Manchester Piccadilly and bound for Bournemouth via the S&DJR line, it was to be diverted away from there from 8th September, thereafter running via Oxford. No. 46157, which was new in July 1930, moved from Saltley to Carlisle Upperby in late June 1962, so this view will probably be just prior to that date. K. Ellis/Colour-Rail.

Tidy looking 'Grange' No. 6842 *Nunhold Grange* hurries towards the Down platform with a working that the reporting number, which looks to be No. 8O63, indicates was bound for the Southern Region. The locomotive had a near six month allocation to St. Philips Marsh shed between April and October 1962, so the view is likely to date from summer of that year. Brian Arman/Colour-Rail.

THE BRISTOL & GLOUCESTER LINE – BERKELEY ROAD TO YATE

The south end of Wickwar station provided several excellent vantage points to photograph trains working hard, powering up the valley from Charfield. Here, on 20th July 1963, 'Castle' Class No. 5063 *Earl Baldwin* was coping well with its ten-coach load, train No. 1C72, a holiday express from Wolverhampton to Minehead. A Stafford Road engine at this date but shortly to transfer across town to Oxley, the July 1937 built 4-6-0 was withdrawn in February 1965. MARK B. WARBURTON

From the other side of the line, '8F' No. 48669 seems to be making light work of its goods train on a hot day circa 1963, as it passes the Wickwar Down Home signal. We saw the 2-8-0 just now heading north at Charfield. NPC

A fine view of No. 6871 *Bourton Grange* from Station Road, heading south with a Stoke to Bath pigeon train on 1st August 1964. New in March 1939, the 'Grange' is in sparkling condition here, a credit perhaps to the Wolverhampton Oxley shed staff, although the engine may also have recently been in for a minor overhaul. It was withdrawn in October 1965. Note the combined 'S' bend and low bridge road sign. MARK B. WARBURTON

Working hard in crisp, clear conditions on 2nd January 1965, ex-GWR 2-8-0 No. 3859 was also leaking steam from various points. The '28XX' had recently transferred from Didcot to Southall, so was probably on something of a roundabout route home, with this express freight, according to the lamp code, bound for Bristol. The engine had less than five months left in traffic. NPC

More impressive smoke effects on a crisp cold January afternoon, as Class '9F' No. 92136 chunters towards the platforms with what would be considered no more than a medium load for a locomotive of its capabilities. Built at Crewe Works and going in to service on 31st July 1957, the 2-10-0 spent its entire career of nine years and three months based at Saltley shed, being withdrawn in late October 1966, twenty-one months after this picture was taken on 28th January 1965. Note that the Up signal is also 'off' for a northbound train. NPC

A green-liveried BR 'Standard' Class '5' paused at Wickwar with an Up Bristol to Gloucester 'stopper' circa 1962. Barnwood had an allocation of six of these 4-6-0s from the spring of 1962 up until the shed closed in May 1964. Even under heavy magnification the number is not completely clear but in September 1962, the six comprised Nos 73019, 73024, 73031, 73068, 73091 and 73092 and of those No. 73031 appears the most likely candidate. Transferred from Bath Green Park in early April 1962, it moved over to Horton Road in May 1964 and was withdrawn from Oxford shed in September 1965. A Down train was also signalled. NPC

Wickwar was unusual in having two station buildings on the Down platform, built at the same time with one set slightly back from the other and separated by the steps leading up from Station Road. Brunel's design was dictated by the narrow site, with the twin structures built up from the retaining wall facing on to the road below and the accommodation split between the two; from this end: gents toilets, ladies toilet and ladies waiting room in the nearer building, with the booking office and booking hall in the further one. Consequently, the only Brunellian features were the shape of the doorways and the chimneys. No canopies were ever provided. NPC

THE BRISTOL & GLOUCESTER LINE – BERKELEY ROAD TO YATE

As the photographs show, the staff here at Wickwar were as adept at providing a fine display of flowers around the station as their counterparts were elsewhere along the line. This was not just down to pride and having the time and interest to cultivate the platform flowerbeds but also because such endeavours were actively encouraged by the annual 'Best Kept Station' competitions held around the BR regions. Looking across the impressive and colourful flowerbed on the Down platform, 'Jubilee' No. 45658 *Keyes* is seen coasting through with a Paignton to Leeds holiday express on 1st August 1964. A week later, the Holbeck-based 'Jubilee' was to pass through again with a similar southbound working, as shown in the title page double-spread for this volume. The road entrance arch to the goods shed can be seen in the left background and beyond that is a glimpse of the old Wickwar Brewery, which was established in the second half of the 19th century by Arnold, Perrett & Co. Ltd. Today, the Wickwar Brewing Co. Ltd are installed in some of the remaining brewery buildings, producing a range of fine ales. Also visible in the background, above the second carriage, is the station masters house, the only railway building to survive here today. MARK B. WARBURTON

SOUTH – STONEHOUSE TO WESTERLEIGH   393

LEFT: 'Jubilee' No. 45605 *Cyprus* heads south with a summer Saturday express in 1963. Train No. 1V40, a 9.05am working from Bradford to Paignton, was run on eight Saturdays only through the summer as a relief to 'The Devonian' and was usually hauled, as here, by a Leeds Holbeck-based 'Jubilee'. Built by the North British Locomotive Co. and new in to service in early April 1935, No. 45605 transferred to Burton-on-Trent in February 1964 but was withdrawn within two or three weeks of arrival there. The nearer poster on the right edge of the picture was extolling the virtues of North Wales. NPC

ABOVE: On 20th July 1963, No. 6827 *Llanfrecha Grange* was photographed passing through with a Stourbridge to Weston-super-Mare holiday express. New in to service in February 1937, the 'Grange' had had two lengthy spells allocated to Bristol St. Philips Marsh but was based at Stourbridge Junction shed at the time of this view. Transferred to Wolverhampton Oxley in April 1964, it was withdrawn from there in September 1965. MARK B. WARBURTON

RIGHT: 'Royal Scot' Class 4-6-0 No. 46113 *Cameronian* calls at the station in summer 1962. New from the North British Locomotive Co. in October 1927, the 'Scot' was based at Leeds Holbeck shed, to where it had transferred from Mirfield in January 1962. However, No. 46113 had clearly here been pressed in to service on a local 'stopper', perhaps because it had worked to Gloucester and was then being sent down to Bristol, where it could take over a holiday express from the West Country that would take it back to Yorkshire. In a fairly grimy state, withdrawal was not far away, off Holbeck shed in mid-December 1962. K. ELLIS/COLOUR-RAIL

THE BRISTOL & GLOUCESTER LINE – BERKELEY ROAD TO YATE

Another 'Jubilee', Bristol Barrow Road shed's No. 45682 *Trafalgar*, heads a Birmingham to Bristol semi-fast through Wickwar on 6th June 1962. New in January 1936 and Bristol-based from November 1947, apart from spending November 1957 allocated to Sheffield Millhouses shed, No. 45682 was withdrawn at the start of June 1964. This view also provides some good detail of the station buildings and the tiny wooden shelter on the Up platform.
GERALD DIXON/COURTESY THE RESTORATION & ARCHIVING TRUST/REF. GD620034

Viewed from the end of the goods yard and watched by some other interested parties on the platform, No. 7019 *Fowey Castle* coasts through with train No. 1C72 in summer 1963. With no other information to go on, the GloucestershireRailwayMemories website came up trumps here in identifying the working as the 8.02am from Wolverhampton to Minehead and Ilfracombe on Saturday 10th August. The Stafford Road-based 'Castle' was to transfer over to Oxley a month after the picture was taken, from where it was withdrawn in early February 1965. NPC

BRITISH RAILWAY HISTORY IN COLOUR: 4B. GLOUCESTER MIDLAND LINES SOUTH – STONEHOUSE TO WESTERLEIGH 395

Left: 'B1' Class No. 61090 of Sheffield Darnall shed has just cleared Wickwar Tunnel with its train and is passing the goods yard as it approaches the platforms in 1961 with train No. 1N65. This was the 6.05am from Paignton to Bradford, which the 'B1' had taken over at Bristol Temple Meads, departing at 10.10am and was then due past here at 10.36. Moving to Mexborough shed in early September 1962, the 1946-built 'B1' was withdrawn from there twelve months later. There is a rare view of a wagon inside the goods shed, albeit a steel mineral that would have delivered coal for the yard and therefore not have been unloaded inside.
Brian Arman/Colour-Rail

Right: Saltley-based 'Black Five' No. 45260 was photographed speeding past the Up side platform shelter in 1961. Built by Armstrong, Whitworth & Co. Ltd for the LM&SR in October 1936, this was a much travelled engine, with a total of no less than twenty-one allocations between Nationalisation in 1948 and its withdrawal from Lostock Hall shed at the start of August 1968. Colour-Rail

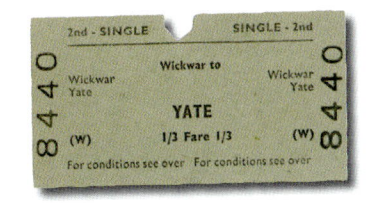

Left: The flowerbeds on the Up platform were equally well looked after, as this view of 'B1' Class No. 61338 hammering through circa 1963 shows. Based at Leeds Neville Hill shed from June 1963 to June 1964, the train number is not decipherable but this will be a West Country holiday express that the 4-6-0 had taken over at Bristol Temple Meads and was bound for Leeds or Bradford. Built by the North British Locomotive Co. for British Railways and entering service on 20th August 1948, No. 61338 was withdrawn from Wakefield shed in January 1965. Colour-Rail

RIGHT: Barnwood shed's 'Standard' Class '5' No. 73028, which we saw earlier on a Bristol to Gloucester local at Berkeley Road, powers through with train No. 1N84 on 8th August 1964. This is a much longer express working, which again is mentioned on the GloucesterRailwayMemories site, being the 2.15pm from Bristol to York which despite rampant dieselisation on the Midland main line from 1961-62, was still steam-worked on Saturdays. The house in the left background, which still remains today, is on the far side of Station Road, which can be seen curving away up the hill in the distance beyond the end of the Down platform. NPC

RIGHT: 'Black Five' No. 44666 starts away with a Birmingham to Bristol local circa 1963. This is another engine that we have seen before, heading south at Standish. In the background there is a glimpse of the signal box and up on the bank above it the station masters house again. The view is not dated but is prior to November 1963, when the yard sidings and the trailing connection just visible by the box were all taken out. The nearer trailing connection, just in front of the locomotive, was removed on 2nd November 1965. COLOUR-RAIL

LEFT: A more elevated viewpoint here on 20th July 1963, looking from part way up the public footpath which also ran by the station master's house and was no doubt well used by successive generations of those venerable gentlemen. 'Black Five' No. 45268 is heading through with a Derby to Weston-super-Mare express. Built by Armstrong, Whitworth & Co. Ltd in October 1936, this was another Saltley-based engine at this date but transferred to Stoke-on-Trent in April 1964. It was another locomotive that survived until the end, being withdrawn from Carnforth shed at the start of August 1968.
MARK B. WARBURTON

BRITISH RAILWAY HISTORY IN COLOUR: 4B. GLOUCESTER MIDLAND LINES SOUTH – STONEHOUSE TO WESTERLEIGH

From a similar spot to the last picture but on the railway side of the fence, 'Jubilee' Class No. 45614 *Leeward Islands* was working hard as it stormed through with the Saturdays Only 6.35am train from Walsall to Kingswear. The picture is undated but the yard connections and sidings look little used, so the date is probably 1963, with the locomotive on its final allocation, to Derby shed. New from Crewe Works in August 1934, it had transferred to Derby from Burton-on-Trent in January 1963 and was to be withdrawn in January 1964. PAUL RILEY/COURTESY THE RESTORATION & ARCHIVING TRUST/REF. PR3935

A picture reproduced from one of the larger 52mm transparencies which a handful of photographers used – they are rare in comparison to 35mm slides, so I can only assume that they cost significantly more. Sadly, this one carried no information on the mount but the locomotive is identifiable as ex-GWR No. 6825 *Llanvair Grange* and the date can be pinned down reasonably accurately too. New in February 1937, the locomotive moved from Laira to Reading in September 1962 and then on to Bristol St. Philips Marsh in April 1964 but was to be withdrawn from there during the week ending 15th June. With the daisies and buttercups in the foreground in full bloom, we are thus probably seeing No. 6825 here with a Bristol-bound freight during the last couple of weeks of its working life. The view also provides some detail of the goods shed, on the right. NPC

A fine view of the south end of the yard, looking towards the north portal of Wickwar Tunnel, with 'B1' Class No. 61167 throwing a smokey trail over its carriages as it heads through with a Paignton to Bradford summer Saturday express on 20th July 1963. The siding in the foreground shows evidence of still being in use and possibly the others too. No. 61167 was built by Vulcan Foundry right at the end of the L&NER era, in May 1947 and was based at Mexborough shed at the date of this view but had moved to Canklow by the time it was withdrawn in December 1964. There is a good view of thr station masters house high up on the right and Wickwar's Holy Trinity church can just be glimpsed through the trees above the engine. On the left is part of the old brewery complex. Beer brewing here ceased after it was taken over by the Cheltenham Original Brewery Co. Ltd in 1924, with the premises being used to make cider instead but that stopped circa 1970. MARK B. WARBURTON

THE BRISTOL & GLOUCESTER LINE – BERKELEY ROAD TO YATE

LEFT: For passenger services, this was the new order on the Birmingham to Bristol main line from the summer of 1962 but most photographers chose still to concentrate on steam hauled trains. Soon after the introduction of diesel haulage on the regular express services, Sulzer Type '4' No. D39 was photographed passing through Wickwar with train No. 1V44, the 12.52pm from York to Bristol, which was due in to Temple Meads at 6.21pm. New in to service from Derby Works on 20th July 1961, at the date of this view No. D39 was based at Bristol Bath Road, which had been closed to steam in September 1960 and converted as a diesel depot. It was allocated to Line Power Controller, Derby in January 1966 and then to Nottingham Division in June 1968. Under TOPS the locomotive became Class '45' No. 45033 in January 1975 and it was withdrawn from service on 4th February 1988. K. ELLIS/COLOUR-RAIL

RIGHT: Wickwar closed to goods traffic in November 1963 and to passengers on the same day as the other stations on the main line, 4th January 1965. John Strange paid a visit to the site on a snowy day in January 1966, where he found the goods shed in the process of being demolished. Not the best of conditions for taking colour pictures, with the result that these views are of rather indifferent quality, they nevertheless provide rare detail, particularly here of the interior construction of the goods shed roof. JOHN STRANGE

LEFT: Looking north, with the bracket signal on the left now minus its last remaining arm and the closed signal box awaiting its fate. In the distance, the buildings had already been cleared from the platforms and there is a grey Morris Minor 6cwt van parked on the right. Today, there is a modern industrial unit and offices built on this site which is not unlike a railway goods shed in design. JOHN STRANGE

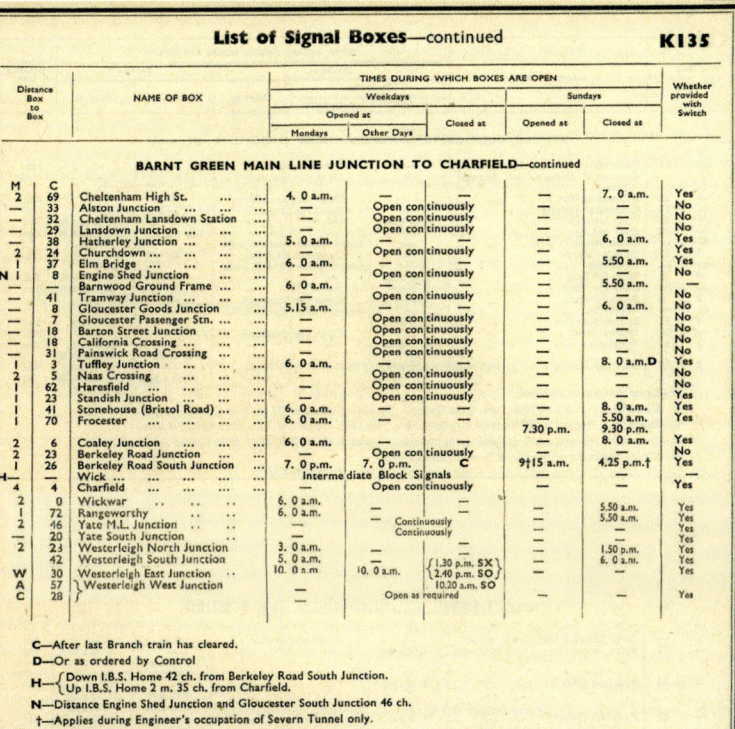

ABOVE: Wickwar signal box was a Midland Type '1' cabin opened on 4th October 1908 and closed on 2nd November 1965. The 25 inch OS survey of 1881 shows a signal box just off the south end of the Down platfrom but the 1901 survey shows a cabin close to the position of that seen here. It is possible, therefore that there were three signal boxes here over the life of the station. The man holding the nameboard in position is only doing so for photographic purposes, as the boards on Midland boxes were positioned at either end just below the eaves, where a gap can be seen in the paintwork. JOHN STRANGE

TOP LEFT: Railwayana collectors look away now! If neither of the Wickwar signal box nameboards survive, then this is why but was this one actually burnt? Did one of them get saved? JOHN STRANGE

ABOVE LEFT: The opening hours for the signal boxes on the Midland main line as far south as Westerleigh, from the *1961 Working Time Tables*. Note that the boxes from Wickwar southwards and at Westerleigh were in the *Bristol District WTT*, so this is a 'cobbled' together version.

LEFT: A frontal view of the box shortly before it was demolished. The hut at the base of the steps housed the signalman's privy. JOHN STRANGE

Two views of another of the ex-GWR 'Grange' Class 4-6-0s, polished No. 6851 *Hurst Grange* of Oxley shed, heading towards Wickwar Tunnel with train No. 1C23, the Saturdays only 6.55am from Wolverhampton to Newquay and Penzance, in the summer of 1963. Unusually at this date, there were a number of wagons in the loop siding next to the Down main line. New in November 1937, No. 6851 was withdrawn from Tyseley in August 1965, two months after transferring there. Note the colour light signal alongside the north portal of the tunnel. PAUL RILEY/COURTESY THE RESTORATION & ARCHIVING TRUST/REF. NO'S PR1640 & PR1740

'Black Five' No. 45040 heads back in to sunlight after exiting the south portal of Wickwar Tunnel in 1960. The train reporting number can just be deciphered as No. W220, which on Saturdays was the Down 'The Pines Express'; Mondays to Fridays, this train ran as No. 1H41. The 'Black Five' was delivered to the LM&SR by Vulcan Foundry in October 1935 and was another Saltley-based engine when seen here. Moving to Oxley in April 1965, it was withdrawn from Crewe South shed in July 1967, four months after being assigned there. Wickwar Tunnel was by far the largest engineering feature on the Br&GR line. Trial bores were drilled in June 1840 and construction commenced in April 1841, the shaft being dug through a bed of mountain limestone at the south end which required no lining and, as can be seen, no portal either. The northern end was through Pennant stone and the centre part through sandstone, all of which did require lining. The tunnel is 1,401 yards in length and is 28ft in height to the apex of the bore. M.E.J. DEANE COURTESY DR SIMON FOSBURY

An Up express heads towards Wickwar Tunnel behind 'Black Five' No. 44658 on 25th August 1962. Built by BR at Crewe Works and entering service on 31st May 1949, No. 44658 was based at Nottingham at the date of this view, so this could be train No. 1M22, the 2.40pm off Temple Meads which was bound for the engine's home city. A career of reasonable length, considering its late build, came to an end when the 'Five' was withdrawn from Wigan Springs Branch shed in November 1967. This picture and the one on the previous page were taken from Bridge No. 47, an aqueduct and footbridge built with the line in 1840, which is shown in the following three views and is still extant today. The cutting sides are also still largely kept clear of trees and bushes and note the colour light signal at this end too. NPC

'Jubilee' No. 45579 *Punjab* heads south with train No. 1V27, the Saturdays Only 6.40am from Leicester to Paignton. The locomotive transferred from Burton-on-Trent to Derby in June 1963, so the picture is likely to have been taken soon after that or in the early summer of 1964, prior to its withdrawal in mid-August of that year. The footbridge can just be glimpsed in the left background through the steam, whilst the photographer was standing on West End Bridge (No. 46), which carries West End Lane across the line.
PAUL RILEY/COURTESY THE RESTORATION & ARCHIVING TRUST/REF. NO'S PR3940

BRITISH RAILWAY HISTORY IN COLOUR: 4B. GLOUCESTER MIDLAND LINES SOUTH – STONEHOUSE TO WESTERLEIGH 405

Viewed from the cutting side just north of West End Bridge, 'Peak' Class '46' No. 46045 heads a Down express out of Wickwar Tunnel and beneath the footbridge on 22nd June 1976. New in to service from Derby Works on 27th September 1962 as No. D182, the locomotive was based at Gateshead at the date of this view. Withdrawn on 1st November 1984, it was subsequently bought for preservation and, restored to its original identity, is now based at the Midland Railway, Butterley, although at the time of writing is part way through a five year stay at the Nene Valley Railway. MIKE SPICER/COURTESY THE RESTORATION & ARCHIVING TRUST/REF. NO'S MSZZ4277

A short while later, an unidentified Class '37' trundled by with a Down freight of steel mineral wagons loaded with what looks to be concrete sleepers. MIKE SPICER/COURTESY THE RESTORATION & ARCHIVING TRUST/REF. NO'S MSZZ4278

RIGHT: Looking south from West End Bridge on 25th August 1962, as 'Jubilee' No. 45656 *Cochrane* hurried by with a thirteen coach West Country holiday express heading back north, possibly to Bradford, the engine being based at Sheffield Darnall by this date. The summit of Wickwar Bank was around two miles further on, to the south of Yate, so the next five miles for the crew of No. 45656 was easy going. We saw this engine passing Coaley earlier on, again in August 1962 but with a different Up express. NPC

LEFT: No. 7014 *Caerhays Castle* with another north-bound holiday express. The number chalked on the smokebox door is not clear but could be H31, whilst the engine was based at Stafford Road at this date, so this is probably a Paignton to Wolverhampton train. An early BR build, completed at Swindon Works in July 1948, No. 7014 covered much of the old GWR system, being based during its career at both of the ex-GWR Bristol sheds, Swansea Landore and Old Oak Common, before heading to the West Midlands in June 1962. Withdrawal, from Tyseley, took place in early February 1962. NPC

BELOW: Ex-L&NER 'B1' Class 4-6-0 No. 61162 hurries towards Wickwar Tunnel with train No. 1N65. This was the 6.05am from Paignton to Bradford, which we saw passing Wickwar a little earlier on another occasion with a different 'B1' at the head. The date is likely to be the summer of 1961, when the locomotive was based at Sheffield Darnall shed; it moved to Staveley Great Central in May 1962. New from Vulcan Foundry in May 1947, it was withdrawn in December 1964. PAUL RILEY/COURTESY THE RESTORATION & ARCHIVING TRUST/REF. PR2681

A slightly wider aspect of the same scene, with the photographer standing on the side of the shallow cutting to photograph Class '9F' No. 92155 heading north with a train of vans on 24th June 1961. Again this is a locomotive that we have encountered before, heading north near Coaley in 1963. There was a small underbridge taking a stream beneath the line about 100 yards beyond the pw hut, so Hall End Bridge in the background was No. 44 in the *Bridge Register*. It carried Hall End Lane which leads to Hall End Farm, in the left distance, and then joins with West End Lane a short way past that. Note the brick-built permanent way hut on the right, no longer in existence although Network Rail do appear to have a pw storage and access site here today. The telegraph pole route has also gone but, apart from that, this is a view which has changed remarkably little in the near sixty years (at the time of writing) since these pictures were taken. NPC

ABOVE: From the same spot, 'Britannia' Class 'Pacific' No. 70053 *Moray Firth* was captured heading by with train No. 1M34, the 10.05am from Kingswear to Wolverhampton, on 28th August 1965. The Oxley-based 'Brit' was another engine previously seen at Coaley, in equally poor condition and minus its nameplates although it still had around eighteen months left in traffic. JOHN GRAINGER

BELOW: Eleven years later, on 22nd June 1976, 'Class 46' No. 46011 was recorded as it roared past the exact same point with an Up express and causing a hawk to wheel away from the line just as the photographer clicked his shutter. Interestingly, note that whilst the brick-built pw hut had gone by this date, it had been replaced by one of concrete panels with a flat roof, which has also since been removed. MIKE SPICER/COURTESY THE RESTORATION & ARCHIVING TRUST/REF. NO'S MSZZ4277

LEFT: A closer view of Hall End Bridge, as BR 'Standard' Class '5' No. 73047 heads through on 25th August 1962. New from Derby Works in December 1953, this was an Eastern Region allocated engine, whilst the train reporting number 1E5? (the last digit is unreadable) marks this as a service bound for that region too. Transferred back to the London Midland Region in early July 1964, No. 73047 was withdrawn from Shrewsbury shed five months later at the start of December. NPC

ABOVE: The crew of ex-GWR '28XX' 2-8-0 No. 2876 lean out of their cab and smile for the benefit of the photographer, as they head by with a short train of ICI H tank wagons on 15th August 1964. Built at Swindon in January 1919, the engine was on its final allocation when seen here, based at Newport Ebbw Junction shed, from where it was to be withdrawn at the end of the year. The view is looking from Hall End Lane, which parallels the line for a short distance after crossing Hall End Bridge, in the distance.
JOHN GRAINGER

RIGHT: Saltley-based 'Black Five' No. 44945 breasts the top of Wickwar Bank with the Bromford Bridge to Avonmouth oil tanks on 23rd February 1963. These are Class 'B' Esso TSVs of 1958-1959 vintage – the sort modelled in Airfix kits in the mod-1960s. This view includes the Rangeworthy Down Home signal on the right, whilst the 4-6-0 was seen much earlier at Eastgate. NPC

THE BRISTOL & GLOUCESTER LINE – BERKELEY ROAD TO YATE

Without doubt the most obscure location on the whole Bristol & Gloucester line was Rangeworthy, which gets no mention at all in Maggs' or Peter Smith's books. For the first near century of the line's existence there was only an occupation crossing here. However, the LM&SR opened a new signal box on 25th January 1942, on the Up side of the line about 50 yards south of the crossing, as a wartime break-section box, located 1 mile 1,604 yards from Wickwar box and 2 miles 1,011 yards from Yate Main Line box, a section that was previously 4 miles 855 yards long, all of which was on a long climbing gradient from Wickwar. The box was built of red brick with a flat concrete roof, to the standard LM&SR ARP design, capable of withstanding the bomb blast of a near miss. It had a frame of just ten levers with a Home, Distant and detonator lever for each direction and one for the trailing crossover in front of the box, so seven working, one lever and two spaces. The adjacent crossing was used by nearby Hall End Farm as a short cut and was the scene of an accident on 28th June 1949 (documented on the Railways Archive website): *The 5.15 pm ordinary passenger train from Bristol to Birmingham, travelling on the Up line at about 50mph, collided with a private motor car at the occupation level crossing known as Hardwicke Crossing, near Rangeworthy signal box, and the leading bogie wheels of the engine were derailed. The car, a 1935 model 10hp Austin saloon, was carried by the engine for a distance of 140 yards, and then fell down the embankment. The sole occupant was the wife of the owner of the farm served by the crossing, and she received cuts and bruises and suffered severely from shock; she was given first aid by passengers in the train and conveyed by ambulance to hospital with the minimum of delay, where she was detained. There were no other casualties'*. The crossover was taken out when the box closed on 20th October 1969 and the occupation crossing is also now closed. Here, 'Jubilee' No. 45676 *Codrington* passes the box with an Up express and it may well be that this picture also provides a more accurate date for the bottom one on page 400; No. 45676 was based at Saltley shed from March to late November 1963, so both pictures are likely to have been taken in July/August of that year. PAUL RILEY/COURTESY THE RESTORATION & ARCHIVING TRUST/REF. No's PR3941

LEFT: 'Royal Scot' No. 46137 *The Prince of Wales's Volunteers (South Lancashire)* passes Rangeworthy signal box with an Up train on 22nd July 1961. New from North British Locomotive in October 1927, this was a much travelled engine, which had no less than fifteen allocations during its BR career, from 1948 to withdrawal in early November 1962. It was based at Derby at the time it was seen here but the train number is only partially readable, again being 1E5? In the summer of 1961, there were two trains due through here within minutes of each other which that could equate with: No. 1E58, the 11.12am from Bournemouth to Sheffield or No. 1E59, the 10.40am Exmouth to Cleethorpes, due past at around 2.20pm and 2.45pm respectively. After careful study of the picture under heavy magnification, I would plump for the first of those. NPC

RIGHT: Now preserved 'Jubilee' No. 45690 *Leander* of Bristol Barrow Road shed heads through Lime Kiln Bridge (No. 43) with a Down train on 5th March 1961. The bridge, which carries Limekiln Lane across the railway, was rebuilt to the form seen here in 1901. NPC

BELOW: Another 'Royal Scot' was photographed on 22nd July 1961, No. 46157 *The Royal Artilleryman*, heading south near Rangeworthy Bridge (No. 42) with train No. 1O95, the Down 'The Pines Express'. Much detective work has gone in to pinning down the exact locations of these photographs to get them in the right sequence travelling southwards and the pylon just seen in the background was a big help here. No. 46157 had transferred from Crewe North to Saltley just weeks before this picture was taken. Built at Derby Works in July 1930, the engine was withdrawn from Carlisle Kingmoor shed in early January 1964. NPC

We now begin a run of photographs all taken from or near Rangeworthy Bridge, most looking north and featuring Down trains, on a succession of summer Saturdays in 1964. We have previously seen British Railway's last steam locomotive, '9F' No. 92220 *Evening Star*, in much better condition than this, with the 2-10-0 clearly suffering from priming problems. Probably caused by impure water in the boiler, the resultant foaming had made rather a mess of the engine's lovely lined green paintwork. *Evening Star* was based at Cardiff East Dock shed at the time of this 25th July 1964 view, transferring there from Bath Green Park in October 1963. Incidentally, Rangeworthy Bridge actually carries Tanhouse Lane over the line but rather unusually was not named after the road. JOHN GRAINGER

LEFT: On the same day, No. 7012 *Barry Castle* was seen heading south with an unidentified train, although with the engine being based at Wolverhampton Oxley shed at this date, it is likely to be a holiday express bound for Paignton, Ilfracombe or Newquay. A week later, John Dagley-Morris was to photograph the same engine heading north on a Newquay to Wolverhampton train (page 372).
JOHN GRAINGER

RIGHT: Passing trains in this 25th July view, with No. 6924 *Grantley Hall* heading south and crossing with an unidentified Up train. A war-time build at Swindon Works in August 1941, the 'Hall' was based at Reading shed at the date of this view but there are no clues as to the nature or destination of its train. Moving to Oxford in November 1964, it was withdrawn from there twelve months later. JOHN GRAINGER

LEFT: We have seen No. 7019 *Fowey Castle* numerous times already but here it is again with train No. 1V52, the 6.55am from Wolverhampton to Penzance on 1st August. JOHN GRAINGER

On 1st August, No. 7024 *Powis Castle*, which we saw earlier at Charfield, was captured heading south with train No. 1V53, the 8.02am from Wolverhampton to Ilfracombe. On the far side of the copse of trees, which remains today, a branch running back from the Up line (the junction for which was by the centre of the train) had once curved round to the west to serve the short-lived Rangeworthy or Old Wood Colliery. The branch opened circa 1883 but had closed in 1888, with the signal box, signals and all associated track being removed in August 1893. The brick-built pw hut has gone but otherwise this view has changed little today. JOHN GRAINGER

BRITISH RAILWAY HISTORY IN COLOUR: 4B. GLOUCESTER MIDLAND LINES SOUTH – STONEHOUSE TO WESTERLEIGH

RIGHT: Mark Warburton had stationed himself at Wickwar on 1st August (page 385) and thus both he and John Grainger photographed No. 6871 *Bourton Grange* heading south with the pigeon special from Stoke to Bath. JOHN GRAINGER

LEFT: Two weeks later, on 15th August, 2-8-0 No. 3844 was seen heading south on a mixed freight, with an insulated container on a 4-wheeled 'Conflat' wagon at the front of the consist. No. 3844 was one of the later members of the '28XX' Class, built at Swindon in April 1942 and based at Westbury shed at the date of this view. Moving to Bristol Barrow Road in mid September 1965, it was withdrawn just a couple of weeks later. JOHN GRAINGER

RIGHT: Looking south from alongside the bridge on 15th August, with 'Black Five' No. 44805 heading north with train No. 1V79, the 7.50am from Paignton to Newcastle. This Wolverhampton Oxley engine has also been seen several times previously in these pages. For those wondering why we are in a run of ex-GWR types, with this the only ex-LM&SR engine to be featured at this particular location, the explanation lies in the LMR's dieselisation of all services bar a handful of the holiday expresses by this date. JOHN GRAINGER

THE BRISTOL & GLOUCESTER LINE – BERKELEY ROAD TO YATE

This final view in the sequence shows No. 7023 *Penrice Castle* heading north with train No. 1M35, the 11.05am from Ilfracombe to Wolverhampton, probably on 15th August again. A week earlier, on 8th August, No. 7023 had passed this way with train No. 1M34, the 10.05am from Kingswear to Wolverhampton. A BR build at Swindon Works in July 1949, *Penrice Castle* had been fitted with a double chimney in May 1958 and was based at Oxley shed at the date of this view. Its paintwork is looking a little shabby here, whilst the engine was clearly burning some inferior quality coal and this was to be its last summer of work, withdrawal taking place in early February 1965. In the distance Folley Bridge (No. 41) can just be seen, which carries a seemingly un-named lane across the line. JOHN GRAINGER

BRITISH RAILWAY HISTORY IN COLOUR: 4B. GLOUCESTER MIDLAND LINES SOUTH – STONEHOUSE TO WESTERLEIGH 417

ABOVE: The hardest two views to pin down the location of along this section of line were these two but I'm fairly sure that they are looking west from lineside a few yards north of Folley Bridge, with the houses just visible in the right background facing on to Engine Common Lane. 'Black Five' No. 44825, seen earlier at Charfield, passes by with train No. 1V31, the 7.43am from Nottingham to Plymouth on 29th August 1964. JOHN GRAINGER

BELOW: At the same location nearly a year later on 25th June 1965, 'Britannia' No. 70045 *Lord Rowallan* heads south with train No. 1V53, which in this year's summer time table was the 8.00am from Wolverhampton to Ilfracombe. New in to service from Crewe Works on 14th June 1954, the Oxley-based 'Brit' was withdrawn from Carlisle Kingmoor shed at the close of 1967. Note that it was already minus its nameplates here. JOHN GRAINGER

Working from GoogleEarth, this proved a very difficult bridge to find, until I realised that it is Yate Colliery Bridge (No. 40), which carries Broad Lane across the railway but today, with the expansion of Yate since the 1960s, has been bypassed by a new bridge built just to its south carrying the B4059 Goose Green Way. The bridge still stands but the road over it is now a foot and cycle path. A month after the previous picture, on 24th July 1965, another 'Britannia', No. 70053 *Moray Firth*, which we have seen a couple of times already, has just come through the brick arch with train No. 1V53 again. Ilfracombe, the destination of this and various other holiday expresses from the West Midlands and other places, is no longer rail served, the line on from Barnstaple having been closed in 1970. JOHN GRAINGER

No. 6999 *Capel Dewi Hall* trundles by with train No. 1M37, the 11.25am Newquay to Wolverhampton, which here on Saturday 7th August 1965 was loaded to eleven coaches. No. 6999 had taken over the train at Temple Meads, having earlier that day gone down to Bristol with relief train No. 1V50. This Hawksworth 'Modified Hall' Class 4-6-0 was another BR-built engine, entering traffic from Swindon Works on 10th February 1949. It had recently transferred from Severn Tunnel Junction to Oxford when seen here and yet again displays the sad and sorry condition in which many of these engines appeared during their final weeks in service; it was withdrawn at the end of the year, at the end of WR steam. The location is a couple of hundred yards to the south of the bridge seen above, with the houses of Windsor Drive in the background. Built in the early 1950s, the first signs of Yate's growth from rural village to Bristol commuter town, they are now completely surrounded by a modern estate which here now reaches right down to the railway. JOHN GRAINGER

A slightly wider aspect of the same location later that day, with 'Britannia' No. 70045 *Lord Rowallan* again at the head of an unidentified Up train. No. 70045 had been attached to the front of the train at Temple Meads, where it had arrived earlier in the day with the regular summer Saturday Wolverhampton to Ilfracombe service, train No. 1V53. Note some depot 'wag' had chalked a new name on the smoke deflector, something 'FC'; one would think possibly 'Wolves', this being an Oxley-based engine at this date but it is not clear enough to read. The shed had three 'Brits' in 1965, which were all regulars on these summer Saturday holiday expresses in their final year of steam haulage, the other two being No. 70053 *Moray Firth* and un-named No. 70047. The expresses ran via the Honeybourne line and they were also to be the last time-tabled steam passenger trains to traverse that route, on Saturday 4th September 1965, with No's 70045 and 70053 both in action that day. JOHN GRAINGER

No. 7029 *Clun Castle* heads north past Windsor Drive, Yate, with the SLS's 'GWR Cavalcade' rail tour of 17th October 1965. This had started from Birmingham Snow Hill at 10.17am behind 0-6-2T No. 6667, with 0-4-2T No. 1420 and 0-6-0PT No. 6435 taking over at Worcester Shrub Hill for the leg to Bristol, a move designed to take them both south as they were then bound for the Dart Valley Railway. However, No. 1420 was removed at Gloucester and replaced by No. 7029, which some reports state was apparently intended only to work the return leg from Bristol. The 'Castle' departed Temple Meads with the return leg at 4.00pm and passed Yate South Junction at 4.22pm, so is thus seen here around a minute later. Note the fresh ballast awaiting spreading and packing on the Down line, whilst the pw ganger was clearly not interested in the passing train. NPC

'Black Five' No. 45186 heads briskly away from Yate with train No. 1M84, the 2.15pm Bristol to York express on 29th August 1964. This was another of Saltley's large complement of 'Black Fives' but not one that we have seen before, built by Armstrong, Whitworth & Co. Ltd for the LM&SR in September 1935. From Nationalisation in 1948, it spent most of its time allocated to Saltley but with short spells over the years at Derby, Sheffield Millhouses, Leicester Great Central and Derby again, before transferring away to Wolverhampton Oxley in early April 1965. No. 45186's final posting was to Crewe South in early March 1967, from where it was withdrawn six months later. In the right background can just be made out part of the large factory of Parnall (Yate) Ltd, by this date manufacturers of domestic appliances. In 1925, George Parnall & Co. acquired the buildings and aerodrome of No. 3 Aircraft Repair Depot just to the north of Yate (and to the left of the line here) and relocated their aircraft manufactory from Park Row, Bristol. They built their last aircraft in 1939 and then went on to make gun turrets, as well as parts for Spitfires and Mosquito fighter bombers, with the factory becoming a Luftwaffe target during the Second World War as a result. Sadly, fifty-four people were killed in raids in February 1941. Parnall (Yate) Ltd became part of the Avery Group in 1962, which was acquired by GEC in 1979 and today the factory is owned by the Whirlpool Corporation. JOHN GRAINGER

BRITISH RAILWAY HISTORY IN COLOUR: 4B. GLOUCESTER MIDLAND LINES SOUTH – STONEHOUSE TO WESTERLEIGH 421

Looking north towards the location of the previous picture, 'Jubilee' No. 45605 *Cyprus* enters Yate on 10th August 1963 with train No. 1V40. We saw this Leeds Holbeck-based engine passing through Wickwar a little earlier, hauling this same train, a relief to the Down 'The Devonian' but on a different occasion. The train is just passing the junction with the Thornbury Branch, which was controlled by Yate Main Line signal box, the earliest still in use on the Br&GR main line, opened on 9th March 1886; it was reduced to ground frame status on 20th October 1969 and taken out completely on 10th May 1971. On the Up side of the line in the left distance are the Admiralty sidings, which were brought in to use on 18th August 1918 and removed in July 1964. Parnall's factory on the right is much reduced in size today and much of the site is now housing. NPC

Burning some very poor quality coal, 'Jubilee' No. 45569 *Tasmania* heads past Yate Main Line box with train No. 1O91, the 7.32am SO Nottingham to Bournemouth express, which would take the Bath line at Mangotsfield and proceed via the Somerset & Dorset route. The picture was probably taken in the summer of 1962, with the train being retimed to start at 7.35am the following year. New from North British Locomotive in August 1934, this was another Leeds Holbeck-based 'Jubilee', examples of which were reularly rostered for these trains. It was reallocated to Patricroft shed in April 1964 but withdrawn almost immediately. The first carriage behind No. 45569's tender is a Gresley Brake Composite of mid-1930s vintage and there appear to be other Gresley coaches further back in the consist. On the left, a Class '4F' 0-6-0 can be seen coming off the Thornbury Branch with a train of coal empties and beyond there are wagons to be seen again in the Admiralty sidings. Several of Parnall's aircraft designs were for naval use but they had very limited success with any of their aeroplanes and only one went in to extensive production but with the Bristol Aeroplane Company. PAUL RILEY/COURTESY THE RESTORATION & ARCHIVING TRUST/REF. NO's PR3943

SECTION 13

THE THORNBURY BRANCH

'Hymek' No. D7008 has come off the Thornbury Branch at Yate Main Line Junction with a train of loaded stone hoppers on 18th May 1967 but has then pulled in to the siding that stopped just short of Station Road bridge. The group in the foreground is likely to be the participants leaving what had been a brake van trip along the branch. New in to service from Beyer, Peacock on 24th October 1961, the diesel-hydraulic was withdrawn on 1st January 1971. M.H. Yardley/Colour-Rail

The Act for the Thornbury Branch received the Royal Assent on 14th July 1864, together with the Midland's rather more important Mangotsfield & Bath Act, with the two lines being jointly financed and having the same engineer. This explains how Sidney Crossley, the MR's chief engineer and builder of the iconic and immense Settle & Carlisle line, came to be in charge of the construction of a minor branch line in south Gloucestershire which was built over the same period in time.

Shortly after the Act had been granted, the owners of the iron mine at Frampton Cotterell began pressing for the construction of a branch just over a mile in length to their pit, running from a junction with the Thornbury line at Iron Acton. Requiring a separate Act, this was granted Royal Assent on 5th July 1865. Tenders for the construction of both branches were invited and three were received in July 1866, with the lowest, that of Eckersley & Bayliss for a shade under £70,000, being accepted. Work began in June 1867 but was held up by certain landowners opposed to the construction, with compulsory possesion being necessary in places. However, by March 1868 the line from Yate to Iron Acton and then on to the mine at Frampton was almost complete and it duly opened for traffic at an unrecorded date in May.

The rest of the line to Thornbury took a little longer, due partly to the need to dig two tunnels, at Tytherington and Grovesend, of 224 yards and 167 yards length respectively. However, there were further hold-ups after August 1870, partly it would seem due to the ending of the contractors' partnership, which was dissolved in June 1871, with Bayliss agreeing to carry on and complete the work alone. Construction of the station buildings and crossing cottages was sub-contracted out.

The completed line was inspected by Lt Col. Hutchinson of the Board of Trade in August 1872, with the MR agreeing to undertake certain remedial works as a result, and the line was then opened for traffic on 31st August. The new branch was 7 miles 20 chains long, running from a double junction with the MR main line at Yate but then quickly becoming single which it remained for the rest of the way to Thornbury. Intermediate stations were provided at Iron Acton and Tytherington but neither had loops for crossing trains. Both had wooden station buildings but the terminus at Thornbury was a rather more stylish affair, built of stone with a tiled roof and the typically elaborate Midland bargeboards of the period.

The branch passenger service was never frequent, beginning with just two trains a day each way, mornings and evenings, although this was soon increased to three by the addition of a mid-day train. The journey time was a leisurely 30 minutes. In the decades that followed, some services were run as mixed trains on the same time allowance but passenger only trains were now taking a more sprightly 22 minutes for the journey. During the 20th century, the service was increased to four trains daily, the first and the last of the day running through to Temple

Meads, some of which cleared the branch in around 15 minutes. No bay platform was ever provided at Yate for branch trains and the stock was stabled overnight at Thornbury. Bus competition began making inroads to the already sparse, largely commuter traffic from 1906, with the A38 providing a far quicker and more direct route in to north and central Bristol. Accordingly, it is not surprising that the passenger service was an early casualty, being withdrawn on 19th June 1944, when the branch was being used for war-time ambulance trains delivering patients to a United States Army hospital at Leyhill, 5 miles north-east of Thornbury, which had been built with stone from Grovesend Quarry.

The first goods traffic was iron ore from the mine at Frampton Cotterell in 1870 but this was to be short-lived, the pit closing in 1878 although the rails were not removed until 1895. General goods traffic was never heavy, with coal and agricultural supplies being the main inward loads, and services over the years were sustained by the heavy amount of mineral traffic generated by the quarries the branch served. Nevertheless, this was not enough to sustain it and with goods services being withdrawn from Thornbury on 20th June 1966, the stone traffic was deemed unremunerative and that too ceased on 24th November 1967, with the track being lifted the following year

Ironically, the branch was to be reinstated due to road construction, specifically the building of the M5 Motorway through south Gloucestershire and also the first Severn Bridge. Grovesend Quarry, now owned by the Amey Roadstone Corporation (ARC) and renamed Tytherington Quarry, would supply the roadstone and the relaid branch was reopened on 3rd July 1972. Bridge decks along the route had to be strengthened and the level

The Thornbury Branch, as shown on the 1 inch OS for 1960. The three closed stations are indicated by white circles and the two tunnels sandwich Grovesend Quarry. The Frampton iron mine branch swung west and then due south away from Iron Acton, the pit being indicated by the hatching beneath the double 'll' in Cotterell.

Looking west from Hazell's Bridge (No. 3), which carries Yate Road over the line, as Class '4F' No. 44534 approaches with a short freight circa 1960. New from Crewe Works in September 1928, this was a Bristol Barrow Road engine from 1959 up until its withdrawal in November 1964. In the background is the wonderfully named Strawberry Gardens Bridge (No. 4), which carries Bridge Road over the line, whilst the property to the right is the still extant 'Bridge House'. David Pollard/NPC

crossings rebuilt to modern standards, whilst the line now only ran as far as a headshunt abutting the A38 at Tytherington. ARC now saw the potential to develop the quarry as a major supplier of roadstone and crushed stone for making concrete and began supplying customers and railheads north of the M4, up to 100 miles away from the quarry and so began the line's second coming. It has not been without hiccups, however; fluctuations in demand saw the branch temporarily closed in the early 1990s and it was then mothballed again in 2013. The good news is that, after a test run in 2017, the branch has recently been completely refurbished and regular stone trains began operating again from the quarry (owned by the Hanson Group since 1989) in early 2019.

With passenger services having been withdrawn prior to Nationalisation, locomotive variety on the branch in the BR era was fairly limited, with Class '4F' 0-6-0s the most common form of motive power. Ex-GWR pannier tanks appeared occasionally, whilst for the last two years WR 'Hymek' diesel-hydraulics worked most of the daily freight trips.

Little remains of the branch stations, the notable survivors being the crossing keepers cottages at Iron Acton and Latteridge, and the station masters house at Tytherington. The overbridges remain as built but a number of underbridges were significantly and none to subtly reconstructed for the heavier stone trains. Proposals to reopen the branch to passenger trains, which would run under the A38 again to the outskirts of Thornbury, are highly unlikely to come to anything on the grounds of cost, as well as signalling and pathing difficulties, and the fact that Bristol has invested heavily in the MetroBus system, which will probably be extended out to the town at some stage instead.

TOP AND ABOVE: Two views of Class '47' No. 47070 as it hauls a stone train towards Yate on 9th September 1975. The views are taken from Robin Hood Bridge (No. 5), a triple arch span carrying Nibley Lane over the railway. In the top picture the train has just passed the Advance Warning Board (a black cross on a white background) for Station Road Crossing at Iron Acton. The lower picture moments later looking the opposite way shows the '47' about to head round the curve towards Strawberry Gardens Bridge. BOTH BILL POTTER/KRM

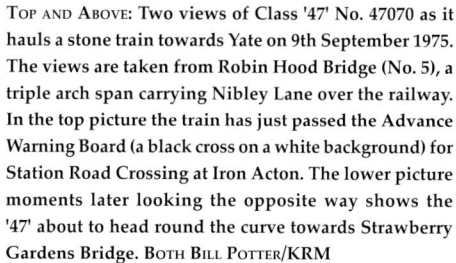

LEFT: Iron Acton siding was latterly almost always served from Up trains, although it was permitted for a locomotive to propel up to five wagons and a brake van from Yate. Shunting the siding involved blocking Station Road level crossing for a period, although it was far from being a busy thoroughfare. Here, in summer 1960, Class '4F' No. 44523 has uncoupled from its train to pull forward and then reverse in to the siding to collect a wagon. GERALD PEACOCK

No. 44523 reverses slowly in to Iron Acton siding, as the fireman rides on the steps ready to jump down and couple up to the empty wagon being collected. The rest of its train has been left on the running line alongside the remains of the station platform whilst this manoeuvre is performed. Iron Acton had a wooden station building identical in design to that provided at Tytherington, which we shall see shortly, but which had been demolished in the late 1950s. The siding here was actually formed by a stub of the branch to Frampton Cotterell iron mine and the only facilities provided were a weighbridge and hut, and a loading gauge. There had also been a small signal box, opened in 1877, which gained a new frame in 1907 after removal of the iron mine branch but was reduced to ground frame status in 1928. It was the only signal box on the branch apart from Yate Single Line Junction, opened in 1886 and closed in 1905 and latterly the only signals were the Fixed Distants for the level crossings. GERALD PEACOCK

INSET TOP: A condensed index of local trip workings to and from Thornbury, Westerleigh Sidings and Yate, from the *Working Time Table of Classes 7, 8, 9 and Local Freight Trains, Bristol District, 17th June 1963.*

'Hymek' No. D7012 pauses at Iron Acton whilst the secondman opens the gates on 10th June 1966. The siding was out of use by this date and heavily overgrown, although it was not closed officially until 3rd September 1967. In the background is Iron Acton Road Bridge (No. 7), a three arch stone-built structure which carried Bristol Road over the line. Today, it is referred to by Network Rail as Pagford (Old Bristol Road) Bridge. This was the return working of the trip, which had departed Yate with twelve empty hoppers and a brake van 45 minutes late at 12.15. The hoppers were dropped at Grovesend Quarry and six full ones collected. Four minutes was allowed in the schedule for each crossing to be negotiated. JOHN RYAN

The Friday 10th June 1966 visit to the branch was an organised brake van trip, which the photographer recalls was probably organised by the Branch Line Society, hence the other members stood here watching progress. Closure of the line to general goods traffic and thus completely to Thornbury was scheduled for 20th June and this was the one branch in the area that John had not yet travelled. This view is looking west, with the siding hidden beneath grass and weeds; the course of the original iron ore branch curves away southwards beyond the piles of coal, deliveries of which were now by road by this date. The crossing keeper's cottage remains today. JOHN RYAN

RIGHT: The rebuilt Station Road level crossing at Iron Acton on 9th September 1975, looking west towards Robin Hood Bridge. The bridge itself is today of lesser importance, with a new road having been built by-passing Iron Acton. Named Bristol Road, it is the reason why the route over the bridge has been renamed Old Bristol Road. The rail approach to Station Road crossing is protected by advance warning boards and colour light signals, whilst road users are faced with flashing lights when a train approaches. No barriers were provided for what is a little used stretch of road. BILL POTTER/KRM

ABOVE: Looking north-west from Robin Hood Bridge in 1960, as No. 44523 trundles by with Trip 810, the Saturdays only return working from Thornbury to Yate. The consist would appear to be entirely empty wagons which had delivered coal to the terminus. The view behind the train is of the line curving away through green fields and hedgerows. GERALD PEACOCK

LEFT: A new by-pass curving round Iron Acton to the north and west was opened circa 1970, so when the line was relaid in 1972 a new level crossing was required. The road had been laid over the track bed at a slightly higher level, which required the railway to be raised up to cross it. This was a much busier road, so the crossing was equipped with automatically operated half barriers, which when open for road traffic as they are most of the time, made it easy to spot from Robin Hood Bridge on 9th September 1975. BILL POTTER/KRM

Trips along the branch were leisurely to say the least, with train crews having to operate the crossing gates in the years after the passenger service ceased. In 1960, as the train comes to a halt near the end of the long one and a quarter mile straight section southwards from near Rangeworthy, the fireman of No. 44523 climbs down to open the gates at Latteridge level crossing. There were double gates here, as some sections of the line were laid out to allow for the possibility of double tracking at some stage, a forlorn hope which never came close to reality. However, as we saw at Stonehouse Wharf Crossing in Volume 4A, it was only necessary to open one of each pair of gates to allow the train to pass through, which then stopped again on the other side for the guard to get down from his brake van and close them. There is a glimpse of the crossing keeper's cottage on the right, which remains as a private residence today. No. 44523 was another Barrow Road '4F', although had only just transferred to there from Bath Green Park a few weeks before these pictures, and was built at Crewe Works in August 1928, a month before classmate No. 44534 which features in David Pollard's photographs on the branch. GERALD PEACOCK

Because the passenger service had been withdrawn so early, illustrating the two stations on the Thornbury Branch was always going to be the big challenge for the Midland lines south of Gloucester. I was thrilled therefore, when John Ryan's box of slides which covered his trip of 10th June 1966 included this wonderful shot looking east at Tytherington, where the station building was still intact some twenty-two years after passenger trains had last called here, although it remained open and staffed for parcels until 1st August 1949. The secret of its survival was the fact that it was rented to the local scout troop from after that date, who held it up until the branch closed in 1967. The 'Hymek' is partially straddling the bridge over Itchington Road, which in the *Bridge Register* is, presumably mistakenly, named Hitchington Bridge (No. 12). Seen here still in as built in 1867 condition, it is one of the bridges substantially rebuilt for the heavier loads carried by modern wagons. Tytherington had had a single siding on the south (right) side of the line just behind where the photographer was standing, which had been lifted in October 1963. Short branches had also run in to quarries on both sides of the station, Church Quarry on the north side (left), which was closed circa 1944, and West Quarry to the south, the line to which was also lifted in October 1963. Note the approach road on the left, at the bottom of which was the station master's house, still extant today. JOHN RYAN

INSET LEFT: Tytherington Tunnel nameboard was snapped as the train passed through on its way to the quarry on 18th May 1967. M.H. YARDLEY/COLOUR-RAIL

BELOW: A little later, 'Hymek' No. D7008 shunts Grovesend Quarry sidings. The view is looking west towards Grovesend Bridge (No. 15), which has three stone arches and carries Itchington Road – on its way from Itchington and to the A38 – over the line. At this date, the quarry sidings were controlled from two ground frames, Hardwick's Siding at the east end and Grovesend Quarry at the west end, and it is the latter which features on the left here. After relaying in 1972, the two new ground frames provided were known simply as Grovesend Quarry No. 1 and No. 2 respectively. After dropping the empty wagons here on the outward trip, No. D7008 made a special visit to the closed Thornbury station with the brake vans, collecting the loaded wagons on the return journey and then heading back to Yate Main Line Junction where we saw it first. M.H. YARDLEY/COLOUR-RAIL

ABOVE LEFT AND RIGHT: Class '47' No. 47070 runs round at the quarry on 9th September 1975. Both views are taken from Grovesend Bridge, looking east, left, and west, right. Built at Crewe Works and new in to service as No. D1654 on 23rd January 1965, the locomotive was renumbered under TOPS in February 1974. Based at Cardiff Canton at the time of these views, it has since carried the numbers 47620, 47835 and 47799, the names *Windsor Castle* and *Prince Henry* and is today preserved at the Eden Valley Railway. BOTH BILL POTTER/KRM

LEFT: A general view of the loading facilities at the reopened Tytherington Quarry, looking east towards Yate on 25th September 1976. On the right is the loading hopper with the stone conveyor leading up to it, whilst behind are the block of six bins holding the crushed stone ready to be loaded. The run round loop on the right is on the course of the original branch to Thornbury. These facilities were still as seen here after the quarry and line were mothballed in 2013 but may have been altered or replaced for the most recent reopening.
D.L DOTT/COLOUR-RAIL

ABOVE LEFT AND RIGHT: On 26th September 1959, ex-GWR pannier tank No. 9769 arrived at Thornbury station with the RCTS (Bristol Branch) 'Bristol & South Gloucestershire Rail Tour', made up of three corridor coaches. Departing Temple Meads, the tour travelled first to East Depot and Canon's Marsh, returning then to Temple Meads before heading off to Avonside Wharf, Fishponds, Avonmouth, Henbury, Stoke Gifford, Yate and then Thornbury. However, time was lost almost immediately so arrival here was at least an hour and a half late, and there is some doubt as to whether the rest of the trip, round all three sides of the Berkeley Road triangle, was undertaken before heading back to Temple Meads. Built at Swindon in October 1935, No. 9769 was based at St. Philips Marsh shed at the date of the tour, having transferred over from Bath Road a year earlier. It moved on to Westbury in September 1960 and was withdrawn in March 1963. The engine is seen here after arrival, left, and taking water during running round, right. Note the rear coach was in the by then obsolete red and cream livery. BOTH NPC

Although LM&SR types such as Class '1P' 0-4-4 tanks or 'Jinty' 0-6-0 tanks had been the normal motive power on the branch passenger trains, this view of No. 9769 preparing to depart with the tour gives a good indication of how things would have looked if services had been maintained for another decade and a half. A couple of local lads on bicycles watch this historic moment, as the last ever passenger train left Thornbury station. NPC

An unidentified '4F' coasts in to the station with a daily goods trip, comprised entirely of loaded coal wagons, in October 1960. The steep climb out of the station towards Grovesend Tunnel, which could cause a heavy train to slip to a standstill, is apparent in this view. M.E.J. DEANE, COURTESY DR SIMON FOSBURY

No. 44553 gently lets off steam after arriving with the daily trip from Yate on Saturday 10th June 1961. Under the instructions in the 1963 *Working Time Table* on the next page, this would be Bristol Trip No. 810, under train reporting No. 9F38, leaving Yate at 1.00pm and due here at 1.55pm, with 10 minutes allowed for shunting at Grovesend Quarry on the way. The steep drop down from Grovesend Tunnel is again well shown in the distance but of most interest is the glimpse of Thornbury engine shed, a wooden structure erected around the time of opening in 1872 but which was deemed 'temporary'; as with the station building at Stroud, it was never replaced. Closed on 19th June 1944 when the passenger service was withdrawn, the track to it, which ran back from the turntable road and crossed the line in to the goods yard, was lifted in December 1948, although for some reason the rails inside were left in place. From 1st October 1946, the shed was rented out to the local coal merchant for stabling his lorry, and it seems to have remained standing until the branch closed in 1967. A siding ran back near to it from the goods yard, at a slightly higher level, on which wagons were positioned for coaling and also for loading ashes from the locomotives. The smart red motor just pushing its way in to the picture on the left is an Austin A40 'Farina', the chrome strip on the bonnet suggesting an early example of a model which came out in late 1958. MARK B. WARBURTON

Local Trip Working—continued

BRISTOL 809
Ex LM. Class 4 (0-6-0)
Enginemen
Barrow Road
809A on duty 4.55 a.m. off duty 1.10 p.m. D

	arr. a.m.	dep. a.m.	
Barrow Road Shed		5‖10	LE MO
Westerleigh Sidings	5‖30		
Barrow Road Shed		5‖10	LE MX
Bristol (St. Philips)	5‖15	5‖25	EBV
Westerleigh Sidings	5†45	6.15	TTHSX 9F32
Yate	6.30	8.6	
Rangeworthy	8.15	8.16	
Wickwar	8.22	8.30	
Charfield	8.42	10.40	
Wickwar			R
Westerleigh Sidings	11.15		
Westerleigh Sidings	5†45	6.15	TTHO 9F38
Yate	6.30	8.0	
Grovesend	8.30	8.40	
Thornbury	8.55	9.40	
Grovesend	9.50	10.5	
Yate	10.40	11.0	
Westerleigh Sidings	11.15		
	p.m.	p.m.	
Westerleigh Sidings		12.5	SX 7B43
Fishponds	12.25	12†40	EBV 0F32
Bristol (St. Philips)	12†50	12‖55	LE
Barrow Road Shed	1‖0		
	p.m.	noon	
Westerleigh Sidings		12.0	SO 9F34
Bristol (St. Philips)	12.34	12‖40	LE
Barrow Road Shed	12‖45		

BRISTOL 810
Ex LM. Class 4 (0-6-0)
Enginemen
Barrow Road
810A on duty 9.0 a.m. off duty 6.0 p.m. SX
810A on duty 6.35 a.m. off duty 7.35 p.m. SO
810B on duty 3.45 p.m. off duty 11.45 p.m. SX
810B on duty 3.15 p.m. off duty 11.15 p.m. SO
810C on duty 10.20 p.m. D, off duty 6.20 a.m. MX & SUN

	arr. a.m.	dep. a.m.	
Barrow Road Shed		9‖15	LE SX
Yate	9‖35		
Shunt as required			
	p.m.	p.m.	
Yate		1.0	9F38
Grovesend	1.30	1.40	
Thornbury	1.55	2.35	9F38
Grovesend	2.45	3.20	
Tytherington	3.30	3.40	
Iron Acton	3.55	4.5	
Yate	4.15		
Shunt as required			
Yate		6.30	SX
Westerleigh Sidings	6.43	7.20	9F38
Bristol (TM)			R
West Depot	8.15	9.52	9F38
Pylle Hill	10.2	R10.20	
Westerleigh Sidings	11.5		
	a.m.	a.m.	
Westerleigh Sidings		2.5	MSX 9F38
West Depot	3.0	3†10	EBV
Westerleigh Sidings	4†0	4.55	Q 6F38
Bristol (St. Philips)	5.28	5‖33	LE
Barrow Road Shed	5‖38		

BRISTOL 810 (continued)

	arr. a.m.	dep. a.m.	
Westerleigh Sidings		2.20	SO 9F38
Bristol (T.M.)	3.18	3†28	EBV
West Depot	4†20	4.55	Q 6F38
Westerleigh Sidings	5.28	5‖33	LE
Bristol (St. Philip's)	5‖38		
Barrow Road Shed		6‖50	SO LE 0F35
	a.m.	a.m.	
Westerleigh Sidings	7‖25	7.30	9F38
Yate	7.46		
Shunt as required			
Yate		10.5	
Grovesend	10.35	10.45	
Thornbury	11.0	11.30	
Grovesend	11.40	11.55	
	p.m.	p.m.	
Yate	12.30	1‖0	LE
Barrow Road Shed	2‖0	4‖15	LE
Bristol (St. Philips)	4‖20	4.45	(Assist.)
Westerleigh Sidings	5.10		
Shunt			
Westerleigh Sidings		7.20	9F38
West Depot	8.15	9.52	
Pylle Hill	10.2	R10.22	
Westerleigh Sidings	11.5		
	a.m.	a.m.	
Westerleigh Sidings		3.0	SUN 9F38
West Depot	4.15	5.10	
Bristol (T.M.)			
Bristol (St. Philips)	5.35	5‖40	LE
Barrow Road Shed	5‖45		

LEFT: Details of the local trip workings No's 809 and 810, to and from Thornbury, Westerleigh Sidings and Yate, which were all covered by Bristol Barrow Road enginemen, from the *Working Time Table of Classes 7, 8, 9 and Local Freight Trains, Bristol District, 17th June 1963*. The trips varied as the letter notations indicate, with locomotives first heading 'light engine' (LE) off shed, with some then being Mondays only (MO) or Mondays excepted (MX), Tuesdays, Thursdays, Saturdays excepted (TTHSX), Tuesdays, Thursdays only (TTHO), Saturdays only or excepted (SO or SX), Mondays, Saturdays excepted (MSX) or Sundays only (SUN). Some days just an engine and brake van was required (EBV), whilst some trains only ran if required (Q), *i.e.* if there was any traffic. Shifts were all of eight hours duration bar one which was nine and all trips were rostered for a Class '4F' 0-6-0.

BELOW: Although the Class '4F's largely ruled the roost now, there were occasional visits from WR pannier tanks, such as Class '57XX' Nos 3659 and 9680 in 1964 and 1965 respectively, and an unidentified Class '94XX' 0-6-0PT in 1965. However, any variety otherwise had to be supplied by Barrow Road's large fleet of '4F' 0-6-0s that were used on the trips, with No. 44411 here now being the fourth different member of the class that we have seen to date, with one more yet to come. The '4F', having arrived with a daily goods trip circa 1960, will turn here and, unusually, will then drop off the empty hopper wagons at Grovesend Quarry on the way back to Yate. At the rear of the platform is an Austin A35 of the 1956-59 period and the houses in the left background, on Summerleaze, still remain today. M.E.J. DEANE, COURTESY DR SIMON FOSBURY

BELOW: Driver and fireman put their backs to it as No. 44523 is swung on the Thornbury turntable in the summer of 1960. Although turning was effected by means of a handle inserted in to the capstan, it could still require some effort with the locomotive only just fitting on the 34ft diameter table. GERALD PEACOCK

INSET LEFT: A closer study of the turntable in autumn 1966, which had not been used after steam had ceased at the end of the previous year. There were winding capstans at either end. NPC

Pictured on the same day, No. 44523 shunts coal wagons in the spacious goods yard. As well as house coal for domestic use, four to five wagonloads of coal was also delivered here for Thornbury gas works every week up until it closed circa the mid 1950s, which was then carried up to the works on the north side of the town by a local haulier. In the centre background, just beyond the end of the platform, there is a glimpse of the livestock pens, which given how well laid out the rest of the yard was, were positioned very awkwardly along a short siding running back from a headshunt at the end of the platform road. GERALD PEACOCK

From 1961, when construction began of both the Severn Bridge and Oldbury nuclear power station, large quantities of cement and iron bar began being delivered to Thornbury goods yard for onward road transport to each site. Here, in the summer of 1961, No. 44205 prepares to leave with a train of empty 'Presflo' cement wagons and hoppers for Grovesend Quarry. A rake of loaded 'Presflos' had been dropped in to the siding on the left, where a cement lorry is parked waiting to load. The locomotive would have been a very rare 'cop' for any local spotters; new in November 1925, it was based at Barrow Hill shed at Staveley, in Derbyshire, spending virtually all of its BR career in the East Midlands – note the overhead wires warning flashes on the tender. It was withdrawn at the beginning of March 1963. GERALD PEACOCK

RIGHT: A page of views of Thornbury station and goods yard, during the occasion of the brake van trip behind 'Hymek' No. D7012 on 10th June 1966. Here, locomotive and brake van sit alongside the platform. The distinctive water tower, a cast iron tank mounted on six slim pillars of blue engineers brick, was provided at the same time as the locomotive shed. The water was piped from a spring at Grovesend. Arrival of the trip here was timed at 1.07pm and only seven minutes were spent before returning. JOHN RYAN

ABOVE: Despite the box van on the left and the amount of coal visible in the merchant's yard beyond the goods shed, the rails show little sign of any recent use, having a thick coating of rust. There had been four sidings in the goods yard, two on the left which ended at buffer stops, whilst the two running through and to the left of the goods shed met to form a loop on the other side. One of the sidings on the left had gone, possibly when the coal and ash siding for the engine shed, which ran back from it, had been lifted along with the line to the shed in December 1948. There is a small mystery here – where had the loaded stone hoppers collected from the quarry been hiding in the top picture? JOHN RYAN

LEFT: No. D7012 waits to leave as the local coal merchant's lorry heads out of the yard in the centre background, down on to Thornbury High Street. Note only the platform road has any sheen on the rails. Departing at 1.14pm, arrival back at Yate was at 13.58pm. JOHN RYAN

A fine panoramic view of the station, looking east up the bank towards Grovesend and Yate, in August 1966, after the final withdrawal of goods services. Showing the west elevation in full, although suffering from neglect, the building still exuded an air of style, with its peaked Roman tiled roofs, decorative ridge tiles and bargeboards, and locally sourced, grey freestone walls. The arches in the two chimneys were a particularly attractive touch. The design comprised twin pavilions either side of a central booking hall, with a waiting area at the front, which was glazed and faced out on to the platform, whilst the gents toilets were housed in an extension at the far end which can be seen in a couple of the other views. The station was not signalled, so no box was ever provided. There was a single ground frame, positioned on the north side of the line at the entrance to the goods yard, which can be seen in the centre distance here. Note, however, that the engine shed had been demolished. The car on the right is a fairly new looking Morris Oxford Series VI, which were produced from 1961 to 1971. This may have looked like the end but, amazingly, one more train was to venture down here prior to the arrival of the demolition contractors … . *NPC*

ABOVE: ... and here it is! Our third and final sighting of No. D7008 on 18th May 1967 indicates that not only was this an organised trip, with an extra brake van attached to accommodate the fortunate few, but that the train was permitted to venture beyond the quarry to pay a final visit to Thornbury station. A small gaggle of enthusiasts stroll along the weed-grown platform in the background. The line from Grovesend Quarry to Thornbury had closed on 20th June the previous year, so the next trains to call after this would be those of demolition contractors Thomas Ward in September 1968. Two further 'Hymeks', No's D7014 and D7041, were to make appearances on the first of these.
M.H. YARDLEY/COLOUR-RAIL

ABOVE: Thornbury was not a station frequented by railway photographers, so this colour record of it is invaluable, even post closure shots such as this view of the station building taken on 20th October 1967. NPC

LEFT: Taken on the same day, I had originally intended to leave this view of the turntable and water tower out, different though the aspect was, only to realise that it provided a rare glimpse of the station master's house in the background. Slightly divorced from the rest of the station site and at a lower level, we only really get to see the roof of it here but enough to make out that it bore a strong similarity to the station building in design. The last station master to reside here was William Bray, from circa 1950 to 1956, after which the post was abolished and the local ganger, Ron Davis, moved in with his wife Mary. They moved out in 1979, the house having been purchased by the local council so that it could be demolished as part of the redevelopment of the whole station site. NPC

SECTION 14

THE BRISTOL & GLOUCESTER LINE
YATE TO WESTERLEIGH WEST JUNCTION

Leaving a trail of filthy smoke, Class '9F' No. 92230 heads north with an Up train of vans on 21st August 1965. Note that although the box is generally known as Yate Main Line Junction, the nameboard reads only Yate Main Line. Built at Crewe Works and in to service on 31st August 1958 at Banbury shed, the 2-10-0 was based at Newport Ebbw Junction at the date of the picture but was shortly to transfer to Horton Road, in October. However, it was then placed in store the following month. NPC

From Yate to the ex-Great Western main line at Westerleigh is a distance of just one and a half miles and this short journey is the final one we shall make along the old Bristol & Gloucester Railway main line in this volume. The journey southwards beyond the bridge under the Paddington to Bristol main line, from Westerleigh to Temple Meads station via Mangotsfield and Staple Hill will be covered in the volume on Bristol. However, this short section is also potentially one of the most interesting, covering as it does the various junctions, connecting loops and a flyover at Westerleigh, an area where the railway today has been much simplified since the 1960s.

These junctions and connecting loops had only come in to being shortly after the dawn of the 20th century, following the construction by the GWR of the London, Bristol & South Wales Direct Railway, a new main line running from Wootton Bassett to the Severn Tunnel via Filton and Patchway, which is often referred to as the 'Badminton Line'. Built under an Act of 7th August 1896, the new line was thirty-one miles in length and was opened throughout for goods traffic on 1st May 1903 and to passengers on 1st July. The Midland line was crossed by means of a three arch viaduct, of stone abutments and piers, with brick arches, which the Midland numbered 32A in the *Bridge Register* but that was owned and maintained by the GWR.

The GWR now saw the opportunity to establish a direct route to their new main line from the Severn Bridge, the railway across which and as far as Berkeley Road had been jointly owned with the Midland since 1894, whilst the GWR already held running powers over the MR line south of Standish Junction. The importance of this was further emphasised with the opening of the Honeybourne line on 1st August 1906, which then gave the GWR a direct route from Birmingham to Bristol, the very thing they had lost out to the Midland on some six decades earlier. They wasted little time in starting to run a new direct express, which the Midland contested in court on the basis that the new connections at Westerleigh were only for trains running via the Severn Bridge but the ruling eventually went in favour of the GWR. The new loop at Berkeley, permitting direct running southwards from the Severn Bridge, was opened on 9th March 1908.

The GWR and Midland lines met at Yate South Junction, the GWR Down line crossing the MR on a flyover to join their Up line. The Midland line past Nibley to where it is crossed by the GWR Badminton Line is covered here, as is the route from Yate South Junction to Westerleigh West Junction, although this was a GWR line. However, it is integral to the route that we have travelled from Gloucester and the trains that we have seen on the way.

The new lines at Westerleigh formed a triangle with three new junctions, North, East and West, allowing GWR trains to run direct to either Bristol or towards Swindon and London. These connections were opened on 1st May 1903, complete with three new signal boxes: Westerleigh North Junction, Westerleigh East Junction and Westerleigh West Junction. However, the dispute with the Midland over running rights meant that the most important connection, at Yate South Junction, was not opened. A box had been provided there in 1897, to control the connection to the sidings laid in for the contractors S. Pearson & Son Ltd, who were building the new lines, but this was closed in July 1903.

From 4th February 1907, the lines were officially out of use whilst the dispute with the Midland went to court, reopening on 9th March 1908 along with the new loop at Berkeley and, finally, the junction with the Midland at Yate South. It may well be that the box here was that provided in 1897, which had simply been mothballed since 1903. However, from the outset, the East Curve was far less used than the West Curve, which was only of use for trains coming over the Severn Bridge or freights from Sharpness Docks that were then heading eastwards. Swindon and all points east on the GWR main line were served by the much shorter route via Standish Junction and the Stroud Valley.

Yate and the junctions with the ex-GWR main line at Westerleigh, as shown on the 1 inch OS for 1960.

Accordingly, the East Curve was taken out of use on 18th December 1916 but then reinstated again on 18th February 1918, closed again on 10th July 1927, reopened during the war on 16th August 1942 and closed for the final time on 4th January 1950, although it was not physically removed until around 1965. After being run down for several years, the Midland main line via Mangotsfield was closed to passenger services in 1969 but a single line remained open to service Bath gas works until 31st May 1971. Retained for the civil engineers use to Mangotsfield after that, this was subsequently cut back to the 122 miles 65 chains point (from Derby), where the line goes under the M4 Motorway. Here, on the site of the old Westerleigh yard sidings closed in 1965, Avon County Council first opened a refuse terminal in 1985 served by a single siding, whilst in 1991 a large oil storage depot was established here. With the ex-GWR line now the dominant route at Yate South Junction, the layout was much simplified and the WR Down line was completely realigned with the Up line, the rails over the flyover being lifted in 1971 and the bridge demolished.

With No. 6435 leading No. 7029 *Clun Castle*, the 'GWR Cavalcade' rail tour approaches Yate on the outward leg of the journey. Most unusually, the train is crossing from the Up main back to the Down main but I have been unable to find any reference to why the train was on the Up line in the first place. The likelihood would seem to be that Sunday engineering operations had necessitated the train running wrong line for a distance but where it had made the original crossing is not known; in any case this would have required a reversal, as all the crossovers on the route were trailing. The other possibility is that the train had been set back in to the single remaining siding on the Up side to allow something else to pass. Note that the loading bay siding in the foreground ran behind the box. NPC

'Black Five' No. 45444 heads a Down express through Station Bridge (No. 38) and in to Yate station at an unknown date. This is probably the best view that we have of the antiquated arrangement that existed at several of the cramped goods yards on the Br&GR, which harked back to the very earliest days of the railways. Whilst the sidings north of the road bridge serving Parnalls remained open until 1967, the goods shed and yard were closed in 1963 and the rails seen here were lifted over the weekend of 23rd-24th January 1964. Built by Armstong, Whitworth & Co. Ltd in December 1937, this was an engine that moved home quite often from the mid-1950s but, under heavy magnification, it appears to be carrying a 16A Nottingham shedplate on the smokebox door. It transferred to there from Woodford Halse in mid-June 1963 and then moved on to Fleetwood at the start of December 1964. With all this information, we can therefore confidently place the photograph in the summer of 1963, whilst the train is highly likely to be the one remaining through working to Bournemouth, No. 1O91, the 7.35am from Nottingham which now ran via Bristol, Westbury and Salisbury. No. 45444 was withdrawn from Lostock Hall in early August 1968. PAUL RILEY/COURTESY THE RESTORATION & ARCHIVING TRUST/REF. No's PR3925

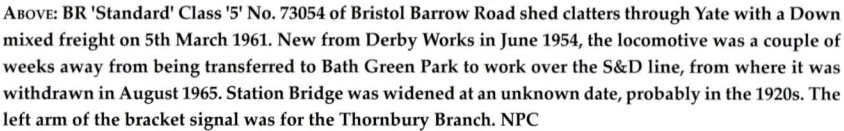

THE BRISTOL & GLOUCESTER LINE – YATE TO WESTERLEIGH WEST JUNCTION

Above: BR 'Standard' Class '5' No. 73054 of Bristol Barrow Road shed clatters through Yate with a Down mixed freight on 5th March 1961. New from Derby Works in June 1954, the locomotive was a couple of weeks away from being transferred to Bath Green Park to work over the S&D line, from where it was withdrawn in August 1965. Station Bridge was widened at an unknown date, probably in the 1920s. The left arm of the bracket signal was for the Thornbury Branch. NPC

Right: The pub sign for The Railway Hotel, Station Road, Yate, seen here on 10th June 1966, depicted a Johnson Midland 'Spinner'. Sadly the pub is no more, the building having recently been demolished despite a campaign to save it. Planning permssion for the flats development on its site was refused in June 2018! John Ryan

Below: 'Black Five' No. 44660 starts away from Yate with train No. 1M09, an Up Nottingham relief, again in the summer of 1963. No. 44660 was a BR build, at Crewe Works in May 1949 and was based at Saltley shed. A late build, it was also an early withdrawal, from Saltley in September 1964, a working life of just over fifteen years, very short for one of these usually long-lived Stanier 4-6-0s. This view also shows the south end of the cramped goods yard, with its short loading bays and wagon turntable, prior to the tracks being lifted. Paul Riley/Courtesy the Restoration & Archiving Trust/Ref. No's PR3919

BRITISH RAILWAY HISTORY IN COLOUR: 4B. GLOUCESTER MIDLAND LINES SOUTH – STONEHOUSE TO WESTERLEIGH   445

An overall view of Yate looking south from Station Bridge on 10th August 1963, as yet another of the ubiquitous 'Black Fives', No. 45272 of Saltley shed calls with an Up train, probably a Bristol to Birmingham service. I have found no reference anywhere to the apparent S25 reporting number on the front of the smokebox, so have no idea what it means, whilst the locomotive was previously seen heading north at Standish Junction. The goods shed matched others on the Br&GR in design, with twin arches in the end walls for rail and road access, the latter again later being bricked in; the building survives today in commercial use. The large station masters house in the left background also still remains but the only platform on this side of the bridge at the reopened station is on the Up side, the Down platform being staggered north of the bridge. NPC

446 THE BRISTOL & GLOUCESTER LINE – YATE TO WESTERLEIGH WEST JUNCTION

A fine overall study of Yate station, taken in late afternoon autumn sunshine circa 1962. This was another handsome Brunellian building, in red brick with stone quoins and window and door surrounds, tall chimneys turned through forty-five degrees and an all round canopy which, for once, BR appears not to have messed about with. It is likely that the section at the far end, nearest the footbridge, set back a little and without a canopy, was a later extension, although the large scale OS shows it to have been in place by 1880. The shelter on the Up side matched the main building in style but with the usual flat roof these smaller buildings sported. The footbridge (No. 37), of cast iron columns and wrought iron girders, was added in 1889 and note the Yate totem in Western Region brown and cream on the lamppost on the right. Another 19th century legacy was the height of the platforms, which necessitated a step up or down for passengers joining or leaving trains, whilst no bay was ever provided for Thornbury Branch services, which instead ran through to and from Bristol. NPC

LEFT: We now start a short run of views taken from a vantage point just to the west of Station Bridge, the first during the long winter of 1963, on 24th February. In the icy cold conditions, 'Black Five' No. 44810 of Saltley shed throws off a fine head of steam as it heads through with a Bristol to Birmingham freight. Built at Derby Works in 1944, the locomotive was withdrawn from Stoke shed in early August 1966. NPC

BELOW: On 10th August 1963, 'Hall' Class No. 5967 *Bickmarsh Hall* was photographed with what was probably a Bristol to Birmingham local; for some reason it was carrying an out of date WR three digit reporting number but the 'H' would otherwise signify that it was bound for Birmingham. New in March 1937, No. 5967 had recently transferred from old Oak Common to Westbury, from where it was withdrawn in June 1964. NPC

RIGHT: On the same day, 'Black Five' No. 45301 was seen heading through with train No. 1M00, an up holiday relief probably bound for the East Midlands. The locomotive was an unusual visitor here, having transferred from Llandudno Junction to Cricklewood East shed around three months earlier. New from Armstrong, Whitworth in January 1937, No. 45301 was withdrawn from Annesley shed in early July 1965. The car on the left, which appears in most of these views, is a Ford Cortina Mark 1 'Super' of circa 1965, whilst the BR lorry which also does is a circa 1955 Austin 'Lodestar' 3-tonner in 'blood & custard' livery. NPC

RIGHT: There is no clue as to the order in which these pictures were taken but next we have No. 7014 *Caerhays Castle* with what could be train No. (H)22, from Paignton to Wolverhampton. It certainly seems from these views that some on the Western Region were still wedded to the old reporting numbers. The other question I have is did many of these trains stop here and if so, given they were holiday expresses from the West Country returning folk home, why? It certainly looks from the pictures as though some of them called here – note the driver looking back along the platform from the cab in this view. NPC

LEFT: The final picture in this sequence has 'Jubilee' No. 45653 *Barham* at the head of train No. 1N40, the 10.20am from Newton Abbot to Bradford. This is not a 'Jubilee' that we have seen before, although it was a Saltley-based engine at this date. New from Crewe Works in January 1935, it moved to Blackpool Central at the end of April 1964 and then to Newton Heath a month later, from where it was withdrawn at the start of April 1964. NPC

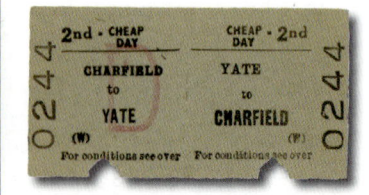

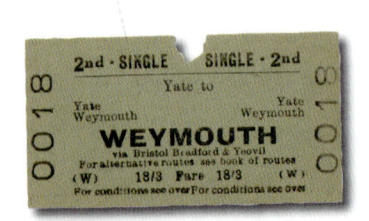

RIGHT: Having crossed back over to the Down line, No. 6435 and *Clun Castle* head through the station with the 'GWR Cavalcade' tour of 17th October 1965. From this angle it can be seen how the north end of the station building was set back from the main part, hence the thought that it may well have been a slightly later extension. NPC

Left: 'Black Five' No. 44806 certainly does not appear to be preparing to stop at Yate as it powers through with train No. 1M18 in the summer of 1963. This is another train that I have not found in the *Working Time Table* but the locomotive was shedded at Nottingham at this date – and had been since November 1957 – so this is likely to be a holiday relief from the West Country to the East Midlands. New from Derby Works in July 1944, No. 44806 moved to Burton-on-Trent in September 1964 and then on to Speke Junction and finally Lostock Hall, surving to the end of steam in early August 1968. Note the Yate nameboard on the right also in WR cream and brown.
PAUL RILEY/COURTESY THE RESTORATION & ARCHIVING TRUST/ REF. NO'S PR3920

RIGHT: A snapshot of the station building and the station masters house from an Up train circa 1962. NPC

BELOW: A sad view from August 1969, over four and a half years after the station had closed to passengers on 5th January 1965. The platforms had been removed but otherwise the buildings were still intact, although the canopy on the main building had also been removed. They are shown as still *in situ* on the 1976 50 inch OS, so were probably demolished circa 1980. In the distance, Yate South Junction and signal box can be made out, the box closing on 10th May 1971 when the junction was remodelled. The WR Up line can be seen branching away behind the bracket signal, which is indicating that a train was due heading that way. The WR Down line can be seen joining the Midland Up line just by the box. NPC

An unidentified '4F' 0-6-0 heads south through Yate South Junction with a mixed freight in 1960. The roof of the box can just be made out in the distance, above the rear of the train. On the right, the WR Up line climbs away towards Westerleigh North Junction, whilst the WR Down line was still some way off to the left or west at this point, behind the trees. On the right is the open expanse of Westerleigh Common, which is bisected off to the right by Westerleigh Road. The huge growth experienced by the town from the 1970s has seen all of the land to the east of Westerleigh Road built on but the common fortunately has been spared and remains as an amenity for the community. The single line serving Westerleigh oil terminal (the council refuse depot closed in the early 2000s, although a line still runs to the site) now drops down where the twin tracks of the Midland formerly ran, whilst the WR line on the right is double track, the Down line to the west having become redundant as a result and been lifted. GERALD PEACOCK

LEFT: The first of three views taken at Nibley on 9th June 1962, in time order, first showing Ivatt Class '4' 2-6-0 No. 43040 drifting southwards with a Gloucester to Bristol 'stopper'. New from Horwich Works in July 1949, the engine was based at Saltley but would transfer to Trafford Park three months after the picture was taken and was withdrawn in November 1966. NPC

BELOW: We have seen very few double-headers in this volume, not least because the gradients on the Midland main line through Gloucestershire presented few problems and loadings were well within the capabilities of the locomotives rostered to haul them. Therefore, this view of BR 'Standard' Class '5' No. 73140 and 'Jubilee' No. 45658 *Keyes* heading south with train No. 1V36, the 7.32am from Bradford to Bristol, is unusual. *Keyes* was a regular on this route that we have seen several times already but No. 73140 would have been a rare visitor, based at Derby shed at the date of this view and, from new in November 1956, spending all of its career at depots in the East Midlands, the North West and North Wales. The likelihood is that the 'Jubilee' was ailing and the 'Standard' had been attached to assist, with the train number hastily chalked on its smokebox door. NPC

BELOW: Class '8F' No. 48177 heads beneath the bridge that the GWR built at the turn of the century for their new connecting chord. No. 36A in the *Midland Bridge Register*, it comprised stone abutments and pillars with an iron girder span of 52ft or 82ft on the skew, and was owned and maintained by the GWR. Today there is no sign that it ever existed bar a very short length of the old trackbed on the right. New from North British Locomotive in March 1942, the 2-8-0 was based at Saltley at the date of this view but would transfer to Westhouses shed near Alfreton around a week later. It was withdrawn from Oxley in early March 1967. The photographer was standing at the top of the shallow cutting between Nibley Road Bridge (No. 36) and the GWR bridge. Not shown in any of these or the following pictures taken around this area, Nibley Road Bridge comprises wrought iron girders resting on stone abutments and does still remain today, spanning the branch to Westerleigh oil terminal. NPC

On the evening of the previous day, 8th June 1962, Saltley 'Black Five' No. 45260, an engine we saw earlier at Wickwar, heads north with an Up parcels train. NPC

Another Saltley 'Black Five' but one that we have not met previously, No. 44663, brings a southbound express beneath the WR line on 25th August 1962. The train number is not sharp but looks to begin 1O, so this could well be a Birmingham New Street to Bournemouth train, bound for Bath and the S&DJR line over the Mendips. Built by BR at Crewe Works and entering service in June 1949, No. 44663 was withdrawn from Heaton Mersey in early May 1968. NPC

By this date, it was left to the WR expresses to provide the locomotive variety on the LMR line, as here on the evening of 4th August 1962, when No. 5999 *Wollaton Hall* of Westbury shed was seen cruising northwards with an unidentified holiday express. The engine, which was new from Swindon Works in June 1940, is likely to have been an unusual 'cop' for any Gloucester-based 'spotters', as it would not have been used to working on this route. Furthermore, although it looks in reasonable fettle here, it had only weeks left in service, being withdrawn in the September. Note the solitary chocolate and cream carriage near the rear of the train. NPC

THE BRISTOL & GLOUCESTER LINE – YATE TO WESTERLEIGH WEST JUNCTION

Class '4F' No. 43951 pounds north through snowbound countryside at Nibley with a train of coal empties on Sunday 17th February 1963. The three-arch bridge carrying the ex-GWR Bristol & South Wales Direct Railway of 1903 over the Midland line can be seen in the centre distance. The engine had been based at Saltley but had transferred to Nottingham around five weeks before this picture was taken, so these empties are likely to be heading back to the Nottinghamshsire coalfield. Built by Armstrong, Whitworth in 1921, the 0-6-0 was withdrawn from Nottingham shed in September 1964. NPC

Class '8F' No. 48350 also leaves behind an impressive trail of steam as it forges northwards with a mixed freight on the same day. Built at Horwich Works and new in to service in April 1944, the 2-8-0 was withdrawn from Trafford Park in September 1967. It had been a long time resident of Toton shed at the date of this view, so this is likely to be a Westerleigh Sidings to Toton freight, train No. 6M05, running on a Sunday possibly because of the extreme weather conditions. NPC

BRITISH RAILWAY HISTORY IN COLOUR: 4B. GLOUCESTER MIDLAND LINES SOUTH – STONEHOUSE TO WESTERLEIGH 455

It is difficult to believe having seen the heavy snow lineside in the previous two pictures but this was the view in the opposite direction on the same day! No. 6903 *Belmont Hall* of Pontypool Road shed heads to Bristol with a train of South Wales coal. The train number had been chalked on the smokebox door but it is not clear what it is supposed to be but presumably this is a working that ordinarily would have been routed through the Severn Tunnel, so the likelihood is that it was closed for maintenance. No. 6903 was built at Swindon Works in July 1940 and was withdrawn from Banbury shed in September 1965. NPC

ABOVE: A fortnight later, on Saturday 2nd March 1963 and most of the snow had gone as 'Black Five' No. 44819 steamed beneath Bridge No. 36A with a Gloucester to Bristol 'stopper'. The engine was based at Derby at this date but transferred to Blackpool Central ten weeks later, so would have been a rare visitor here. New from Derby Works in November 1944, it wa withdrawn from Wigan Springs Branch in November 1967. NPC

The driver of Class '8F' 2-8-0 No. 48734 whistles up having just received the road from the Yate South Junction signalman, his northbound mixed freight having been held by Nibley Road Bridge as a faster train on the WR line was allowed through, circa 1963. DAVID POLLARD/NPC

The photographer then swung round to take the 'going away' shot moments later, as No. 48734, still whistling, made its way towards the WR flyover and Yate South Junction under a darkening late evening sky. The season is clearly late summer, probably July, whilst the shadows indicate that the sun is low in the west, so I am therefore going to have a stab at this being train No. 6M03, a Bristol to Bescot freight, which departed at 7.43pm Mondays to Thursdays or 7.50pm on Fridays and Saturdays, and would be passing here probably around 8.30pm. Note too the coal piled high in the tender at the start of the engine's journey. Built at the ex-North Eastern Railway works at Darlington in October 1945, the 2-8-0 was on its final posting and would be withdrawn from Bescot at the start of October 1964. The 'door to door' container looks very new. DAVID POLLARD/ NPC

THE BRISTOL & GLOUCESTER LINE – YATE TO WESTERLEIGH WEST JUNCTION

LEFT: This slide carried no details but I am fairly certain that we can identify the train exactly courtesy of the Gloucestershire Railway Memories website. 'B1' Class 4-6-0 No. 61090 was photographed by Stephen Mourton at Hatherley near Cheltenham on 22nd June 1963, heading north with train No. 1E69, the 12.45pm from Bristol to Sheffield and this is almost certainly the same working a little earlier in the day. One of the class built by the North British Locomotive Co. Ltd, No. 61090 spent much of its career alternating between Sheffield Darnall and Mexborough, being based at the latter at the date of this view and from where it was withdrawn excatly three months after the picture was taken. This is the second time that we have seen the engine, the first time being at Wickwar two years earlier. NPC

RIGHT: We now enter 'Black Five' heaven in the summer of 1964, by which date there was little variety to be found in the class of steam engine to be found at the head of passing LMR trains. However, most of them are examples of the class that we have not seen before. In the early evening of Tuesday 9th June, No. 44981 of Saltley shed drifts south with a Gloucester to Bristol local, possibly train No. 2B74, the 5.40pm off Eastgate, which would pass here at around 6.50pm. New from Crewe Works in July 1946, No. 44981 moved to Holyhead shed in June 1965 and was withdrawn from Shrewsbury in January 1967. NPC

LEFT: No. 44732 heads north with what is likely to be train No. 2M74, the 6.30pm from Bristol Temple Meads to Birmingham, which was due past here at around 6.55pm. There is a parcels van just visible on the rear of the train. The locomotive was a BR build, at Crewe Works in February 1949 and was based in the north west, so was some distance from home with what was a local working for this area and would also explain why we have not seen it before. It was withdrawn from Wigan Springs Branch in July 1967. NPC

Just over a week later, on Wednesday 17th June, No. 44690 of Derby shed was photographed at the head of a short mixed freight. This is another of the Stanier 4-6-0s that we have not encountered previously and was another BR build but at Horwich Works in October 1950. Moving to Rose Grove shed in early March 1966 it was an end of steam withdrawal at the start of August 1968. This is another late afternoon/early evening working, possibly train No. 5M25, the 5.20pm Bristol to Water Orton goods. NPC

Fortunately, WR trains heading up from Bristol were able to provide a little additional colour, as here on Saturday 8th August 1964, when No. 5955 *Garth Hall* of Bristol Barrow Road shed was seen with train No. 1M69, a Weston-super-Mare to Wolverhampton holiday relief, another working noted on the GloucesterRailwayMemories website. New from Swindon Works in December 1935, No. 5955 was converted for oil burning during the post-Second World War coal crisis and renumbered as No. 3950, in which form it ran between October 1946 and October 1948. It had been transferred from Swindon to Barrow Road only days before this picture was taken and was withdrawn from the Bristol shed in April 1965. NPC

RIGHT: Saltley-based 'Black Five' No. 45280 sweeps by with train No. 1N84, the 2.15pm from Bristol Temple Meads to York, which by this date was steam worked only on Saturdays, as here on 22nd August 1964, diesels being in charge of it Mondays to Fridays. The locomotive was seen previously in Volume 4A, heading north at Standish Junction in 1962. Note the Up express heading east on the WR main line in the right background. NPC

ABOVE: A touch of LMR variety here on the same day, as grubby 'Jubilee' No. 45602 *British Honduras*, which was seen departing Eastgate two weeks earlier at the start of Volume 4A, made its way north with train 1N40, the 10.20am from Newton Abbot to Bradford. This was a regular working for a Leeds Holbeck-based 'Jubilee' in the early 1960s. NPC

BELOW: Finally at this location, in a warm summer haze on Saturday 24th July 1965, 'Britannia' No. 70053 *Moray Firth* sweeps by, heading back to Wolverhampton with a train from Ilfracombe. This is our fifth encounter with this 'Brit', sadly every one of them showing it in this very neglected condition. NPC

As well as Western engines on the old Midland line at Westerleigh, in the BR era it was also quite common to see ex-LM&SR motive power traversing the ex-GWR lines. Here, on 8th August 1962, '4F' No. 44160 of Saltley shed heads back to Birmingham with a train of vans from Avonmouth. New from Crewe Works in February 1926, the '4F' had a ten year stint at Saltley, from May 1954 to April 1964, when it was transferred north to Gorton in Manchester. It was withdrawn from Workington in early December 1965, two months short of its fortieth birthday. Viewed from the south-west side of the railway, this is an LMR Up train but it is on the WR Down line and is just crossing the bridge over the Midland, which it will join at Yate South Junction. NPC

No. 4956 *Plowden Hall* heads 'light engine' down the slight gradient from the bridge over the Midland line, just visible behind the tender. One of the early members of the class, built at Swindon Works in September 1929, No. 4956 was allocated to Horton Road shed from early February to the end of June 1962, so this view is likely to date from the late spring of that year. The engine was withdrawn from Westbury shed in July 1963. GERALD PEACOCK

'Castle' Class No. 5063 *Earl Baldwin*, which Mark had photographed at Wickwar in July 1963, crosses over the Midland line with an Ilfracombe to Wolverhampton train on 10th August 1964. By this date the engine had moved from Stafford Road over to Oxley shed. MARK B. WARBURTON

'Black Five' No. 45263 heads towards the flyover with an LMR Up train on 4th August 1962. Another of Saltley's fleet but a class member that we have not seen before, the 4-6-0 was built by Armstrong, Whitworth in October 1936 and withdrawn from Heaton Mersey in October 1967. The train is passing the Yate South Junction Distant signal and the locomotive is crossing a short metal span over a farm track, which has been removed along with the rest of the chord since closure. NPC

Without doubt the most illustrated locomotive within these two volumes is Class '4F' No. 44045, which we have seen just about everywhere. Here it is again, in a fine portrait showing the 0-6-0 heading north 'light engine' over the occupation bridge circa 1960. Note the stay post for the signal. GERALD PEACOCK

The first of four views taken at the same spot, clearly a good vantage point which attracted several photographers. This section of line has proved extremely difficult to identify; I had originally thought it was on the Midland south of the flyover but finally realised that it is on the low embankment carrying the ex-GWR line from Westerleigh North Junction towards the flyover. On 28th June 1963, immaculate (probably ex-works) No. 6917 *Oldlands Hall* heads north with a train of equally clean looking carriages, including four in WR chocolate and cream (a pity they were not next to the engine!). In 1962, the WR decided to dispense with the GWR style carriage livery introduced six years previously, on the basis that it was proving impossible to keep them in uniform rakes. It was felt that mixed livery trains such as this looked untidy, so the decision was taken to paint all coaching stock in maroon. The colours were a sad loss to the 1960s railway scene – although corporate blue and grey was not too far away – and sights like this were soon to disappear. New in June 1941, the 'Hall' was based at Oxley shed at the date of the view so this is likely to be a Paignton, Ilfracombe or Newquay to Wolverhampton holiday express. Moving to Banbury in late January 1965, the locomotive was withdrawn in the September. NPC

'Black Five' No. 45407 strides north away from Westerleigh North Junction with a Paignton to Nottingham train on Monday 10th August 1964. Built by Armstrong, Whitworth in September 1937, the 4-6-0 was based at Burton-on-Trent at this date and was another end of steam withdrawal in early August 1968. MARK B. WARBURTON

Yet another 'Black Five', No. 44804 of Derby shed, skips by on Saturday 22nd August 1964, with what is probably a Paignton to Derby train – the train number is only faintly visible but could be 1M23. It was the bit of road in the foreground which finally enabled me to pin down the location, with the photographer standing on the corner of Nibley Lane as it turns sharply south after crossing Nibley Road Bridge. NPC

THE BRISTOL & GLOUCESTER LINE – YATE TO WESTERLEIGH WEST JUNCTION

RIGHT: A final view of a train crossing the low embankment, with '8F' No. 48327 in silhouette as it passes by with an Up LMR goods on 9th October 1965. New from Crewe Works in March 1944, this was a Heaton Mersey engine at this date, so was some distance from home and something of a rare 'cop' here. It was withdrawn from Patricroft shed in early June 1968. NPC

LEFT: We now begin a short run of pictures taken on the WR Up line from Yate South Junction to Westerleigh North Junction. An unidentified Class '9F' 2-10-0 heads past the Starting signal for Yate South Junction (lever 3), with the Fixed Distant for Westerleigh West beneath – fixed because of the sharp curve approaching that junction. Taken circa 1965, the locomotive is in the 921 number series but the last two digits are not clear. The Midland line can just be seen dropping away on the left and the signal in the background was the Yate South Junction Down main line Starting signal to Mangotsfield North. DAVID POLLARD/NPC

RIGHT: No. 5996 *Mytton Hall* heads past the same signal with a train of vans circa 1960. Built at Swindon in June 1940, the 'Hall' was based at Worcester at the time of this view and is probably bound for the yards at Stoke Gifford. It was a relatively early withdrawal, off Oxley shed in August 1962. Incidentally, this was not a single line as such (which by general implication is a reversible line) but what was known as Branch No. 1, Branch No. 2 being the 'flying junction', as it was known, on the Up side from Westerleigh. GERALD PEACOCK

BRITISH RAILWAY HISTORY IN COLOUR: 4B. GLOUCESTER MIDLAND LINES SOUTH – STONEHOUSE TO WESTERLEIGH 467

The only member of the 'Manor' Class that we have seen within these pages was No. 7814, in appalling condition passing Wickwar, so it is a pleasant surprise to see tidy looking No. 7808 *Cookham Manor* here, rounding the Up chord or Branch No. 1 with a mixed freight. The engine was based at Tyseley shed from January 1961 to September 1962 and this view of it is likely to date from that period. New in March 1938, it was withdrawn from Gloucester Horton Road shed on 31st December 1965 and was purchased for preservation shortly afterwards by a member of the Great Western Society. It is currently a static exhibit at Didcot Railway Centre. GERALD PEACOCK

No. 6851 *Hurst Grange* is seen a little further round the Up chord on 6th June 1961, at the head of a short train of rails carried on bogie bolster wagons, with a barrier wagon at the front. The engine was based at Oxley shed from October 1960 to July 1965. New in November 1937, it was withdrawn in August 1968. NPC

At the date of this view showing 'Black Five' No. 44965 passing Westerleigh North Junction with train No. 1X39 on 8th August 1962, the point rodding from Westerleigh North Junction Signal Box (the roof of which is visible above the centre of the train) had recently been dismantled. The engine was based at Saltley, whilst the 'X' in the train number (*WR WTT 1962-63*: '*For inter-Regional excursion, military and special trains*') indicates that this could be a military special conveying soldiers north. Built at Horwich Works in August 1946, withdrawal of the 4-6-0, off Bolton shed, took place in April 1968. NPC

BRITISH RAILWAY HISTORY IN COLOUR: 4B. GLOUCESTER MIDLAND LINES SOUTH – STONEHOUSE TO WESTERLEIGH

Also looking in very tidy condition was '28XX' 2-8-0 No. 2871, pictured rounding the curve from Westerleigh West Junction and passing the closed Westerleigh North Junction Signal Box circa 1961. Built at Swindon Works in November 1918, the engine moved to Westbury shed in February 1961, with this view likely dating from its time at that shed, prior to moving on to Taunton in the September. It was withdrawn from there in May 1963. The rails of the East Chord were still *in situ* on the far left but had not been used since 1950, with the North Junction box being closed on 4th January; however, the track was not lifted until around 1965. Note the point rodding for the junction still in place in the foreground. GERALD PEACOCK

We end our tour of the Midland in Gloucestershire on Western Region metals at Westerleigh West Junction, as '4F' 0-6-0 No. 44123 heads on to the London to Bristol main line with a mixed freight. The picture is undated but the engine, which we have seen several times already at Haresfield, on the Nailsworth & Stroud Branch and at Berkeley Road, was based at Barnwood and is here sporting an 85C shedplate on its smokebox door; Barnwood was recoded from 85E to 85C on 10th September 1960, so the date is post that but probably only be a few weeks. Westerleigh West Junction Signal Box had opened with the London, Bristol & South Wales Union line on 1st May 1903 and was closed on 10th May 1971. Between 1927 and 1942, when the East Chord running between North Junction and East Junction was out of use, it was renamed Westerleigh Junction Signal Box but did not revert to that name after closure of the chord for the fourth and final time in 1950. DAVID POLLARD/NPC

BRITISH RAILWAY HISTORY IN COLOUR: 4B. GLOUCESTER MIDLAND LINES SOUTH – STONEHOUSE TO WESTERLEIGH

Taken on the same day, No. 5911 *Preston Hall* of Cardiff Canton shed comes off the West Chord with an unidentified passenger working. New in June 1931, No. 5911 was withdrawn from Canton in September 1962. DAVID POLLARD/NPC

A rare sighting in this locality of ex-WD 2-8-0 No. 90365 of Woodford Halse shed, with a Woodford to South Wales freight. Built by North British Locomotive in September 1944 as WD No. 8514 and renumbered as WD No. 78514 four months later, the engine gained its BR number in May 1951. It was withdrawn from Doncaster shed in June 1965. Both lines cross Westerleigh Road on separate bridges just behind the signal box. DAVID POLLARD/NPC

Class '8F' No. 48659 comes off the West Chord at Westerleigh West Junction and on to the three-arch viaduct over the Midland line to Mangotsfield with a trainload of coal circa 1965. Built at the Southern Railway's Eastleigh Works in November 1943, the 2-8-0 had transferred from Crewe South to Bescot in mid-September 1964 and then moved to Saltley in mid-March 1966, from where it was withdrawn two months later. This spectacular picture is taken from the top of the Up Home bracket signal for the junction, positioned at the west end of the viaduct, which would suggest that the camera was in the hands of a railwayman. The shadow of both him and the signal can be seen on the ground in the left foreground. The large house on the left is a late 17th century Grade II listed building, first listed in 1952 as 'Bridge Farmhouse', although it appears on the 1951 25 inch OS as 'The Sign of the Dolphin' and is now listed as that; it was apparently formerly a public house called 'The Dolphin'. For those who wonder about the process of putting together these colour volumes, not only is this the last but one picture in the book but it was also the very last picture acquired for it, bought off the internet three days before the files were despatched to the printers! NPC

A different aspect of Westerleigh West Junction for our final view, as No. 6816 *Frankton Grange* heads on to the WR main line with a mixed freight for Bristol circa 1960. This is taken on the same day as the pictures a couple of pages earlier and again helps to confirm the date, as the locomotive is sporting an 82B St. Philips Marsh shedplate on its smokebox door. Transfer to that shed occurred in late September 1960, so the picture is probably not long after that. New from Swindon Works in December 1936, the 'Grange' finished its service in July 1965. DAVID POLLARD/NPC

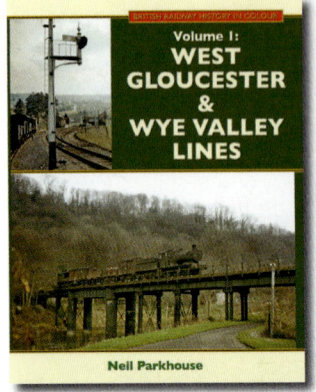

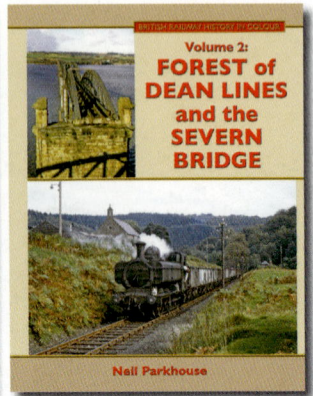

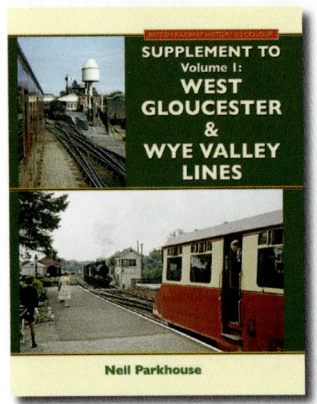

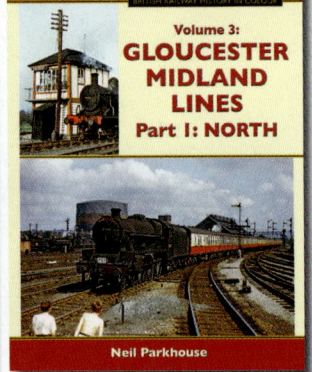

COLOUR IMAGES WANTED FOR THIS SERIES

There are still locations that I have little or nothing of for the planned further volumes in this series, whilst I am always interested in finding images for my collection from anywhere in the county. Anyone with colour slides or photographs of Gloucestershire railways that they would like to share with a wider audience and that I could possibly use in future volumes is invited to contact me directly at the Lightmoor office address at the bottom of the Contents page or by email: neil@lightmoor.co.uk

BOOKS IN THIS SERIES:

VOLUME 1: WEST GLOUCESTER & WYE VALLEY LINES (2ND ED.)
328 pages. Laminated board covers.
ISBN: 9781899889 76 1. £30.00 + £4.00 p&p.

VOLUME 2: FOREST OF DEAN LINES AND THE SEVERN BRIDGE.
328 pages. Laminated board covers.
ISBN: 9781899889 98 3. £30.00 + £4.00 p&p.

VOLUME 3: GLOUCESTER MIDLAND LINES PART 1: NORTH
280 pages. Laminated board covers.
ISBN: 9781899889 76 1. £30.00 + £4.00 p&p.

SUPPLEMENT TO VOLUME 1: WEST GLOUCESTER & WYE VALLEY LINES
48 pages. Laminated card covers. (Note: These pages are contained within the 2nd Ed.)
ISBN: 9781899889 39 9. £7.50 + £2.50 p&p.

VISIT **WWW.LIGHTMOOR.CO.UK** TO ORDER